SAGE was founded in 1965 by Sara Miller McCune to support the dissemination of usable knowledge by publishing innovative and high-quality research and teaching content. Today, we publish over 900 journals, including those of more than 400 learned societies, more than 800 new books per year, and a growing range of library products including archives, data, case studies, reports, and video. SAGE remains majority-owned by our founder, and after Sara's lifetime will become owned by a charitable trust that secures our continued independence.

Los Angeles | London | New Delhi | Singapore | Washington DC | Melbourne

ADVANCE PRAISE

'Many years ago, as a senior copywriter in one of New York's largest ad agencies, I presented a concept for a beauty brand. And yes, it actually had an idea attached to it, which was rare for beauty ads in those days. But I'll never forget my male creative director's response. He said straight-faced without a touch of irony, "I don't buy it; women don't think like that." So I applaud Professor Jethwaney on her book exploring how and why women are depicted so one-dimensionally in advertising. Whether it's Mumbai or New York, it needs to change. And I know the guy to whom I'll be sending a copy.'

Michele Aglira, *Creative Director, Publicis Conseil, Paris*

'Excellent and well researched, your book looks at advertising through a gendered lens. Without being prescriptive, it brings to the fore many problems inherent in the portrayal of women in advertising. The book is a timely reminder of the need to start a serious discourse around the subject of stereotyping women in advertisement and the risks this may have, by subliminally influencing mindsets of people. It forces the readers to re-examine their response to women's portrayal in advertising and to ask the question "why"'.

Zulaikha Haq, *Gender and Women Rights Activist, Afghanistan*

'A monumentally path-breaking book which, on the one hand, raises consciousness of women in slumber and, on the other, challenges conscience of the advertising world by linking a mirror of reality with a window of opportunity for enlightened choices. Each chapter is provocative and fascinating with contemporary debates and scholarship of ideas. This work will bring immense clarity of thoughts and sophistication of ideas to a large number of start-up advertising companies, media students and the established seasoned advertisers by introducing them to a philosophical terrain that brings maturity, ethics and sustainability to a sceptically naive world of monolithic patriarchal mind set.'

Professor Amita Singh, *Public Intellectual, Author, Commentator*

'A highly informative and beautifully written book on advertising nuances and gender by one of the most knowledgeable minds on the subject that I had the fortune to meet. An easy, worthwhile read for those engaged in the advertising industry and in general for everyone to take a peek into the evolving landscape of advertising.'

Mariyam Shakeela, *Maldives, Parliamentarian, Businesswoman, President of Women's Chamber of Commerce*

'Professor Jaishri Jethwaney's new book is a major contribution to gender studies in India. Jaishri has been the leading light and principal coordinator of the media research project of the South Asia Women's Network (SWAN) on the Status of Women in Media in South Asia. She led the segment on gender in advertising among all eight participating South Asian countries. The constant objectification and stereotyping of women through advertising immensely influences societal mindsets, especially among the young. I congratulate Jaishri on her continuing research on this vital issue, this time focused on India.'

Veena Sikri, *Professor and Ambassador, Convener, SWAN*

THE *Beauty* PARADIGM

SAGE Response, our business books imprint, celebrates its silver jubilee this year. As we reflect on this transformational journey that began with a single title, we thank everyone who has helped us to produce content that is topical and relevant across a varied audience of aspiring managers, working professionals, practitioners and students. We feel privileged that eminent management and leadership experts, professionals and stalwarts from academia supported and trusted us with their work. Over the years, SAGE Response has built an enviable list of practice-based, reader-friendly books that provide creative strategies to keep pace with the rapidly changing global scenario. As we grow and evolve with the times, it is our endeavour to continue to publish books that offer innovative solutions, approaches and perspectives to the disciplines that we serve.

THE *Beauty* PARADIGM

GENDER DISCOURSE IN INDIAN ADVERTISING

JAISHRI JETHWANEY

Los Angeles | London | New Delhi
Singapore | Washington DC | Melbourne

First published in 2022 by

SAGE Publications India Pvt Ltd
B1/I-1 Mohan Cooperative Industrial Area
Mathura Road, New Delhi 110 044, India
www.sagepub.in

SAGE Publications Inc
2455 Teller Road
Thousand Oaks, California 91320, USA

SAGE Publications Ltd
1 Oliver's Yard, 55 City Road
London EC1Y 1SP, United Kingdom

SAGE Publications Asia-Pacific Pte Ltd
18 Cross Street #10-10/11/12
China Square Central
Singapore 048423

Published by Vivek Mehra for SAGE Publications India Pvt Ltd. Typeset in 10.5/14 Sabon by Fidus Design Pvt Ltd, Chandigarh.

Library of Congress Congress Control Number: 2021944067

ISBN: 978-93-5479-165-9 (PB)

SAGE Team: Namarita Kathait, Shipra Pant, Shivani A. Damle and Rajinder Kaur
Cover Image, Photos and Book Design Credits: Kamal Bhatnagar and Prabhat Bhatnagar

To all those amazing women, often unknown and unsung, who take a stand to make a difference!

CONTENTS

LIST OF ABBREVIATIONS

AAAI	Advertising Agencies Association of India
ABX	Advertising Benchmark Index
AFE	Alliance for Family Entertainment
AIIR	All India Radio
ANA	Association of National Advertisers
ASA	Advertising Standards Authority
ASCI	Advertising Standards Council of India
BCCC	Broadcasting Content Complaints Council
BCCI	Board of Control for Cricket in India
BFSI	Banking, financial services and insurance
BJP	Bharatiya Janata Party
CCC	Consumer Complaints Council
CCPA	Central Consumer Protection Authority
CEDAW	Convention on the Elimination of All Forms of Discrimination against Women
CII	Confederation of Indian Industry
CSR	Corporate social responsibility
ECD	Executive Creative Director
F&L	Fair & Lovely
FCB	Futbol Club Barcelona
FGDs	Focus group discussions
FICCI	Federation of Indian Chambers of Commerce & Industry
FLO	FICCI Ladies Organization
FMCG	Fast-moving consumer goods
FTC	Federal Trade Commission
GST	Gender sensitivity test
HRD	Human Resource Development
I&B	Information and Broadcasting

ICC	Internal Complaints Committee
ICSSR	Indian Council of Social Science Research
IDIs	In-depth interviews
IIHB	Indian Institute of Human Brands
IIMC	Indian Institute of Mass Communication
INS	Indian Newspaper Society
IPC	Indian Penal Code
ISID	Institute for Studies in Industrial Development
IT Act	Information Technology Act
JWT	J. Walter Thompson
MMTK	Multimedia Tool Kit
MRUC	Media Research Users Council
NCR	National Capital Region
NCW	National Commission for Women
NDA	National Democratic Alliance
NGOs	Non-governmental organizations
PETA	People for the Ethical Treatment of Animals
PG	Postgraduate
PGD	Postgraduate diploma
POSH	Prevention of sexual harassment
SDGs	Sustainable Development Goals
SPI	Suspension pending investigation
SWAN	Sex Workers' Rights Advocacy Network
TVC	Television commercial
UGC	University Grants Commission
UGC	User-generated content
UK	United Kingdom
UN	United Nations
UNESCO	United Nations Educational, Scientific and Cultural Organization
UNICEF	United Nations Children's Fund
USA	United States of America
VC	Vice chancellor
WCB	Women on Corporate Boards
WCD	Women and Child Development
WPP	Wire and Plastic Products

PREFACE

Half the human race, women in general, feel the brunt of inappropriate representation and stereotyping at every possible space. The issue of women portrayal in media, first imperceptibly, then vocally, has been in the public domain for decades. Advertising occupies the 'paid for' space and time in media, and so has a position of power in the media ecosystem. The ad industry, in general, to a large extent has kind of quarantined itself from all the criticism and indictments, living in a world of make-believe that advertising only mirrors reality! If for argument's sake, we agree to that, is it not the responsibility of an institution that causes spell on the mind space of people to be responsible enough to reflect the social change and visible shifting gender roles over a period of time? It also needs to introspect on the fact that it is not just in traditional societies that often have a patriarchal way of looking at things, but even in modern societies advertising narrative has been raising eyebrows. Many celebrity brand ambassadors in the West have raised their voice against being airbrushed in ads to create a perfect picture of them.

In India, the celebrities, in general, with some exception who have refused to endorse fairness products and surrogate advertising, do not even seem to understand the problem but are busy endorsing mindless campaigns. Let us take the instance of the Vectus overhead tank advertisement released in April 2021 that has the husband-wife duo Kareena and Saif Ali Khan endorsing the brand. While the man is talking about the 'anti-bacterial' qualities of the tank, he asks the woman protagonist if she would also say something, to which Kareena, who is standing against the tank, objectifying herself, adds pointing to herself 'Khubsoorat hai, just like me' (It is beautiful, just like me). If a woman like Kareena, who believes, she is modern, evolved and responsible, compares herself with a tank and has agreed to endorse this kind of narrative, there is little hope for a gender sensitive discourse in advertising in India!

As protagonists, celebrities can't get away from the responsibility of retrograde discourse. They have a larger responsibility to at least people who follow them. The new Consumer Protection Act, 2019, has made brand endorsers liable for penalty on wrong and exaggerated claims. The Act talks about the need for 'Due Diligence' on the part of the endorsers. The Act, however, does not include objectification and stereotyping that are part of the Indecent Representation of Women (Prohibition)Act, 1986. Does one really need a law to be gender sensitive is something each brand endorser and content creator needs to ask herself/himself!

The annual Gender Gap Index released by the World Economic Forum, 2020, reflects India at number 112 from among 153. In India, women are discriminated from the embryonic stage, when more than 46 million lose their lives even before taking birth, according to the United Nations Population Fund's estimate, calling them missing women'.

Advertising that has some great creative minds can contribute positively in mainstreaming gender in the social discourse.

Now, about the book. The research that went on for close to two years had the following research questions and focus.

- RQ1. In what ways are women stereotyped or negatively portrayed in advertisements in various media?
- RQ2. What are the differences between culture-defined gender roles/expectations and women's portrayal in advertising?
- RQ3. In the process of creating an advertisement, what is the role of creative people and marketers/clients in creating negative or stereotypical imagery of women?

- RQ4. Which product categories consistently portray women as sex objects?
- RQ5. Are there any brands that have tried to reflect the social shift and portray women roles based on reality?
- RQ6. What is the extent of implementation of policies and guidelines in the advertising sector that encourages gender-sensitive narrative in the ad content?
- RQ7. Do the course curricula at university level sensitize the future professionals to gender and portrayal issues?
- RQ8. Are the existing policies and legal frameworks adequate to deal with the problem, or do these need addressing for policy change?
- RQ9. Has liberalization of the Indian economy changed the ad narrative?

The book with 12 chapters addresses these and more perspectives on the above-mentioned research focus by digging deep into every area through extensive field survey, in-depth interviews of the ad agencies' top management and chairs of professional bodies, such as Advertising Agencies Association of India (AAAI) and Advertising Standards Council of India (ASCI), and focus group discussions (FDGs) with creative teams and deconstruction of advertisements across brand categories and subgroups, analysing mass communication syllabi and policies and laws to take a 360 perspective of the issue in hand.

As the research was undertaken with a policy perspective, a stakeholder meeting was organized at the request of the author by the Ministry of Information and Broadcasting (I&B) in November 2020, which can be said to be the tipping point. The data presented seemed to please not many from the professional bodies, representing the advertising industry and the media. They had questions on the efficacy and motives behind such a research, which was understandable, as the empirical data was anything but complimentary on the gender narrative. Researchers often hear that, so it was fine. But, lo and behold, one hears that ASCI has become the founder member of UN's Unstereotype Alliance and it has also commissioned an India-wide research, GenderNext, to gather insights on people's perceptions and issues that need addressing. A great achievement!

The first few steps in a thousand-miles-long journey, indeed, are the most crucial ones!

CREATIVE CONCEPT

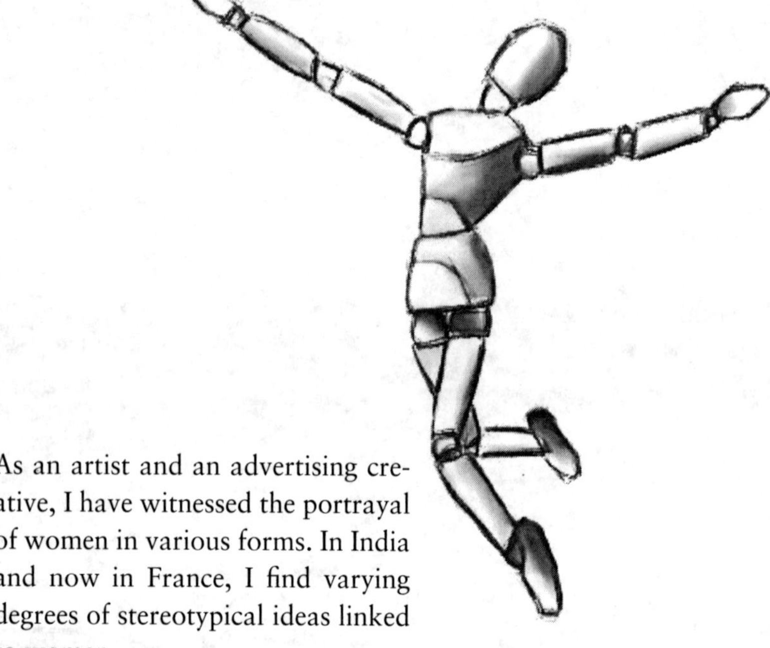

As an artist and an advertising creative, I have witnessed the portrayal of women in various forms. In India and now in France, I find varying degrees of stereotypical ideas linked to women.

However, there is a universal truth about the position of women in advertising, and that is how brands showcase women in order to market their products/services.

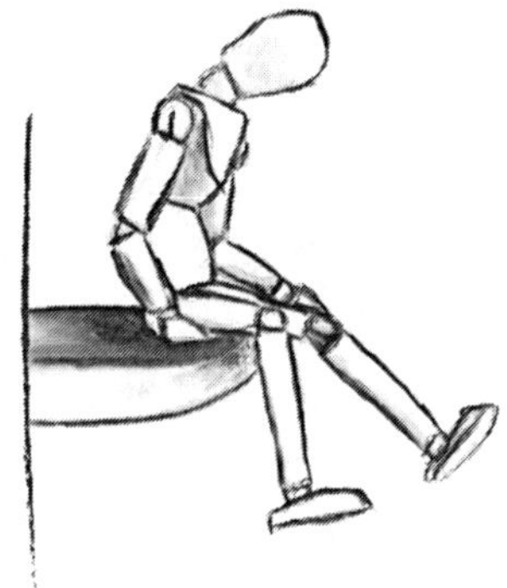

I have been using a wooden model for my studies on the human form. Artistic references are, more often than not, of the female body. Such is the power of women's beauty.

When I looked at the model after reading a few chapters from this book, I realized that I, too, am guilty of trying to showcase women in some form or another.

Therefore, instead of using this wooden model to portray a woman, I decided to use it to represent society's endless attempts to depict her.

- Kamal

ACKNOWLEDGEMENTS

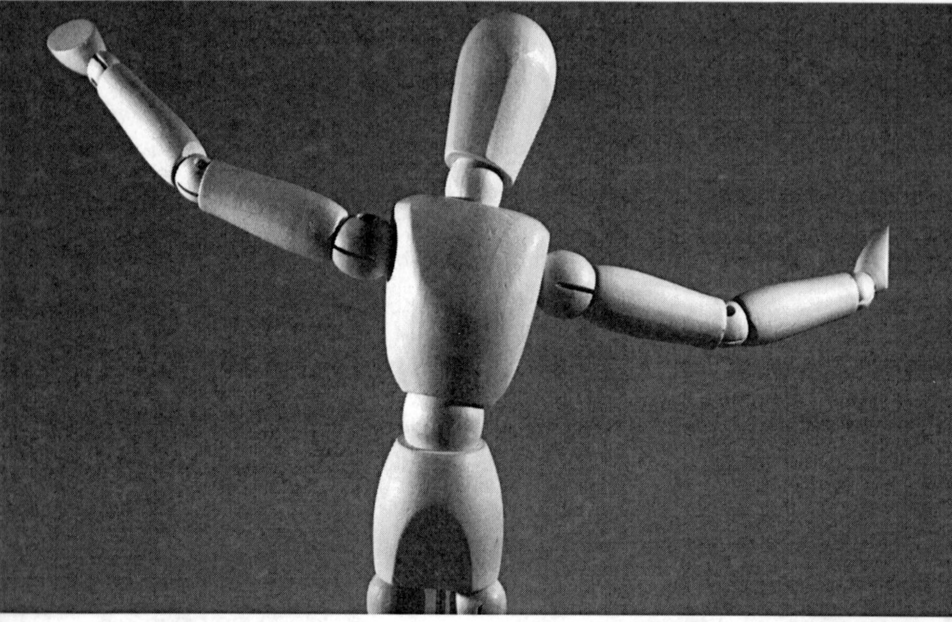

The book is slim, but the work behind it has been mammoth! The trajectory included a pre-research round table with industry stalwarts and academics, a national advertising conference that saw the coming at one place, people who matter, with their candid views and new ideas, a post-research round table, a faculty meet, a stakeholder meet at the Ministry of I&B, a policy paper, a multimedia toolkit, hundreds of interviews and many FGDs. For content analysis, it meant going through reams of papers on policies, laws and hundreds of syllabi, and the toughest of all—choosing over 1,150 campaigns from among over 5,000 campaigns to scientifically cull out the sample for deconstruction. In this long journey, many people joined, some to work, others to advise and critique and many to cheer up!

The foremost on my list are P. V. Narayanamoorthy, Tilak Mukherji and Chintamani Rao, the three industry veterans, who

I consulted at various stages. The confidence of the research team was heightened from their very constructive critique and advises that came aplenty. With Avijit Dutt, I had many informal discussions, especially on deconstruction of ads.

Kunal Sinha, Parveen Ahluwalia and Supriya Mukherji were my teammates throughout the research period, and I have no hesitation in acknowledging that without them, a work of this kind could not have been accomplished. Two youngsters, Suan (Paite Gualnam) and Komal Sachdev, were research associates, besides dozens of field researchers, who all deserve my grateful thanks.

Among the three of us including my colleagues Professor Seema Goyal and Dhanunjai, we conceptualized and thought through the innovative advocacy tool, the interactive Multimedia Tool Kit and Gender Sensitivity Barometer, which, to my mind, has been one important outcome of this seminal study. Rakesh Gupta very patiently turned all the research data into graphs and charts. Puja Mehta worked silently and diligently on copy editing of the text, never losing her patience on deadlines. They all have been indispensable for the research and deserve my appreciation.

Both, late Professor S. K. Goyal and Professor Murthy, vice chairman and former director, respectively, at the time the research study was undertaken, were very gracious in providing all the infrastructure and logistic support and an academic environment at Institute for Studies in Industrial Development (ISID) that scholars yearn for. All faculty colleagues, an important part of the internal peer-review, gave many suggestions that have enriched the study.

My grateful thanks are due to Professor V. K. Malhotra, Member Secretary, Indian Council of Social Science Research (ICSSR) for appreciating the importance of this research and fully funding it. I am grateful to the ICSSR Review Committee comprising Professors Asha Shukla, Amita Singh and K. G. Suresh for giving constructive suggestions during the various review meetings.

Professor and Ambassador Veena Sikri and Professor Gita Bamezai deserve my special mention and appreciation for making me a part of the UNESCO–SWAN project on the subject that later led to my taking this seminal India-specific ICSSR project.

I cannot thank enough Mr Atul Tiwari, IAS, Additional Secretary, Ministry of I&B, and Mr Amit Kumar, Director, and other officers for facilitating stakeholder meet at Shastri Bhawan, Ministry of I&B, by inviting people who mattered. This, to my mind, was the trigger that has had a cascading effect in the industry body taking the gender issue seriously.

Dr Maithili Ganjoo, Dean, Manav Rachna University, has been a friend from academics. One time, we thought of doing the book together, but our schedules did not match. The folder on my laptop still has the name SAGE-JJ-MG. I hope there shall soon be another opportunity to work together on a project in the near future!

Reaching out to advertising people, holding discussions and conducting FGDs was not easy at all! The entire credit for facilitating the process and being at the spot goes to some of my former students, now holding leadership positions in the industry, including Ashish Chakravarty, Anita Bose, Sohini Gooptu, Atul Purohit and Anand Bhushan, in particular. A big thanks to all of them.

Kamal Bhatnagar, another former student, winner of many awards and nominations including at Cannes and the One Show, now working out of Paris, has conceptualized the visual representation of women in the society for the book. I am including his process of thinking as presented to me. Incidentally, Kamal was the creative director on the very empowering Bournvita campaign 'Taiyaari Jeet ki' (preparation for victory). With his team at the Ogilvy and a very positive client who decided to show a different aspect of Indian motherhood, one who tells her child that he/she doesn't deserve to win if his/her practice was not good enough. Years later, and in its latest rendition, this new-age mother still challenges her child with a new logic, 'Mere bete ko jeet ki aadat tab lagegi, jab who mujhe harayega; tab nahin jab mein usse jeetne doongi' (my son would get used to winning only when he defeats me, and not when I let him win). Parents often lose in the game to let their children win. However, in this ad, the protagonist thinks otherwise; the child has to defeat the mother—who is an athlete herself, in the race to be a habitual winner and not win just because she lets him. Kamal proves that he is a feminist at heart!

His brother, Prabhat Bhatnagar, who kind of revolutionized digital viral marketing in India long before the birth of social media and the ex-founder of Digivaasi, a creative digital studio based out of Delhi, has carried forward his ideation and prepared the photographs, including the cover.

Professor Mahrukh Mirza, Vice Chancellor, and Dr Tanu Dang and Dr Neeraj Kumar, both faculty at the KMC University at Lucknow, deserve huge appreciation and thanks for not only facilitating field research in Lucknow but also organizing a conference on the research subject at the university with more than 500 students, faculty and the VC himself attending it. Tanu also organized a round table with the mass communication faculty from various universities at the campus, for deliberations on the course curricula which forms an important part of this research.

One of the most important names that I have intentionally kept almost at the end for a special mention is Sam Rufus, long-time friend, visiting faculty at Indian Institute of Mass Communication, who has taught creativity for over three decades, for suggesting the title of the book, *The Beauty Paradigm: Gender Discourse in Indian Advertising* (sending me many titles, explaining each, logically). Sam, active on the advertising scene for many decades, in my view, is one of the creative genius who ideates logically, scientifically, many a time using props to explain. His classes, some of which I had the privilege of attending were a sheer joy!

It has been an absolute pleasure working with Manisha Mathews, Namarita Kathait, Shipra Pant and other team members from SAGE! Deeply appreciate their enquiring mind, eye for detail and above all diligence.

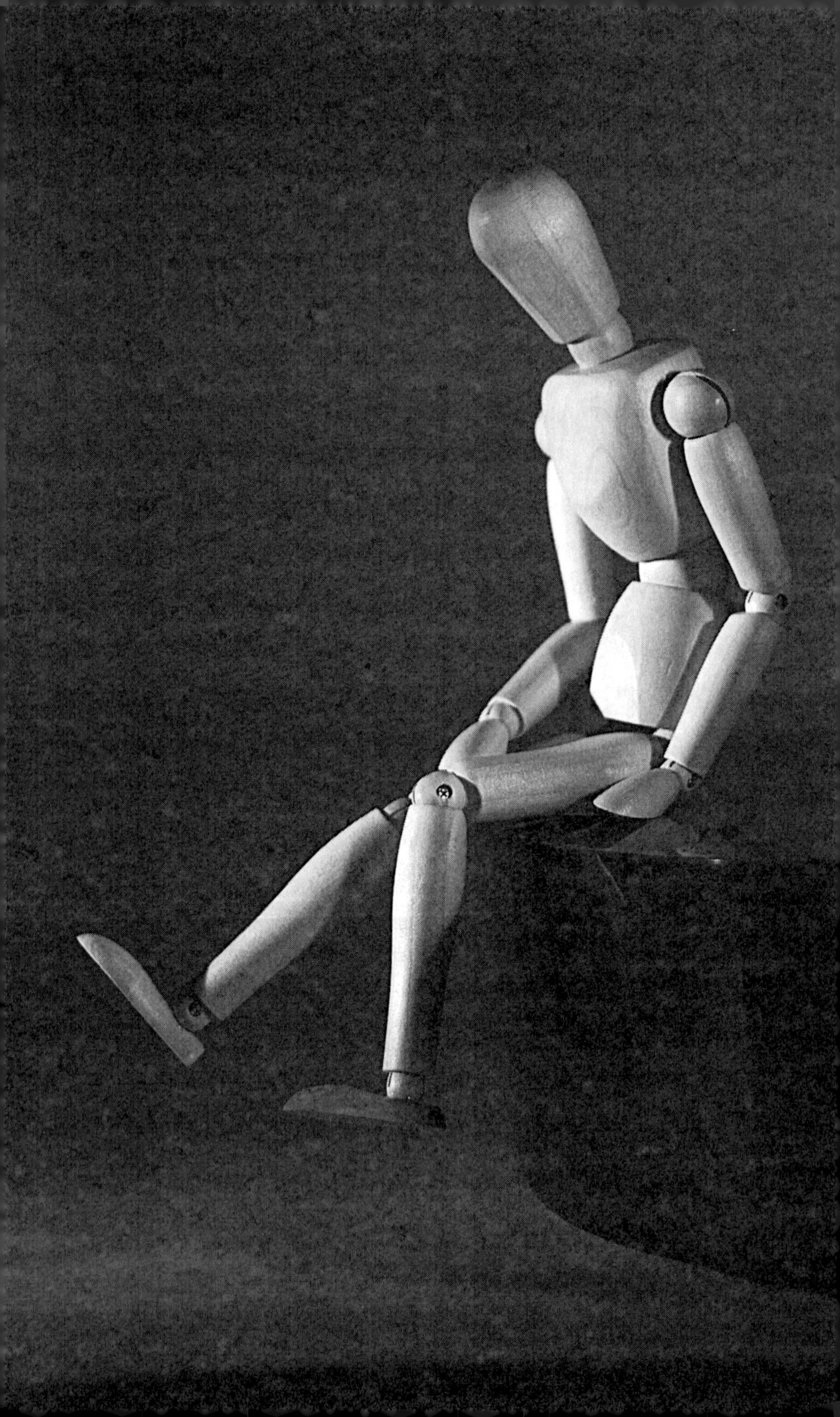

CHAPTER 1

IS ADVERTISING AS GUILTY AS IT IS MADE OUT TO BE?

What really decides consumers to buy or not to buy is the content of your advertising, not its form.

David Ogilvy

Advertisements have made us smile, cry, introspect and question at different times. Some ads remain in our memory for years, for both good and bad reasons. We have often wondered how a 30- or 60-second ad makes us buy something we did not need, or changed our mind on an issue, making us feel good about it! Those who like advertising feel that ad space is the only 'happy' space amidst the discordance and cacophony attached to news and entertainment programmes appearing on various media vehicles. Advertising is a multi-billion industry that moves both the markets and the minds. Six large, mostly Western conglomerates control more than 75 per cent advertising globally. Change, as they say, is the only constant but surprisingly the basic crux of advertising has not really changed over a period of time, despite that everything else around us has changed so drastically. Even now, ads almost always showcase people who are attractive, good-looking with perfect bodies and, of course, successful, making it aspirational for the viewers.

Advertising is a mediated phenomenon that needs a medium to carry it, like newspapers, radio, television, digital space, outdoor medium, etc. We do not buy newspaper to read ads or switch on radio or television to watch ads, but by default or design, we end up getting attracted to at least some of them. At the same time, it is also not uncommon for us to zap channels when ads appear in a programme or flip pages of newspapers and magazines to avoid ads, which are often seen as irritants and unavoidable disturbances. Some premium paid television channels now publicize 'ad-free' movies and programmes as their unique selling proposition to attract subscribers to their channels.

In order to attract the attention of the discerning viewer, the creative teams in the ad agencies and media-planning experts use many strategies to catch our attention, which include the use of various appeals, attractive imagery and media innovations. As ads jostle between news items and entertainment programmes, among the many tactics that the advertisers have often used, two are making use of the female form to attract men and male gaze, as many empirical studies point out. Women find place even in ads for brands for which they may not even be direct consumers.

ADVERTISING THROUGH THE LENS OF FEMINISM

The feminist thought in the 1960s, in retrospect, drew attention to the representation of women in media and called for a systematic investigation into the area of female role stereotypes in popular media. Particularly, it was suggested that advertising in popular media was a primary means for introducing and promoting female-role stereotypes and sexism, calling attention to a systematic investigation into this area. Scholars believe that whereas the 1960s and the 1970s largely experienced development of the feminist perspective, the 1980s and the 1990s coincided with the emergence of a viewpoint that gradually weakened the arguments of feminist thought. During the 1990s, issues of 'sexuality' rather than 'gender' became the focus of discourse and debate. During this period, sexual imagery of women was viewed as radical and cutting-edge rather than unfair and exploitative. Researchers, in order to examine such role portrayals in these studies, have applied content analysis methodology frequently.

Research in different countries and at various points of time is reflective of the exclusive and gender-insensitive nature of societies. Scholars believe that it is inevitable because, in general, social thoughts like philosophy, history, science or even theory are also gender insensitive, which has a concomitant impact on the policies as well as on governance and dispensation of justice. Media, a part of the social milieu, too, remains largely gender insensitive in its approach and narrative. Advertising, as a marketing tool, draws its references from various persuasive theories that look for appeals and symbols that largely cater to men and male gaze.

Advertising is criticized for voyeurism, misogyny, objectification of women's body and for following a patriarchal approach in its discourse. In order to better understand the issue of portrayal, let us operationalize feminism, voyeurism, misogyny, objectification and patriarchy to make a start.

Feminism means different things to different people. Often, it is used as a pejorative term against women who reflect their mettle and do not shy away from speaking their mind. In the beginning, the word feminism was used to mean, 'What related to females,' but it is believed that in 1837, radical French philosopher Charles Fourier coined the expression *féminisme* in his writing to make a link between women's status and social progress. 'Liberty, unless enjoyed by all, is unreal and illusory,' he said (Biroglu, 2018). Feminism, as has come to be broadly accepted, is a series of various movements—social, political and economic—that aim to achieve equality of sexes, including equal opportunities for women along with men to education and work (Offen, 1988).

Voyeurism is described as seeking pleasure from secretly watching other people in a sexual situation or more generally watching other people's private lives.[1]

Misogyny is described as the feeling of hatred or strong dislike for women or prejudice against them. A misogynist is seen as anti-feminist, male chauvinist, male supremacist, sexist, etc.

Objectification posits treating people like tools or inanimate objects devoid of feeling, opinion or rights of their own. Advertising, across cultures, is criticized for using women as props and objects to attract attention.

Patriarchy literally means 'rule by the father'. In patriarchal societies, women are expected to play subservient roles to males, including father, husband and sons. In other words, being under the patronage of the male members of the household. The second wave of feminism posited patriarchy as a social, more than a biological, phenomenon.

OBJECTIFICATION: WOMEN AS MERE PROPS

Objectification is a notion central to the feminist theory. It posits treating a person, usually a woman, as an object, the focus being primarily on sexual objectification. Critics believe that the feminist literature of the 20th century and later was hugely influenced by Immanuel Kant's work on sexuality and objectification. Objectification, for Kant, involved the lowering of a person, that is, a being with humanity, to the status of an object. He argued that when a woman was seen as an object of enjoyment in sexual relations, the object was of no use once that enjoyment was over. In this way, the loved person tends to lose what was special to her as a human being—her humanity, and is reduced to a thing, a mere sexual instrument. Kant's notion of objectification, therefore, focused largely on instrumentality: the treatment of a person, as Herman puts it, as a mere tool for the lover's purposes. Objectification, for Kant, involved regarding someone 'as an object, something for use'. (Herman, 1993). When women in general are included in ads not as protagonists for the brand but merely as props only to attract attention or when their body form is compared with objects, they stand objectified as sex objects—vulnerable, submissive and dependent.

Objectification, sexualization and patriarchy loom large in advertising across societies. The citation of two ads that appeared within a time gap of 50 years would prove the point that not much has changed in the ad discourse, despite so much hue and cry on gender equity and sensitivity. A dramatic ad in 1972 from Geritol, a vitamin supplement brand, had a middle-aged, good-looking man showering praises on his wife, who with a huge grin was shown leaning on his shoulder. He praised her on how she looked after the household, took care of their child with perfection and cooked excellent dinner among other chores. All this he ascribed to the energy that she had by taking the supplement. 'And look at her,' he stressed, 'She looks better than any of her friends.' Looking back at the camera, he closes, 'My wife, I think I'll keep her.' The ad drew huge criticism from various sections of society. The National Organization for Women wanted nothing short of pulling off the ad from airways (Cramer, 2020).

To underscore the argument that things have not much changed, recently an ad by KFC that sexualized the narrative attracted so much backlash on the social media that the fast-food giant had to withdraw the ad. In the ad, a young lady in a low-cut blouse was shown compressing her lips and pushing her upper torso as she checked her image in a car window. While she did it, the car glasses rolled down reflecting two young boys ogling at her, much to the discomfiture of their mother. The young lady grinned, asking 'Did someone say KFC?' (Cramer, 2020) Interestingly, in India, the TVS Scooty ad has the same storyline and sequence as in the KFC ad discussed before. The only difference is that in the car, it is a man ogling at the protagonist, while his hapless wife looks on. The ad went on famously running the whole campaign, without much criticism. This is one of the many ads analysed for a research by Indian Council of Social Science Research (ICSSR) on portrayal of women by one of the authors which will be discussed later.

WOMAN IN ANCIENT INDIAN LITERATURE

Indian society reflects a very complex picture of womanhood. There are examples of great, emancipated women in ancient Indian history. For instance, Gargi, believed to be born around 700 BCE, is said to be a philosopher of great intellect who was highly knowledgeable in the Vedas and the Upanishads. She is believed to have participated in intellectual debates with other philosophers. Maitreyi, born in the 8th century BC, is cited as another example of the educational opportunities available to women in the Vedic period and their philosophical achievements. She is often referred to as the precursor of the Indian intellectual women. Both Gargi and Maitreyi have colleges named after them at the University of Delhi.

A general study of various religious scriptures, however, reflects the conflicting status of women. If the Vedas say that feminine energy is the ultimate source of energy and creator of matter in the universe, the Manusmriti belittles women in more than one way and expects that 'as a girl, she should obey and seek protection of her father, as a young woman her husband, and as a widow her son' (Olivelle, 2005).

The Manusmriti, also known as Manav Dharam Shastra, is the earliest metrical work on Brahminical dharma in Hinduism. A couple of quotes on women given below will reflect the status accorded to them:

> *Swabhavevnarinam* ...' – 2/213. It is the nature of women to seduce men in this world; for that reason, the wise are never unguarded in the company of females.
>
> *Avidvamsamlam* ...' – 2/214. Women, true to their class character, are capable of leading astray men in this world, not only a fool but also even a learned and wise man. Both become slaves of desire. (Buhler, n.d.)

Decoding what is reflected above, it can be argued that a woman is seen not only as an object of desire, but also as the seducer, a cause of man's downfall. If a man gets attracted to woman and is led astray, it is because of her 'class character'.

The Rig Veda, on the other side, contains hymns composed by as many as 27 *brahmavadinis* or women seers including Gosha, Godha, Vishwavara and Apala.[2] The philosophical realization respecting women in such ancient times, feel some analysts, was unparalleled in the history of the world (Chaudhuri, as cited in Devi & Subrahmanyam, 2014).

Western scholars Rita Gross and Cynthia Humes in the book *Is the Goddess a Feminist? The Politics of South Asian Goddesses* comment on the ancient- and medieval-era Hindu texts and epics that discuss a woman's position and role in society over a spectrum, such as one who is a self-sufficient, marriage-eschewing powerful goddess, to one who is subordinate and whose identity is defined by men rather than her and to one who sees herself as a human being and spiritual person while being neither feminine nor masculine (Gross, 2000; Humes, 2000).

Critics believe that Indian advertising has failed to reflect the social shift witnessed in modern times. It has not adequately reflected the reality of women coming out of their closet, being financially independent and taking on the world. Some brands have tried, but a lot remains to be done. Advertising invariably tells women how they are supposed to look and behave in order to be acceptable. It is a common practice to brush female images to make them look perfect and use other image manipulation techniques that have come with spurt in computer technology. The commercial nature of ad messages to attract the discerning media consumer most of the time, however, results in eroticization of the female body. 'Women on View: Aesthetics and Desire in Advertising', an exhibition in Berlin in 2019, aimed at examining how the female form has been used in advertising for decades. The exhibition featured photos by some of the best names in fashion and commercial photography to bring home the reality about the 'eroticization of the female body in western advertising' being commonplace (Welle, n.d.).

It is also commonplace in advertisements to find women portrayed as inferior to men in status, intelligence and social hierarchy. Proponents of advertising generally argue that advertising only mirrors society and presents a 'slice of life' to attract the target audience.

There is no denying that the advertising narrative has the additional ubiquitous burden of brand promotion. Advertising, an essential part of marketing, generally aims at persuading the potential consumer to buy a particular brand or service. To this effect, advertisers use all kinds of strategies or tactics in textual and visual narrative to attract the attention of the average flippant media consumer.

Is Indian Advertising Patriarchal in Its Narrative?

Anyone who observes ads notoriously jumping to our screens or flashed on papers would wonder if Indian advertising reinforces stereotypes about women, objectifies them and inappropriately portrays them. Are there any specific brands that are notorious for doing this? More importantly, who and what kind of people would want to write and create such imageries? Advertising, seen as a glam profession, generally attracts young, urban, educated men and women, who are expected to be aware of the issues and controversies surrounding advertisements; why then they go on creating stereotypes and objectify women in ads after ads?

To answer all the above, one needs to understand that creative writers and visualizers are born and live in the same milieu as the rest of the people. They absorb, assimilate and practice within the same social environment; hence, what they write and project cannot be different from what their understanding of the subject is. Women continue to be judged and portrayed, as they are perceived and treated in real life. And importantly, it is not just men who are behind such portrayals. Any ad agency's creative team consists of many members including women too (although in less number). So, it can be posited that it is not a man or a woman but the mindset of an average creative person in a patriarchal milieu.

However, things are surely changing, albeit slowly, and there are many examples to cite. For instance, in a recent ad of Parle 20-20 biscuit brand, in which a young girl and her parents are shown shopping at an apparel store, the girl tries a short dress and asks her mother how it looked. While the mother nods approvingly, the young father sitting at a distance says, '*Kuchch jyada hi chotti nahin hai*' (Isn't it far too short?), to which his wife quips, '*Chhoti dress nahin, chotti soch hoti hai*' (it is not the dress, it is the thinking that is small!), or the Hero Honda ad, 'Why should boys have all the fun,' with cine star Priyanka Chopra as its protagonist. In one of the ads in the series, the protagonist questions the different sets of rules for her and her brother. While she takes her own call, the mother follows the patriarchal narrative. Teaching young children about gender is important, so that they do not fall prey to stereotypes about boys and girls. There is this interesting ad from Colgate toothpaste that shows young boys who are not ready to include the girl in the game on the pretext that if she hurts herself, she would cry. To this, the girl quips, '*Mere girne ki fikr hai ya aapne haarne ki?*' (Are you worried about me falling down or you losing out against me?) There is yet another interesting narrative in the All Out brand's #StandByToughMoms ad that has a benevolent patriarch who stands by his young daughter-in-law when she refuses to give food to her young son at the dining table because he had stolen money from his father's wallet. She becomes an object of ridicule by all, some half a dozen men and women in a joint family set-up, including her own husband, until the patriarch says that the boy had not taken the money but stolen it. Admonishing those who were critical of the mother, he said that if he were in his daughter-in-law's place, he would not have fed him for two days.

When the patriarch spoke with authority, everyone went silent at once, including his own wife and son, the young boy's father. It can be argued that patriarchy may not always be reflected as 'rigorous, dominating, oppressive, exploitative, marginalizing and subjugating women'; it can also be 'benevolent and understanding.' As Soman (2009) puts it, patriarchy, though deeply rooted in the society, operates as a 'set of loose guidelines as habitus, leaving room for improvisation and innovation on the basis of the capital and associated power acquired by women.'[3]

PARADIGM SHIFT IN AD NARRATIVE IN THE 1990S

It is generally argued that Indian advertising has undergone a huge transformation, especially when we compare the ads of the pre-liberalization era to those of the post-liberalization era (i.e., after 1991). Stereotyping of women has always been there when we look at the ads made in pre- and post-Independence times, until the 1980s, but the portrayal, often, was not indecent or offensive. A new phenomenon witnessed in the liberalized economy has been the provocative and bold imagery of women in ads of various brand categories. The reason proffered is the coming of global agencies that used the global concept with some customization, resulting in explicit show of cleavage and bold imagery, what otherwise explains a huge public outrage against the ads that objectified women at various points of time. In 1995, a black-and-white ad in which super models Milind Soman and Madhu Sapre wrapped by a python, wearing nothing but a pair of Tuff shoes, became a talking point on the changing standards of narrative in advertising. The court case, invoking the 1986 Act on the Indecent Representation of Women, went on for decades. In another ad, television star and model Sana Khan was featured in a racy commercial, wherein she was shown washing a man's underwear while making sexual innuendos. The Lux Cozi ad 'Aapna luck pehanke chalo' (wear your lucky charm) was equally sleazy; it showed a woman being drawn to a man wearing

Lux Cozi, standing near a swimming pool. In the 2010 Fastrack ads for bags and accessories, superstar cricketer Virat Kohli and cine star Genelia D'Souza were seen getting intimate in a series of three ads. The brief from the client to Lowe's, the agency that created the campaign, was to 'keep it cheeky and flirtatious' (Das, 2010). It is here that the brand owners, the large corporate organizations, play a key role in deciding what the ads would be like. In a Switzerland-based company CALIDA's ad, model and actor Dino Morea was seen pulling off cine star Bipasha Basu's underwear with his teeth. The ad was eventually banned after several women organizations raised their voice against it. As quoted in the media, Bipasha later claimed that those were some private moments that were not meant to be photographed and used' (Jha, 2020). Ford Motor Company was forced to apologize for an ad that was tag-lined, 'Leave your worries behind with Figo's extra-large boot,' featuring a caricature of three women tied in the rear of a vehicle driven by Silvio Berlusconi, the former Italian prime minister (Lyman, 2013). Various brands of deodorant ads, in general, have put women in a bad light. For instance, the Set Wet Zatak and Wild Stone deodorant ads (2011) showed women lusting over a man who had used the said deodorant. The Ministry of Information and Broadcasting (I&B) found the ad 'indecent, vulgar and suggestive'. The Advertising Standards Council of India (ASCI) was directed to ensure that the advertisement was modified or taken off the air (Irani, 2011). Canadian adult film star Sunny Leone's condom ads in India have always drawn sharp criticism and uproar for being sexually provocative and sensual. Her ad for Manforce condom was reoriented after a public outrage against the ad (Ganguly, 2017). The digital version, however, continues to be steamy. Another advertisement by Leone that was released before a Hindu festival fuelled public's anger for its slogan 'Play with love this Navratri'. Indian authorities, as reported by the media, pulled out many billboards carrying the ad, which was thereafter withdrawn (Brand Equity, 2017). Levi's ad 'Live unbuttoned', essayed by cine actor Akshay Kumar that was followed by a ramp show, wherein his wife unbuttoned his jeans, ended up in litigation for its alleged indecency and bad taste. In retrospect, the 1990s KamaSutra condom ad that had cine stars Pooja Bedi and Dino Morea in a sensual sequence initiated a discussion on inappropriate ads in the Indian Parliament. Defending the ad in his biography, *A Double Life*, the late Alyque Padamsee, often called 'god' by his admirers, argued that the ad was tastefully filmed, without even once mentioning the words sex or condom (Padamsee, 2000). Here, it is important to keep in mind that condom advertising (especially after the Nirodh days, which positioned condom for family planning/population control) has always worked on the enjoyment aspect, which the creative teams defend, and is often based on consumer insights, through a rigorous research process before the ad narrative is finalized. There is no denying that there is a thin line in what is perceived as an 'indecent' act and the state of empowerment. A young woman out on a date carrying a condom in her wallet in the ad can be viewed as promiscuous portrayal versus one of empowerment, depending on where the argument is coming from.

SPACE FOR ALTERNATE NARRATIVE

Sexual liberation and, therefore, its portrayal could sometimes also be seen as how modern women wish to be seen and represented. Some recent films like *Lipstick under My Burkha*, *Parched* and some other Netflix movies seem to have started a new discourse on this aspect. Deepika Padukone's advocacy film *My Choice*, created by Homi Adajania, portrays a modern woman who wishes to be in control of her life and her choices, without being answerable to anyone. Sensual portrayal of women in commercial space can be seen by some as liberating and how there is a narrative for such a perspective within feminism itself. As far as condom and some other lifestyle ads are concerned, invariably the ads target men. The sensuality, therefore, needs to be read as playing into the idea of male fantasy that often ends up in objectifying women. From the advertisers' perspective, such portrayals reflect the modern woman who chooses to do what she wishes to; for critics, such ads belittle women and compromise their self-worth and dignity. There probably is no empirical data to suggest a positive or negative impact of provocative ads, especially those that courted controversy on the sale of the brand. However, in the case of the Amul Macho ad, it was claimed by the company that the controversy resulted in a huge surge in the sale of the brand.

THE QUINTESSENTIAL WOMAN IN THE INDIAN AD DISCOURSE

Is there a quintessential Indian man and woman in the ad discourse in India, we may ask. Chaudhuri (2017) argues that the mention of a typical Indian woman invokes set images, which are 'culturally loaded, filled with allusions'. In the entire process, which is exclusive and hegemonic, 'a specifically upper-caste gender norm has been imposed as the "Indian" norm.' The Indian woman was created to fit in as someone who is compassionate but not necessarily a central figure in the discourse. Man was created as the archetype upper-caste family patriarch, a rationalist, a social reformer, a nationalist with a scientific temper and a fierce culture revivalist with virtues of a Western imperial man (Chaudhuri, 2017, p. 93).

The last few years have witnessed many discussions and debates in both academic and non-academic circles over gender and the way it is portrayed in the media. The #MeToo movement in the US and, later, elsewhere, including India, has brought centre stage, the issue of sexual harassment of women at workplace as also the role of media in creating stereotypes and objectifying women. The argument also proffers that if media can create a certain kind of imagery, then it also has the power and the capability to create a positive narrative about women, based on reality. One has seen, of late, efforts on the part of some ad agencies in creating marquee campaigns to address gender perspective, termed 'femvertising'. The moot point, however, is whether the advertising industry as a whole is making strides towards improving the representation of women or is it only to respond to the heat of the moment to be politically correct; only time will tell. Critics believe that in India, the prevalence of femvertising is not yet sufficiently influencing entrenched gender inequities.

In the next chapter, we will map women's arduous journey throughout history to stepping up and advocating for their cause.

NOTES

1 https://dictionary.cambridge.org/dictionary/english/voyeurism

2 Brihaddevata 11.82–11.84: *Gkosa Godka Visvavara, Apalopanisan Nisat; Brakmajaya Jukur nama, Agastyasya svasaditik; Indrani cendramata ca Sarama Eomasorvasi; Lopamudra ca Nadyas ca Yarn! nm ca ^asvatl Srir Laksa Sarparajnl Vak Sraddka Medka ca Daksina; Eatri Surya ca Savitri krakmavadinya Iritak*. https://archive.org/stream/in.ernet.dli.2015.213298/2015.213298.Brihad-Devata_djvu.txt. Prahlad Kakkar, famous ad film maker, in a UNESCO–SWAN conference on Mainstreaming Gender in Media in 2016, referred to Manusmriti's misogynist text which he said found reflection in how women were treated in the society and reflected in the media discourse.

3 In the quoted text, 'habitus' means mental or cognitive structures through which people deal with the social world. https://quizlet.com/217382783/pierre-bordieu-flash-cards/

REFERENCES

Biroglu, E. (2018). *Who is the first feminist in the history?* Research Gate. https://www.researchgate.net/post/Who_is_the_first_feminist_in_the_history

Buhler, G. (Trans.). (n.d.). *Manusmriti: The laws of Manu* (pp. 11). https://www.islamawareness.net/Hinduism/manusmriti.pdf

Chaudhuri, M. (2017). *Refashioning India: Gender, media, and a transformed public discourse*. The Orient Blackswan.

Cramer, M. (2020, 1 February). In a long history of sexist ads and outrage, it's the apology that's new. *The New York Times*. https://www.nytimes.com/2020/02/01/business/media/kfc-commercial-sexist.html

Das, B. (2010, September 21). Moving on, on the fast track. *Afaqs*. https://www.afaqs.com/news/advertising/28311_moving-on-on-the-fast-track

Devi, N. J., & Subrahmanyam, K. (2014). Women in the Rig Vedic age. *International Journal of Yoga*, 2(1), 1–3. https://www.ijoyppp.org/article.asp?issn=2347-5633;year=2014;volume=2;issue=1;spage=1;epage=3;aulast=Devi

Ganguly, S. (2017). Manforce withdraws controversial condom hoardings from gujarat. *The Economic Times*. https://economictimes.indiatimes.com/industry/services/advertising/manforce-withdraws-controversial-condom-hoardings-fromgujarat/articleshow/60782165.cms?utm_source=contentofinterest&utm_medium=text&utm_campaig=%20cppst

Ganguly, S., & Bhushan, R. (2017, December 12). No child's play: Condom ads banned from 6 am to 10 pm in India. *ET Brand Equity*. https://brandequity.economictimes.indiatimes.com/news/advertising/no-childs-play-condom-ads-banned-from-6-am-to-10-pm-in-india/62031646

Gross, R., & Humes, C. (2000). Draupadi's question. In A. Hiltebeitel & K. M. Erndl's (Eds.), *Is the goddess a feminist? The politics of south Asian goddesses* (pp. 104–111). New York University Press.

Herman, D. (1993). Beyond the rights debate. *Social & Legal Studies*, 2, 25–43. https://plato.stanford.edu/entries/feminism-objectification/

Irani, D. (2011). Men's deo ads an aberration; Axe, wild stone, set wet faced ad council wrath. *The Economic Times*. https://economictimes.indiatimes.com/mens-deo-ads-an-aberration-axe-wild-stone-set-wet-faced-ad-council-wrath/articleshow/10235148.cms

Jha, S. (2020, March 21). When dino morea pulled bipasha basu's 'underwear' with his teeth and landed in trouble (throwback). *International Business Times*. https://www.ibtimes.co.in/when-dino-morea-pulled-bipasha-basus-underwear-his-teeth-landed-trouble-throwback-815607

Lyman, E. J. (2013, March 24). Ford apologizes for ad featuring bound-and-gagged women in berlusconi's trunk (updated). *The Hollywood Reporter*. https://www.hollywoodreporter.com/news/general-news/ford-apologizes-kardashian-hilton-ad-430628/

Offen, K. (1988). On the French origin of the words feminism and feminist. *Feminist Innuses*, *8*(2), 54–51.

Olivelle, P. (Ed.). (2005). *Manu's code of law: A critical edition and translation of the Manava-Dharmasastra* (pp. 98, 146 and 147). Oxford University Press.

Padamsee, A. (2000). *A double life: My exciting years in theater and advertising*. Penguin India.

Welle, D. (n.d.). Sex sells: Objectification of women in advertising. https://www.dw.com/en/sex-sells-the-objectification-of-women-in-advertising/a-47282358

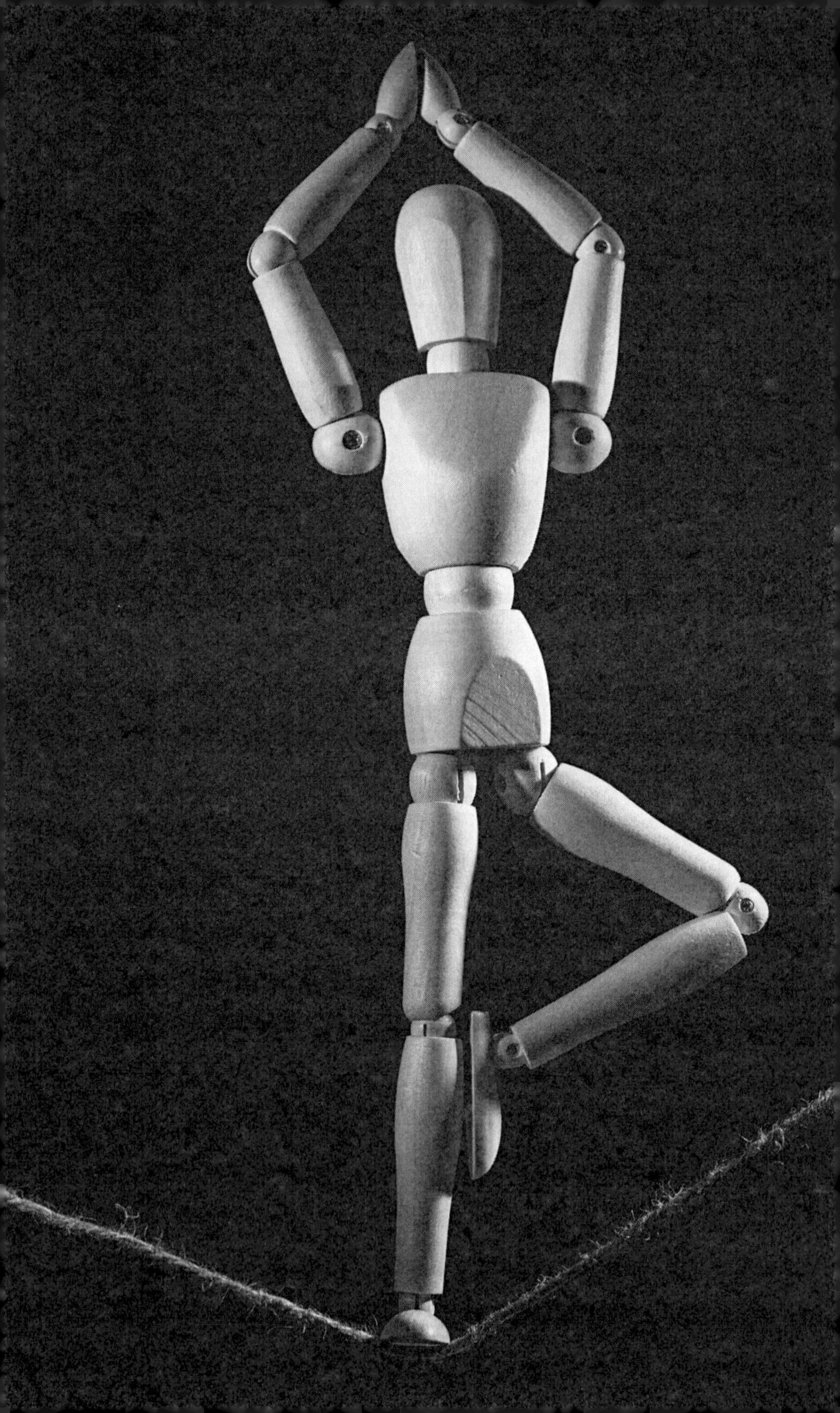

CHAPTER 2

WHAT WOMEN WANT?

The story of women's struggle for equality belongs to no single feminist nor any one organization but to the collective efforts of all who care about human rights.

Gloria Steinem

What Women Want is an interesting 2000 American romantic comedy film written by Josh Goldsmith et al., directed by Nancy Meyers, with Mel Gibson and Helen Hunt playing the protagonists. Gibson essaying the role of Nick Marshall, who by a freak accident, discovers that he has a new power which allows him to hear women's thoughts. And what does he do with this power? He goes on stealing the ideas of his accomplished women colleagues to sell as his own in the ad agency that he worked for. The film went on to be a revenue grosser, despite mixed reviews. Do men need that special power to read a woman's mind may be a difficult proposition to answer, but a literature review of a couple of centuries, especially penned by women writers and activists, reveals that a certain bias has existed against women on their capabilities, status and role within homes and in the public sphere. The inherent bias clearly has, over a period, given an idea to media writers, in general, on how women would be portrayed, especially in the entertainment and commercial space. Before we discuss the role of women in spearheading various movements that led to bringing the issue in the public domain, the role of social reformers and lawmakers and, later, international organizations in contributing to ensuring women some rights, a glimpse of some classic books and other literature would help us in getting a feel of what women have desired and the ignominy and barbs they suffered for speaking their mind on the rights of women.

By presenting women as objects of pleasure to attract the male gaze for commercial interests or due the age-old gender bias in a regressive patriarchal milieu, a whole narrative gets built up against them that does not seem to change, despite some efforts of late by a few to offset it. Writers and creative persons, therefore, need an exposure to literary and historical facts on the various movements to get sensitized on the issues taken up by women and their long and arduous journey to secure some rights and policy interventions in various countries. Creative writers, especially those engaged in popular culture storytelling, have a responsibility towards society as their writings affect mindsets. Any exposure to gender discourse would hopefully hone their critical faculties and widen their perspective.

RANDOM GLIMPSES OF FEMINIST LITERATURE

Mary Wollstonecraft

Way back in the 18th century, Mary Wollstonecraft in her essay *A Vindication of the Rights of Woman: With Strictures on Political and Moral Subjects* (1792)[1] talked about women issues when the word 'feminism' was not even coined. Her work is considered as pioneering in the feminist philosophy. Her views are said to be in response to the works of a number of educational and political theorists of the 18th century, particularly to Jean-Jacques Rousseau. It is believed that she wrote the essay after Charles Maurice de Talleyrand-Périgord submitted his report to the National French Assembly in 1791, which recommended that only domestic education should be imparted to a woman to enable her to become a better homemaker, a wife and a mother.

Wollstonecraft's basic argument revolves around the need for women to be educated in order to earn a position in the society. She argued that if women were educated, it would, in turn, shape their children's future, which was in the national interest. She wished that men took women as companions and not merely as wives. This, she said, would be possible only when women were literate to match the intellect of men. She considered education as a fundamental right that women deserved. Wollstonecraft's critics feel that she did a hurried job as a rejoinder to the report. She was expected to come up with the second version that was to be more articulate, but the task remained unfulfilled due to her demise.

In her argument, she questioned Rousseau's premise that women should be educated for the pleasure of men. Her counterargument was that education for women was meant to strengthen their body and mind.

Some of her critics questioned if her support for women's education can even be termed as a feminist ideology as she did not touch upon gender equality. Her later work, a fictionalized novel called *Maria*, is considered a better take on feminism when compared with her essay. Wollstonecraft directed her criticisms against the revolutionaries who did not acknowledge the right of political participation for women, the Constitution draft designed by them and the thinkers like Rousseau.

Whatever the argument of her critics, there is no denying that Wollstonecraft's work laid the foundation for later works in feminism and gave a direction to what feminism needed to include. Analysts believe that the very title of her essay, *A Vindication of the Rights of Women*, by its own reckoning, was feminist in letter and spirit. She articulated concepts such as reason, natural rights and contract in the context of women's rights, which were used by the thinkers of her age against the issues like church, religion, privileges, etc., in a way to question traditional assumptions about the nature of men and women (Duman, 2012).

Virginia Woolf

Another great crusader of women's rights is Virginia Woolf. Critics see her book *A Room of One's Own* (1929) as one of the pioneering works on feminism in the 20th century. Her work came between the two World Wars and the Great Economic Depression of 1929. Woolf was concerned about the lack of education among women and their dependence on men for economic reasons. In her book, she has quoted various literary and professional sources to express her disdain on how women were perceived as unintellectual and objectified. She has primarily looked at women from the perspective of their literary accomplishments or lack of it and how women were projected in the literature per se. When Woolf talked about *A Room of One's Own*, what she had in her mind was the privacy and freedom a woman must have to be expressive about her life. She exhorted women to be expressive about their life, howsoever good or mean it might be. Unlike men, she argued, women lost the chance to attain greatness in literature as writers because they did not get equal opportunities.

In the book, she brought in a fictitious character named Mary, who visited the British Museum to find out what had been written about women over the period. Virginia Woolf built a strong argument that both history and literature have been male constructs, which have traditionally marginalized women.

In *A Room of One's Own*, Woolf talked about Shakespeare's sister Judith—a fictional character—who was equal to Shakespeare in talent and in genius, but whose legacy was radically different. This imaginary woman never wrote a word and died by her own genius left unexpressed. Her book's last paragraph sums it all:

> As far her coming without that preparation, that when she is born again she shall find it possible to live and write her poetry, that we cannot expect, for that would be impossible. But I maintain that she would come, if we worked for her and that so to work even in poverty and obscurity, is worth a while. (Woolf, 1929)

Simone de Beauvoir

Simone de Beauvoir's book *The Second Sex* (1949) commences with two quotations, which reflect the basis of her argument in the book (Borde & Malovany-Chevallier, 2011).

There is a good principle that created order, light and man; and a bad principle that created chaos, darkness and woman.

—Pythagoras

Everything that has been written by men about women should be viewed with suspicion, because they are both judge and party.

—François Poullain de la Barre

The Second Sex, a well-researched seminal work by Simone de Beauvoir, is considered as one of its kind of feminist literature, an encyclopaedia that has left nothing to imagination, covering the folklore, customs, laws, history, religion and philosophy across many cultures as well as scriptures and personal interview by the author in two continents to understand the state of women. Simone's one sentence, 'One is not born a woman, one becomes one,' sums up her feminist philosophy in the larger context.

Simone influenced the later feminist movements in the West, but not many seemed to acknowledge her contribution to the extent that she always deserved. The translators in the introduction rightly say,

> While no one individual or her work is responsible for the seismic shift in laws and attitudes, the millions of young women who now confidently assume that their entitlement to work, pleasure and autonomy is equal to that of their brothers, owe a measure of their freedom to Beauvoir. (de Beauvoir, 1949)

Toril Moi, writing a review in the *Guardian* on Beauvoir's 100th birth anniversary in 2008, wrote that reading *The Second Sex* changed her life. Moi commented that Simone's analysis of sexism is, perhaps, the most powerful theoretical contribution to feminism. In a nutshell, Simone's thesis suggests helping women in their path to transcendence and subjectivity, which meant that women must go to work, they must pursue and participate in intellectual activity leading to change in their lives, and that they must strive to transform the society into a socialist society, seeking economic justice as a key factor in liberation (Moi, 2008).

Some of her ardent critics felt that what she wrote about the state of women seemed very different from her own personal experience. She met her life partner who was also her first love, the celebrated Jean-Paul Sartre, and remained with him until his end, but declined to marry him when he proposed to her. She had no children of her own, leading critics to comment that her idea about the relationship of a mother to her children bore no testimony to reality. The Vatican placed *The Second Sex* on the list of forbidden books (Francine Du Plessix, 2010).

Kate Millett

Kate Millett's book *Sexual Politics* (1969), based on her doctoral thesis, is considered an important addition to the feminist literature of the 20th century (Millett, 1969). Millett's thesis has posited that sex has a frequently rejected political aspect. She argues that patriarchy plays a vital role in sexual relations. Differentiating between sex and gender, Millett argued that sex is biological while gender is psychological and, hence, cultural. In the book, Millett has also covered major events and the state of women, analysing the writings of various writers including John Ruskin and Sigmund Freud. She also looks at the Nazi perception of women. Millett's core argument in the book is that women are helpless because men, through patriarchy, control the basic mechanism of society.

Some critics feel that Simone De Beauvoir's *The Second Sex* hugely influences Millett's work, which, however, was more intellectually engaging and emotionally invigorating than Millett's work (Rossi, 1997).

Historian Arthur Marwick described *Sexual Politics*, alongside Shulamith Firestone's *The Dialectic of Sex: The Case for Feminist Revolution* (1970), as one of the two key texts of radical feminism (Marwick, 1998).

Patricia T. Clough, however, opined that Millett's work is 'the first book of academic feminist literary criticism' (Clough, 1994).

Nancy Fraser

Nancy Fraser, another contemporary professor of philosophy and politics, has an interesting take on the evolution of feminism. She divides it in three stages (calling it Act), namely in the first Act, she argues that the feminists 'joined with other currents of radicalism to explode a social-democratic imaginary that had occulated gender injustice and technicized politics'. She posits that this phase was characterized by 'the personal is political', the movement exposing capitalism's deep androcentric stance, and sought to transform society root and branch. In the second Act, feminism, according to Fraser, was 'drawn into the orbit of identity politics'. During this phase, feminism's 'transformative impulses were channelled a new political imaginary that foregrounded "differences"'. At the start of Act three, 'reinvigorated feminism', is perceived to 'join other emancipatory forces aiming to subject runaway markets to democratic control', aiming at its structural critique of capitalism's androcentrism, its systematic analysis of male domination and its gender-sensitive revisions of democracy and justice. (Fraser, 2013).

TRACES OF FEMINISM: FROM COLONIALISM TO CONTEMPORARY INDIA

Scholars of feminist movement generally divide the history of feminism in India into three phases. The timeline, however, differs among various scholars. The first phase began in the mid-19th century, when some social reformers and the British colonists initiated a sort of social movement against certain evils that directly affected women. The issues taken up included child marriage, female infanticide and sati *pratha*, the burning of women on the funeral pyre of their husbands. Analysts believe that the first phase of feminism was spearheaded by the English-speaking elite Indian women. Of the many references available, Rokeya Sakhawat Hossain's work from 1905 titled 'Sulatana's Dream' is an important text that radically questions the normative gender roles and patriarchal structure (Hossain, 1905). In her short story, she one day wakes up from a dream to find that the society she knew had changed. Here, the normative is that women are out in the public, while the men were kept within the domain of the house. Not only that but all gender roles had been switched where women ruled the society. As she narrated her discussion with other women in the 'new' society, Hossain deconstructed the different layers of subjugation that women in a patriarchal society had to face.

Thanks to their efforts, organizations such as the All India Women's Conference, the Young Women's Christian Association and the Anjuman-I-Islam[2] were set up to engage with women from various sects and religions. Besides advocating for the women-suffrage issue that they took up with the authorities, these organizations also skilled women in many areas including stitching, baking and embroidering to become efficient home-makers. In this period, there were many other great political luminaries that include Kasturba Gandhi and Sarojini Naidu, who took leading part in the freedom struggle. Others including Tarabai, Ahilyabai Holkar, Razia Begum, Rani Durgavati and Rani Laxmibai were known for their remarkable contribution to the making of our nation. Some of the women who contributed in the upliftment of women include Ramabai Ranade, while in the political sphere, the roles of Sarojini Naidu, Vijaya Lakshmi Pandit and Indira Gandhi have been significant. We shall, in the following paragraphs, take a look at select women writers and feminists who set the tone for the future women's movements in India.

Savitribai Phule from Maharashtra is often remembered as the first true feminist in India. Along with her husband Jyotirao Govindrao Phule, she did pioneering work on women's emancipation, which included improving the plight of widows. She is said to have organized a barbers' strike to bring into focus the shaving of heads of the widows. Savitribai began teaching at an early age of 17, and in 1848, the Phules' set up their first school in India for women at Bhide Wada in Pune. Many more schools followed which brought young girls from oppressed families to get education. The government renamed the University of Pune as Savitribai Phule Pune University in her honour in 2014 (India Resists, 2017).

Kamini Roy—born to an elite father who was a judge, a writer and a leading Brahmo Samaj leader—was the first graduate among Indian women during the British period. A well-known poetess, writer, reformist and feminist, Roy fought for women's suffrage along with others in 1921. In one of her essays in Bengali titled 'The Fruit of the Tree of Knowledge', she wrote about male psychology thus: 'The male desire to rule is the primary, if not the only, stumbling block to women's enlightenment... They are extremely suspicious of women's emancipation. Why? The same old fear – 'Lest they become like us.'[3] Jasveen Kaur Sarna, in her essay 'Kamini Roy: Poet, Teacher and the First Woman Honours Graduate in British India' (2017), writes that in 1921, Roy formed the Bangiya Nari Samaj with Kumudini Mitra and Mrinalini Sen to fight for suffrage and women's liberation. The group comprised elite educated women, all from Brahmo background. Roy was later inducted as a member of the Female Labour Investigation Commission from 1922 to 1923, which worked with the government to oversee the conditions of women (Sarna, 2017).

Girijabai Kelkar, 1886–1980, was a Marathi writer, a feminist, married into an illustrious family of Maharashtra. Encouraged by her husband, she educated herself after marriage and soon became a prolific writer of Marathi literature as well as a playwright. Her play *Purushanche Banda* brought into focus the issues pertaining to women's plight. She is said to have funded

Bhagini Mandal, a women's organization in Jalgaon. She also had the distinction of becoming the president of the All India Hindu Mahila Parishad in 1935 (Anagol, 2006).

Mahadevi Varma (1907–1987) is rightfully considered as one of the tallest literary figures and women's rights activist. Her intellectual and literary prowess earned her the laurel of being one of the four pillars—along with her contemporaries Suryakant Tripathi 'Nirala', Jaishankar Prasad and Sumitranandan Pant—of the great Romantic movement in modern Hindi poetry, known as Chayavad. Besides her immense work in empowering women in the last century, she funded the Prayag Mahila Vidyapeeth to promote education of girls. Of her four-prose works, *Shrinkhala Ki Kadiyan,* which deals with the plight of Indian women, there is an interesting narrative, which reads:

> The day the Indian woman awakes with her full vitality, it would be impossible for anyone to restrict her dynamicity anymore. It is true in the context of her rights that neither she could get it through begging nor she would ever achieve it mere through pleadings for these (her rights) are quite different from objects and commodities to be exchanged. (Verma, 1944)

Mahadevi, according to various analysts of her life and works, was well aware of the fact that for struggle/resistance, 'power' and 'conscience' were needed. She said, 'Our rights shall be relative to our powers and conscience.' Professor Manager Pandey, a renowned critic, writer and professor of Hindi literature, in an article titled 'Shrinkhala Ki Kadiyan: Mukti Ki Raahein', while analysing Mahadevi's essay and some other writings, commented, 'in the Hindu social system woman neither have an independent identity nor an independent personality. It is her relation with a man that gives her a personality, defines her identity and provides her personality a meaning.' He quotes Mahadevi Varma to prove his point:

> As a man pets colourful birds for his entertainment, keeps a cow or a horse for his use in the same manner he takes a woman and thinks, like his tamed birds and animals he has a right over the body of the woman too. (Yadav & Tripathi, 2017)

In the early 20th century, Mahatma Gandhi's entry into the Indian freedom struggle saw the entry of women in active politics, which is taken as the second phase of feminist movement in India. Women were encouraged to participate in the freedom struggle (Kumar, 1998). The pre-Independence period also saw Subhash Chandra Bose inducting women in the Azad Hind Fauj.

Partha Chatterjee (1989), in his essay 'Nationalism, Colonialism, and Colonised Women: The Contest in India', maps out the nature in which the question of women was put forth during the nationalist movement. He argues that for the nationalist, there was a need for establishing their superiority over the West. However, the West had already established their superiority in the material domain, and therefore, the nationalist exerted in the realm of spiritual domain. He argues that, therefore, for the nationalist, 'what was necessary was to cultivate the material techniques of modern Western civilization while retaining and strengthening the distinctive spiritual essence of the national culture'. During such times, many nationalist writers saw the rapid Westernization of Bengali women. It was especially the middle-class men who voiced their concern over how such a process of Westernization threatened the institution of home and family. It is in such a context that Chatterjee argues the development of a new narrative on the 'new' Indian women, who had been cast as the protector of the home, and thereby, the spiritual domain of the nationalist project began to be discussed.

The third phase, which began post-Independence of India, focused on the fair treatment of women at home and workplace. The real spurt to women issues, it is believed, was seen in the 1970s, when educated women looked for jobs in the government, schools, colleges, hospitals and industry. These women were the first generation born after the attainment of Independence in 1947. More and more girls, especially in cities, were seen joining higher education and professions such as law, medicine and engineering, besides competing in the civil services examinations. Kiran Bedi received a lot of media attention for being the first woman in free India to join the Indian police force.

Newspapers, in general, post-Emergency wrote extensively on rights-based subjects including issues relating to women. During this time, Ashwini Sarin, a young journalist from the *Indian Express* newspaper created a kind of journalist coup when he 'purchased' a woman by the name Kamla for a small amount to bring home the issue of trafficking of women for flesh trade on the Morena–Agra and Manipuri–Etah circuits. Late S. Nihal Singh, the then editor-in-chief, said,

> Nothing was done by the authorities to check this organized crime spread over three states. Kamla is the symbol of slavery still prevalent in that area. Our action was the only effective way to tell our readers what was happening around them and that something must be done to get rid of the evil. (Gupta, 2013)

Economic independence was considered by women's rights advocates as an imperative to liberate women from dependence on their menfolk and would bring self-dignity and progress in their lives.

POLICY FRAMEWORK WELCOMES WOMEN CAUSE

The 1970s saw the rise of trade unionism and advocacy movements for civil liberties, especially after the clamping of Emergency by Mrs Indira Gandhi in 1975. Further, in 1974, a document was prepared on the 'status of women' by the official Status of Women Commission, titled *Towards Equality*. It focused attention on the fact that, despite many progressive social legislations and constitutional guarantees, women's status in India had indeed not improved much, especially in many areas like political, economic and social spheres. This document has been the basis for many legislations and development programmes focusing on gender as well as creation of women's organizations and working groups—as discussed later. The United Nations (UN) declared 1975 as the International Year for Women and 8 March as the International Day for Women.

The last 70+ years of Independence has seen many organizations springing up that have espoused the cause of women, both in the cities and at grassroots level. Domestic violence, alcoholism, female feticide, sexual harassment of women at workplace, skewed and unjust family laws, reproductive rights, legislative reforms are some of the issues spearheaded by civil society organizations and non-governmental organizations (NGOs). On the academic front, many universities in the 1970s set up women's studies centres. A pioneer in women's studies, Dr Vina Mazumdar, was the first one in the Independent India to combine activism with scholarly research in women's studies. Vina Mazumdar (1994) argues that women became a point of engagement in politics as well as research and academia during the colonial rule with an objective to both justify social reform and give a backbone for India's cultural pride. She writes that, this however, became redundant in post-Independent India, as the need for justification was no longer necessary. This may have, in some way, led to the sidelining of women's issue and with that the increase in gender disparity between men and women (Mazumdar, 1994).This gap was highlighted in the investigation by the Committee on the Status of Women in India and the subsequent report *Towards Equality* 1975. With this, a new agenda was set to change the status of women, and for that research on women's issue was one area which received the impetus (Mazumdar, 1994). A new programme for women's studies, initiated by the ICSSR, began which, over the years, has seen a lot of seminal work in this arena. This went along with several other processes of bringing about change and empowerment as the larger women's movement also went along. Critics, however, feel that in the beginning, there was a lot of academia–civil society interface, which, over the years, has eroded.

Many UN organizations like the United Nations Children's Fund (UNICEF), United Nations Fund for Population Activities and United Nations Educational, Scientific and Cultural Organization (UNESCO) have also entered the policy dialogue with the government based on milestones articulated in the UN Sustainable Development Goals (SGDs) of which India is a signatory.

EQUAL RIGHTS AND OPPORTUNITIES GUARANTEED BY CONSTITUTION OF INDIA

The Constitution of India provides equal status and opportunities to women along with men. The Indian women received equal political rights for which their Western counterparts had to fight a long battle.

Women-centric Laws

Since the country's Independence in 1947, many laws have been passed to address the issues of equal opportunities for women at workplace and home to address issues of sexual harassment at workplace, domestic violence, dowry, female infanticide and feticide, and property rights among others. Discrimination, however, is so well entrenched in the patriarchal mindset of the society, coupled with ignorance and centuries of subjugation that both the urban and the rural women endure (particularly, the latter, as they suffer in larger measure in every possible way) when it comes to equality. Women, especially in the rural arena, are raped and wronged to settle caste rivalries. Young women choosing to wed out of caste and religion often become victims of honour killing. Who they can marry, what they would wear, how they would behave are issues sometimes discussed in the illegal Khap panchayats, while the state administration is often seen as a mute spectator.

The passing of the two acts, namely Sexual Harassment of Women at Workplace (Prohibition) Act 2013, and the Indecent Representation of Women (Prohibition) Act, 1986, together with many other Acts, including against those against domestic violence, dowry and sex determination as well as the setting up of the National Commission for Women at the centre and other state-level commissions, are pointers to the efforts by myriad women's right organizations in influencing policy and also various governments in addressing women issues.

Having said that, there is no gainsaying that there are laws in place, but it is the implementation which is more often lax. Social transformation accompanied with implementation of laws shall be the key to address women-related issues in India. The feminist literature and movements bear testimony to the fact that feminism is very much home grown and organic in India and not a copy of the West, as is generally alleged. The feminist movement is not against men but about fighting the power structures that are so well embedded in the familial, social, political and economic spheres.

Women Advocacy

Advocates of women rights have come to be known by various nomenclatures, depending on their ideology and what they believe in. For instance, those who believe that women-centric policies and laws would change the lot of women are known as Liberal feminist; those who believe that men are responsible for women's state are known as Radical feminists and those who believe that women's oppression is because of the overall socio-economic and cultural ecosystem are referred as Social feminists. They see building linkages and networking with various groups and mass-based organizations and trade unions as the possible way to mainstreaming women issues and finding solutions (Patel & Khajuria, 2016).

CONTEMPORARY VOICES ON FEMINISM

There are many women in the contemporary India both in cities and grassroots level, in academia, publishing and media who have contributed immensely in keeping the issue in focus. While it is not possible to write about all of them, in the following paragraphs, two such activists are introduced.

Kamla Bhasin, one of the contemporary voices of feminism in India, is a developmental feminist activist, poet, author and social scientist. Bhasin's work focuses on gender, education, human development and media. She briefly taught at a university in Germany and worked in the UN, from where she resigned in 2002 to work full time in her NGO—Sangat. She has relentlessly worked for the emancipation of marginalized communities and tribal women.

Bhasin has written several books and brochures on patriarchy and gender, which have been translated into several regional languages. Her compositions have been used by NGOs to help people understand gender issues. Her book *Laughing Matters*, which she co-authored with Bindia Thapar, also has a Hindi version (*Hasna Toh Sangharshon Mein Bhi Zaroori Hai)*. Her other publications include *Feminism and Its Relevance in South Asia*, *Borders & Boundaries: Women in India's Partition*, *Understanding Gender* and *What Is Patriarchy?*

She has been an integral part of the One Billion Rising movement in South Asia. On one of the occasions of One Billion Rising, organized by the UN in 2016 in Delhi, Bhasin said that feminism in India is not borrowed from the Western concept but is local. She further said that the issues around which feminism in India revolved for the last couple of centuries include sati *pratha*, plight of widows, dowry, foeticide and unequal opportunities for women in education and workplace.[4]

Urvashi Butalia, another Indian feminist writer and academic, has done enormous seminal work in the sphere. Her books and publishing house, first, Kali for Women which she founded with Ritu Menon and, later, Zubaan bear testimony to that. Her book *The Other Side of Silence* (1998) recounts the stories of 70 survivors of the Partition. It emphasizes the role of violence against women in the collective experience of tragedy (Bahuguna, 2019).

Maitrayee Chaudhuri (2017, pp.83–84), professor of sociology, argues that the shift in India's economic policies in favour of globalization has 'accompanied a shift in public discourse as evidenced in the media'. The ads, she writes, effectively and implicitly 'eclipse the image of 'another world' of Indian men and women-poor and battered, tribal and peasant, working class and Dalit from public discourse' (Chaudhuri, 2017). Chaudhuri argument is valid from the sociological perspective, but as the ads often cater to only those who have the purchasing power, so the poor and marginalized are not on the marketer's wish list. By creating a world of 'make believe', the ads do eclipse the stark reality prevalent in the society. Occasionally, however, one does find inclusion of the marginalized in the so-called corporate social responsibility ads by the corporate houses that, in a way, take away the last vestiges of human dignity from those on the fringes. Similarly, the political ads around the election time portray political parties embracing the poor and marginalized in the narrative, but only till the elections lasts.

How do the Indian advertisements fit into the prevailing culture, religious and societal ethos of the country is generally an issue of debate. While there are no straightjacketed answers to that, but it is a fact that advertising draws a lot of dissension not only from women in general but also from traditionalists and conformists, both for different reasons. Chaudhuri (2017) argues that a mention of a typical Indian woman invokes set images, which are 'culturally loaded, filled with allusions'. In the entire process, which is exclusive and hegemonic, she posits, 'a specifically upper-caste gender norm has been imposed as the "Indian" norm'. The Indian woman was created to fit in as someone who is compassionate but not necessarily a central figure in the discourse. Man was created as the archetype upper-caste family patriarch, a rationalist, a social reformer, a nationalist with a scientific temper, the fierce culture revivalist with virtues of a

Western imperial man (pp. 93). One finds such men thriving in advertising (The Complete Man from the Raymond suiting or the *Ghar Aaja* [Come Home] Siyaram suiting ad, to cite a couple of cases in point).

In summation, it can be argued that the long struggle by women across countries over centuries for gender equality and equity, hopefully, would not be in vain, and the voices would continue to be raised against lax laws, passivity in implementation, a general lack of awareness about their rights among women in India, especially in the rural hinterland, and inappropriate portrayal of women in media in its varied forms. The theme for the International Day for Women 2021 #ChoosetoChallenge would hopefully resonate beyond the year and continue to inspire women and men to challenge the status quo.

NOTES

1 https://www.bl.uk/collection-items/mary-wollstonecraft-a-vindication-of-the-rights-of-woman. Wollstonecraft's book is available in PDF at this site.

2 Rokeya Sakhawat Hossain, founder of the organization, wrote several books including *Sultana's Dream* that raises fundamental feminist issues that are part of modern western feminism, without being exposed to it.

3 This has been included in Bhattacharya & Sen (2003).

4 See, https://www.youtube.com/watch?v=HmmvM1NOI1; accessed on 10 December 2018.

REFERENCES

Anagol, P. (2006). *The emergence of feminism in India, 1850–1920*. Routledge.

Bahuguna, U. (2019). What winning the Goethe medal means for feminist publisher Urvashi Butalia. *Scroll.in*. https://scroll.in/

article/843928/what-winning-the-goethe-medal-means-for-feminist-publisher-urvashi-butalia

Butalia, U. (1998). *The other side of silence: Voices from the partition of India*. Penguin Books India.

Chatterjee, P. (1989). Colonialism, nationalism, and colonialized women: The contest in India. *American Ethnologist*, *16*(4), 622–633. https://www.jstor.org/stable/pdf/645113.pdf?refreqid=excelsior %3Aeb30f05e9defd8e51a0f8f3805c44491

Chaudhuri, M. (2017). *Refashioning India: Gender, media and a transformed public discourse*. Orient BlackSwan.

Clough, P. T. (1994). The hybrid criticism of patriarchy: Rereading Kate Millett's 'sexual politics.' *The Sociological Quarterly*, *35*(3), 473–486.

Duman, F. (2012). The roots of modern feminism: Mary Wollstonecraft and the French Revolution. *International Journal of Humanities and Social Science*, 2(9), 75–89.

Firestone, S. (1970). *The dialectic of sex: The case for Feminist Revolution*. Farrar, Straus and Giroux.

Francine Du Plessix, G. (2010, 27 May). Dispatches from the other. *The New York Times*. https://www.nytimes.com/2010/05/30/books/review/Gray-t.html

Fraser, N. (2013). *Fortunes of feminism* (p.1). Verso.

Gupta, O. (2013, 22 November). Indian Express pulls off a smart journalistic coup, exposes a sordid flesh trade. https://www.indiatoday.in/magazine/society-the-arts/media/story/19810531-indian-express-pulls-off-a-smart-journalistic-coup-exposes-a-sordid-flesh-trade-772915-2013-11-22

Hossain, R. S. (1905). Sultana's dream and Padmarag: Two feminist utopias (Trans., with an introduction by Barnita Bagchi). Penguin. http://digital.library.upenn.edu/women/sultana/dream/dream.html

Kumar, R. (1998). *The history of doing*. Kali for Women.

Marwick, A. (1998). *The sixties: Cultural revolution in Britain, France, Italy, and the United States, c.1958–c.1974* (pp. 67). Oxford University Press.

Mazumdar, V. (1994). Women's studies and the women's movement in India: An overview. *Women's Studies Quarterly*, 22(3/4), 42–54. https://www.jstor.org/stable/40004254?seq=1#metadata_info_tab_contents

McArthur, L. Z., & Resko, B. G. (1975). The portrayal of men and women in American television commercials. *Journal of Social Psychology*, 97(2), 209–220.

Millett, K. (1969). *Sexual politics*. University of Illinois Press.

Moi, T. (2008, 12 January). It changed my life. *The Guardian*. https://www.theguardian.com/books/2008/jan/12/society.simonedebeauvoir

Nussbaum, M. C. (1995). Objectification. *Philosophy and Public Affairs*, 24(4), 249–291.

Offen, K. (1988). On the French origin of the words feminism and feminist. *Feminist Issues*, *8*(2), 45–51.

Olivelle, P. (2005). *Manu's code of law: A critical edition and translation of the Manava-Dharmasastra*. Oxford University Press.

Parsons, T., & Robert, F. B. (1995). *Family, socialization, and interaction process*. Free Press.

Patel, V., & Khajuria, R. (2016). *Political feminism in India: An analysis of actors, debates and strategies*. Friedrich Ebart Stiftung.

Rossi, A. S. (1997). *The feminist papers: From Adams to Simone de Beauvoir* (pp. 673). Northeastern University Press.

Sarkar, S. (2014). Media and women image: A feminist discourse. *Journal of Media and Communication Studies*, 6(3), 48–58. http://www.academicjournals.org/app/webroot/article/article1396005138_Sarkar.pdf

Sarna, J. K. (2017, 7 July). 'Kamini Roy: Poet, teacher and the first woman honours graduate in British India. *Feminism in India*. https://feminisminindia.com/2017/07/07/kamini-roy-essay/

Sexton, D. E., & Haberman, P. (1974). Women in magazine advertisements. *Journal of Advertising Research*, *13*, 41–46. http://www.acrwebsite.org/volumes/9532/volumes/v06/NA–06

Srivastava, S. (2008, 24 September). Tupperware sexuality: Consumption, morality and the search for a controllable modernity [Public lecture, Latin American Center on Sexuality and Human Rights (CLAM) delivered at State University of Rio de Janeiro].

Uthara, S. (2009). Patriarchy: Theoretical postulates and empirical findings. *Sociological Bulletin*, *68*(2), 253–272.

Verma, M. (1944). *Shrinkhala ki Kadiyan* (p. 9). https://archive.org/details/in.ernet.dli.2015.541016/page/n47

Wagner, L., & Banos, J. B. (1973). A woman's place: A follow up analysis of the roles portrayed by women in magazine advertisements. *Journal of Marketing Research*, *10*(2), 213–214.

Wollstonecraft, M. *(1792). A vindication of the rights of woman: With strictures on political and moral subjects*. Printed for J. Johnson.

Woolf, V. (1929). *A room of one's own* (pp. 95). Feedbooks. http://seas3.elte.hu/ coursematerial/PikliNatalia/Virginia_Woolf_-_A_Room_of_Ones_Own.pdf

Yadav, A. K., & Tripathi, H. R. (2017). Discourses on identity in Hindi literature with special reference to women's identity (translated by authors). http://jankritipatrika.in/read.php?artID=514

CHAPTER 3

GENDER INSENSITIVITY IN INDIAN ADS—NUMBERS DON'T LIE!

Never write an advertisement which you wouldn't want your own family to read. You wouldn't tell lies to your own wife.

David Ogilvy

There has been, in about last two decades or so, an increasing interest in the study of the representation of gender in media. This expectedly has coincided with a huge proliferation of media including the digital platforms in India and a spurt in mass media teaching in the country. Today, we have more than 300 universities and institutions of higher learning teaching various courses in mass media, leading to interest in gender studies. Another noteworthy development has been the presence of a wide array of the 'influencer' population on the digital platforms and a deluge of sorts of the 'user-generated content'. People, in general, who often remained passive, have begun to articulate their feelings via the social media platforms, bringing the debate on gender centre stage.

This chapter has discussed the findings of an ICSSR seminal study undertaken in 2017–2019 that looked at the portrayal of women in the advertising landscape of India for three decades, which has thrown some disturbing, yet insightful, data on how various brand categories have portrayed women since the 1990s, a period often labelled as the 'era of liberalization', which opened the Indian economy to foreign direct investment in the country leading to the entry of many global brands and advertising companies.[1]

DECONSTRUCTING ADVERTISEMENTS USING GOFFMAN'S CONSTRUCT

The common method of deconstructing advertisements is through content analysis, which can be both quantitative and qualitative on certain predetermined indicators. It, however, makes sense to follow a well-tested theoretical construct to analyse ads for not only getting a better perspective and insight but also having a look at comparative data from various countries. Erving Goffman, an American sociologist of great repute, in his classic study *Gender Advertisements* (1988) systematically deconstructed 500 print ads to enquire into how the images of gender were represented in the American advertisements in the 1960–1970s. Many research scholars in the past have adapted Goffman's theoretical construct across countries to enquire into gender representation in their societies. The research findings reflected here have also used Goffman's construct for analysing the ads.

Before we analyse Indian ads, let us look at some empirical studies on the gender narrative in advertising undertaken by various scholars.

1. Courtney and Lockeretz (1971) did a content analysis of over 700 ads across seven magazines in the US that appealed to the general audience. Among many interesting findings and insights, the study found that while 33 per cent women worked in the US, only 12 per cent women were shown as working professionals in the various ads. The researchers concluded that men and women advertised for different products. Women made independent choices only when shopping for cosmetics, food or cleaning products. When

the ad was for a higher-value product like home appliance, the woman could be in the frame but along with a man. The ads, said the researchers, seemed to reflect as if 'a woman's place was in the home' and 'women do not make important decisions or do important things.'

2. A more detailed analysis by Sexton and Haberman (1974) covered ads over three decades, namely 1950–1951, 1960–1961 and 1970–1971, covering product categories like cigarettes, beverages, automobiles, home appliances, office equipment and airlines. The researchers evaluated the ads on 11 dimensions, which covered the number of persons and types of role portrayals in the ads, their relationship with one another and with the product, and the setting of the ad. This study also revealed that portrayals were changing with more women being shown as professionals and less in family situations.

3. An analysis of advertisements in eight national US magazines, it was found that women were represented in home settings. Men, in contrast appeared in business settings. (Courtney & Lockeretz, 1971).

4. McArthur and Resko (1975) observed that the percentage of males used in television ads was higher even for situations where they were not the primary users of a product or service, reflecting who the decision-maker was.

5. Venkatesan and Losco (1975), in a study of advertisements on the role and portrayal of women from 1959 to 1971, once again confirmed the existence of stereotypical portrayals of women as sex objects, for physical beauty and as dependents.

6. Sarkar (2015), in her study, argues that gender-based promotions of products are most common strategies practised by advertisers to establish a strong connection with

a brand. As an offshoot of such stereotyping in virtual and visual world, the cultural predicament becomes more dominating on how a woman should present herself even in reality. Constant distortion imposes and induces a belief that women have to not only suit 'themselves' but also conform to certain level that is set by cultural standard and popular perception.

7. Lakshmi and Selvam (2016) look at the concept of stereotyping of gender roles and representation of minorities from a critical perspective through discourse analysis of select Indian television advertisements telecast countrywide and uploaded on YouTube Ad Leaderboards. The study analyses ads that conform to stereotyping as well as ones that attempt to challenge it through their portrayal of unconventional portrayals. The study highlights change among the urban middle class due to financial independence of women and the influence of Internet, showing how advertising that caters to them has reflected these changes.

8. Malik (2014) in her paper 'Women's Objectification by Consumer Culture' critically examines how celebrities working for mass media are objectified by being presented as 'sex objects' for global consumption. Her paper proposes to draw attention to American writer Brian D'Amato's critique of women's objectification by consumer culture.

9. Chaudhuri (2017), in her insightful book *Refashioning India: Gender, Media and a Transformed Public Discourse*, argues that Indian advertisements both depict the new trends and accelerate them. In the post-liberalization era, a man thought that looking good was not a woman's prerogative alone. Body baring became a common feature in many ads. As a result, one saw the arrival of the quintessential metrosexual man in advertising and entertainment media.[2]

10. Kilbourne (n.d.), a pioneering researcher and an activist, has been deconstructing advertisements since the 1970s.

Her research and analysis reflect an overwhelming evidence of not just sexualization of female body but also the presentation of unreal images of women, which can be hard for real women, particularly teenage girls and young women, to live up to. Her documentary *Killing Us Softly* explores the same issue and has been serialized four times, with each update incorporating the developments that followed after the previous edition was filmed. In the fourth edition of the documentary, she informs that over the period, female sexualization in advertisement has actually gotten worse. At the end, however, she does mention few small victories such as models in the US fighting against use of Photoshop and airbrushing that provide unrealistic images of female body, leading to many publications in the industry agreeing to not airbrush models anymore. However, a key point that she makes in every edition of the documentary is that most people believe that they do not pay much attention to the ads, while it was interesting to note that a major publication had found that 'only 8 per cent of an ad's message is received by the conscious mind. The rest is worked and reworked deep within the recesses of the brain.' This statistic significantly demonstrates how imagery in ads not only reinforces but also enhances existing stereotypes, particularly about women. This is in conjunction with the fact stated by Kilbourne that such sexist and indecent advertisements 'surround us with unhealthy images and constantly sacrifices our health and well-being for the sake of profit.' What is interesting is that she points at how advertising many a time reduces women to just parts of her body in order to sell products, which ends up dehumanizing women. In this regard, she also tells how the use of sexualization of female body is not necessary to sell the product but simply to attract the attention of the male buyers. Over the period, owing to increasing financial independence and purchasing power, the buyers are now overwhelmingly female. However, the marketing ploy has more or less remained the same.

The research in different countries and at various points of time is reflective of the exclusive and gender-insensitive nature of societies. Critics believe that it is inevitable because, in general, social thoughts like philosophy, history, science and even theory are also gender insensitive, which has a concomitant impact on the policies as well as on governance and justice. Media, a part of the social milieu, too, remains largely gender insensitive in its approach and narrative. Advertising, as a marketing tool, draws its references from various persuasive theories that look for appeals and symbols that largely cater to men and male gaze.

The research reflected in the current chapter, as said earlier, is based on Goffman's six main indicators besides two more indicators, namely 'relative size', 'feminine touch', 'function ranking', 'the family situation/scene', 'the ritualization of subordination' and 'licensed withdrawal'. For the ICSSR study, two additional indicators of 'patriarchy' and 'objectification' were added to suit the Indian social milieu.

On images, Goffman believed that pictures could be divided in to 'public' and 'private' spheres. While advertisements belonged to the public pictures' domain, which are faked, Goffman felt the private pictures taken for personal use are not faked. Advertisements, he reasoned, were targeted at a larger audience with specific marketing objectives, designed in such a manner to receive the desired response. To achieve that, advertisers use all kinds of strategies and tactics to get into the mind space of the discerning consumer. Let us, in following matrix (Table 3.1), understand what all the eight indicators convey.

Goffman argues that the gender roles portrayed in ads are likely to be seen as the norm and a slice of life that was constructed in the ads meant to provide cues to viewers on what an ideal life or situation was like. He cited the example of an ideal family on vacation which might take its cues on what 'having a good time' is from external sources and might, in fact, contrive to look and act like the idealized family on vacation in a Coca-Cola ad.

Table 3.1 Erving Goffman's Theoretical Construct on Gender Portrayal in Advertisements with Additional Indicators of Patriarchy and Objectification

S. N.	Analysis Indicator	What It Conveys
1.	Relative size	Men, often, are invariably shown taller than women in ads to convey their authority and power through size difference. The size, at times, also, is manipulated through camera technique. It is assumed that size difference will correlate with difference in social weight.
2.	Feminine touch	Women, more than men, are pictured using their hands and fingers to trace the outlines of an object or to cradle it or caress its surface or to effect a 'just barely touching'.
3.	Function ranking	In the social context, when a man and a woman interact face to face, often man is shown in an executive position, in other words, in a functional posture and the women in a passive posture, with nothing much to contribute to the narrative.
4.	The family situation	A young boy and girl in a nuclear set-up complete an ideal frame, with the man often doing and initiating activities. The man as a father is shown at a distance to denote that he is the protector of the family. Woman is often in the frame but not an initiator of activity.
5.	The ritualization of subordination	A classic stereotype of deference is that of lowering oneself physically in some form or other of prostration. In contrast, holding the head high is stereotypically a mark of ashamedness, superiority and disdain. The configuration of canting postures can be read as an acceptance of subordination, an expression of ingratiation, submissiveness and appeasement, often left for women.

(Continued)

(Continued)

S. N.	Analysis Indicator	What It Conveys
6.	Licensed with-drawal	Women, more than men, are pictured engaged in involvements which remove them psychologically from the social situation at large, leaving them to it and disoriented in it, and dependent on the protectiveness of others who are present. Turning one's gaze away from another can be seen as the consequence of withdrawing from the thrust of communication.
7.	Patriarchy	Patriarchy posits the dominion of man over woman. It also defines the relationship among women as well. Traditional societies including the Indian society are rigorously patriarchal with well-defined power hierarchies within families and outside. The patriarch in the ads often would have the last word; his word would not be challenged.
8.	Objectifi-cation	'Objectification' broadly means treating a person as a commodity or an object without regard to his/her personality or dignity. Women often are presented as sex objects in advertisements to attract the attention of the potential consumers.

Source: Adapted from Erving Goffman's gender advertisements.

DECODING OF ADS ACROSS BRAND SPECTRUM

A cross-section of over 1,100 ads relating to five brand categories, namely fast-moving consumer goods (FMCG), lifestyle, travel and tourism, banking, financial services and insurance (BFSI), and automobile (four-wheelers, two-wheelers and tyres) formed the sample for deconstruction. The timeline covered ads from 1991 until 2019. The ads were selected across three media, namely print, electronic (TV) and digital by stratified purposive sampling technique based on the following criteria:

1. Inclusion of those brand categories and sub-categories, which are large advertisers.
2. Selection of only those ads within these brand categories that have either a woman protagonist or, at least, one or more women in the frame.
3. Taking the sample of ads post liberalization era in India (1990s onwards).

The systematic analysis aimed at finding:

a) The extent of stereotyping and objectification of women by negative weightage based on content analyses indicators.
b) To enquire if there are any typical brand categories that encourage stereotyping or inappropriate portrayal of woman's role in ads.
c) To find out if there are any patterns across brand categories, media and timelines.

Table 3.2 details various brand categories and within the five brand categories various sub-categories that have been content-analysed.

In other words, 1,167 ads across 5 brand categories, 31 sub-categories and 164 brands across 3 decades and 3 media, namely print, television and digital, comprised the sample population that was taken into account for finding the extent of stereotyping and inappropriately projecting women.[3] The next chapter has analysed randomly the gender perspective across various brand categories and sub-categories.

Table 3.2 Sample Population of Ads

S. No.	Categories	No. of Sub-categories	No. of Brands	No. of Ads			Total
				TVCs	Print	Internet	
1.	FMCGs	10	55	211	107	54	372
2.	Lifestyle	10	59	147	182	127	457
3.	Automobile	3	14	67	32	38	137
4.	BFSI	3	18	46	33	38	117
5.	Travel	5	18	37	18	30	85
Total		**31**	**164**	**508**	**372**	**287**	**1167**

MAJOR FINDINGS AND INSIGHTS

What comes out unambiguously in the analysis of Indian ads across various brand categories is the blatant stereotyping and objectification of women in the ad narrative, in general. The saving grace in the previous decade since 2011, has been an indicator of objectification which has come down by over 19 per cent.

Of the eight indicators, namely relative size, feminine touch, function ranking, the family situation, the ritualization of subordination, licensed withdrawal, patriarchy and objectification, the two dominant indicators across the entire Indian ad spectrum are the ritualization of subordination and patriarchy in a majority of ads across brand categories and sub-categories.

Table 3.3 provides cumulative scores across all the five brand categories across the three media—TV, print and digital, over three decades (1991–2019).

The aggregate data, as detailed in Table 3.3, reflects that among all the three media, TVCs perform the worst across all the three categories in being the least gender sensitive on all the eight indicators. On the indicator of objectification, though the negative score is between 25 and 31 per cent across three decades, but when we look at the micro data of brand categories that advertise frequently, explained later in the chapter, some brands have a very high negative score on this indicator going up to over 90 per cent.

In our analysis, we can see interesting patterns in the data of three decades.

TV

There is an overall better gender sensitivity quotient in the current decade (ads chosen between 2011 and 2019), even if by a few percentage points. A lot, however, still needs to be done to improve it as the figures, though an improvement over the last decades, are still dismal on two important indicators, that is, at

Table 3.3 Parametric Weightages for All Media across Three Decades

Column 1	Relative Size	Feminine Touch	Function Ranking	Family Situation	Ritualization of Subordination	Licensed Withdrawal	Patriarchy	Objectification
TVC[a] (1991–2019)	53.15	66.14	69.49	13.58	91.93	54.92	77.76	28.35
Print ads (1991–2019)	25.54	36.02	33.60	2.69	90.32	53.23	78.49	31.45
Digital ads—still (2011–2019)	19.86	49.83	19.86	4.88	85.71	38.33	63.41	25.44

Note: [a]Television commercial.

about 94 per cent on subordination and over 80 per cent on patriarchy. On objectification of woman, there is a drop of 19 per cent in the current decade for all the ads put together on television, which is a significant improvement. Subordination and patriarchy come as the dominant indicators in Indian ads across three decades and three media.

Television has the highest negative weightage at about 92 per cent against the indicator of subordination and about 78 per cent against the indicator of patriarchy, followed by print and digital, respectively, as Figure 3.1 reflects.

When we look at Figure 3.2, there is the same old story of putting women in subordinate roles and regressive patriarchal narrative, with 90 per cent ads with patriarchal narrative emerging from the automobile sector, the highest among the five brand categories. Banking and financial service ads were the other worse offenders on the indicator of subordination in almost 96 per cent ads and over 78 per cent on patriarchal narrative. The stock-market ads have also consistently ignored women as potential buyers of financial products, as there were hardly any ads that had women playing the protagonists.

Figure 3.1 Parametric Weightages across Media

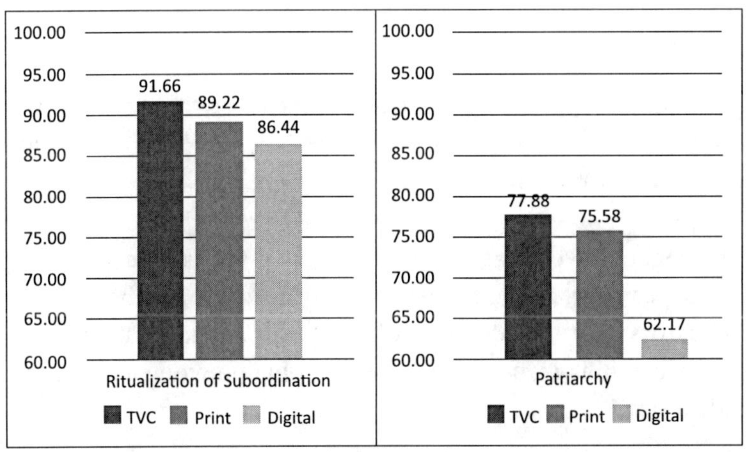

Figure 3.2 Parametric Weightages Evaluation for All Five Categories on TV

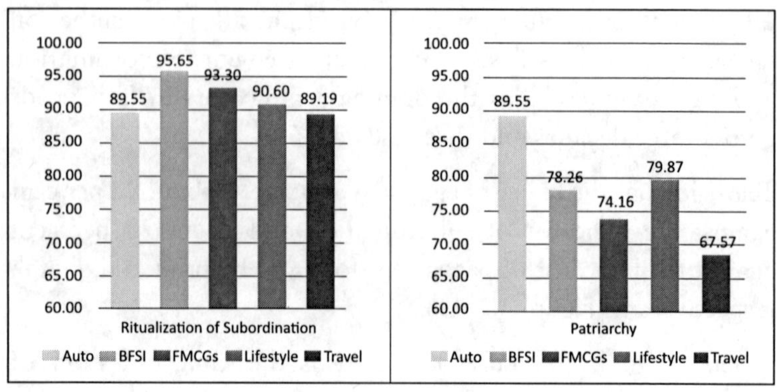

MICRO DATA ANALYSIS

As the FMCG and lifestyle categories have a larger bandwidth of product line, therefore, the absolute data may be a bit misleading. Within these brand categories, let us take a look at the micro data of some lifestyle and beauty products in the TVCs as reflected in the following figures to see how they stand on various indicators.

Contraceptives

Sixty contraceptive ads of various brands were analysed on the eight indicators. As shown in Figure 3.3, the findings do not come as a surprise.

The negative weightage on contraceptive ads is from the least at 73 per cent to the highest at 100 per cent on the various indicators that reflect both objectification and indecency as prescribed in law and blatant stereotyping on women across all indicators.

Figure 3.3 Parametric Evaluation for Contraceptive (Lifestyle) on TV: 1991–2019

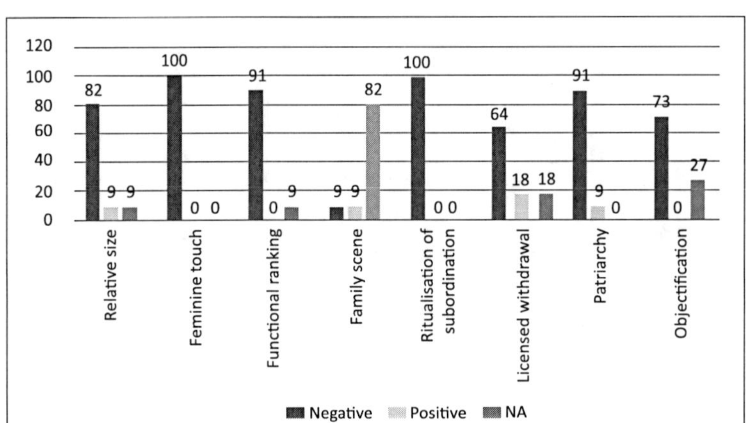

Deodorants

In the category of deodorants, 34 ads were analysed (see Figure 3.4). The negative weightage across eight indicators ranges from 43 per cent to 93 per cent. On all dominant indicators, the ads perform poorly. Even on indicators like feminine touch and functional ranking, not considered dominant in most ads, the negative weightage is over 90 per cent.

Tobacco

In tobacco ads that take the surrogate route, 38 ads were analysed including 11 TVCs (see Figure 3.5). The stereotyping of women in this category is quite blatant. Most of the tobacco-based products have men in masculine roles.

Alcohol

This is yet another surrogate category that objectifies and stereotypes women with a high weightage as reflected in Figure 3.6

Figure 3.4 Parametric Evaluation for Deodorant (Lifestyle) on TV: 1991–2019

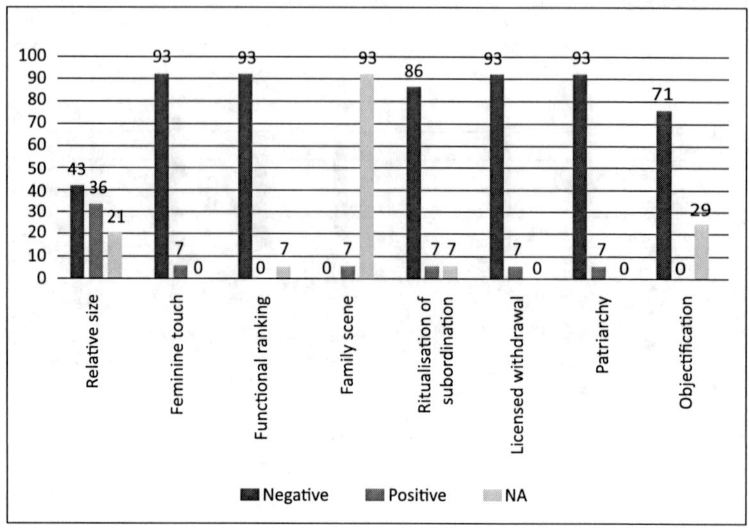

Figure 3.5 Parametric Evaluation for Tobacco (Lifestyle) on TV: 1991–2019

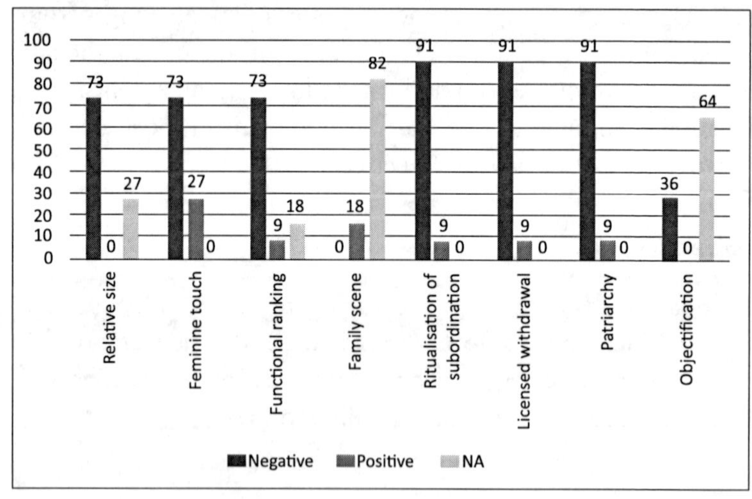

Figure 3.6 Parametric Evaluation for Alcohol (Lifestyle) on TV: 1991–2019

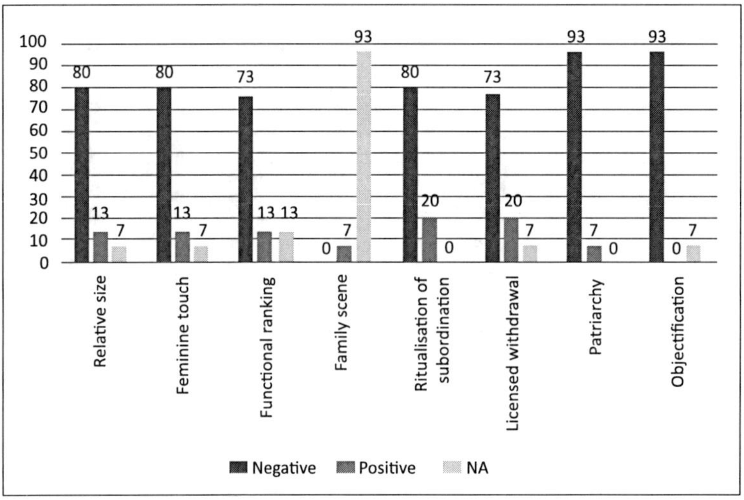

at 73 per cent at the lowest and 93 per cent at the highest score on various analyses indicators.

Beauty Segment

In the beauty segment under the FMCG sector, 67 ads pertaining to face creams and soaps have been included for analysis.

The negative weightage across indictors in beauty products is 49 per cent at the lowest and 97 per cent at the highest (see Figure 3.7). In this category, there is over 97 per cent negative weightage on objectification and subordination and over 77 per cent on patriarchy, which in a way posits that despite being women-oriented, there is a strong undercurrent of patriarchal narrative in this segment also.

Table 3.4 provides the data on negative weightage of serial offenders in lifestyle and FMCG brands at a glance.

Indian ads, on most of the indicators of analysis, have performed poorly, with different negative weightages, though some positive

Figure 3.7 Parametric Evaluation for Beauty Products (FMCG) on TV: 1991–2019

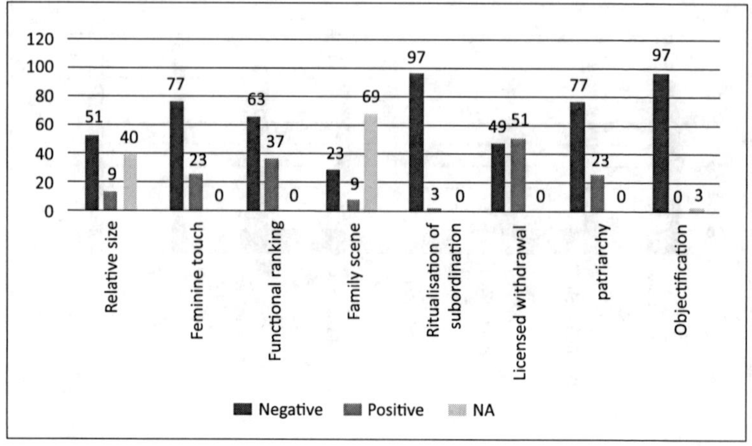

Table 3.4 Parametric Weightages Across Three Decades in Five Sub-categories

Catego-ries	Sub-categories	Ritualiza-tion of Subordina-tion	Objectifi-cation	Patriar-chy
Lifestyle	Contracep-tive	100.00	72.73	90.91
	Alcohol	80.00	93.33	93.33
	Deodorant	85.71	71.43	92.86
	Tobacco	90.91	36.00	90.91
FMCGs	Beauty products	97.14	97.14	77.14

change in the current decade is perceptible. Portraying women inappropriately is by and large restricted to some lifestyle brand categories such as deodorants, apparel, contraceptives, alcohol and tobacco. As these categories are big advertisers, so naturally, the ads are also frequently visible in the public domain, earning the ad sector its share of criticism for being insensitive to gender.

Reflection of large happy families, a common thing in Indian advertising for decades, has now been relegated to the backyard. The narrative has now moved on from the ideal joint family to that of a nuclear family and, at times, single-parent scenario, echoing the reality of postmodern social ethos. The research revealed that more and more ads with family scene now have nuclear or single parents as protagonists. It is not necessarily the single woman but also not uncommon to find the man in custody of the child, doing household chores.

If on the one hand some brands have experimented with projecting an independent and bold woman, a reflection effectively projected by filmmaker Homi Adajania in his ad, 'My Choice' made for the *Vogue* magazine, the role essayed by cine star Deepika Padukone, but the quintessential compassionate and caring woman has not really left the Indian ad narrative. Man continues to be the provider and the decision-maker. The 1990s has also seen the emergence of the 'metrosexual man', a portmanteau of metropolitan and heterosexual, on the advertising landscape. Such a man is conscious of his looks and attitude and spends time and resources to groom himself. We shall talk about this man in a separate chapter in detail.

In the next chapter, we shall take a medley of ads to dig deep into the narrative and imagery.

NOTES

1 The study funded by ICSSR, 'Portrayal of Women in the Indian Advertising Content: Issues and Concerns', was undertaken by the present author. As part of the research work, a number of papers were published in some refereed journals. Jethwaney (2019) carries some data published here in this chapter.

2 Metrosexual, a term coined in 1994, refers to a man (especially one living in an urban, post-industrial, capitalist culture) who is especially meticulous about his grooming and appearance, typically spending a significant amount of time and money on shopping as part of this.

3 The study has not looked at specific media vehicles that carried the ads within the media, that is, specific newspapers and magazines, television channels and digital platforms, as the purpose was to content analyse the ads and not necessarily define which media vehicles these ads appeared, which can be an area of a future study to match the media vis-à-vis target audience.

REFERENCES

Chaudhuri, M. (2017). *Refashioning India: Gender, media, and a transformed public discourse*. Orient Blackswan.

Courtney, A. E., & Lockeretz, S. W. (1971). A woman's place: An analysis of the roles portrayed by women in magazine advertisements. *Journal of Marketing Research, 8*(1), 92–95.

Goffman, E. (1988). *Gender advertisements*. Harper & Row. https://www.academia.edu/16756770/Erving_Goffman_Gender_Advertisements_1988 _

Jethwaney, J. (2019, December). Portrayal of women: An empirical study of advertising content in India from 1991–2019. *Communicator, LIV*(4), 3–28.

Kilbourne, J. (n.d.). What are advertisers really trying to sell us? https://www.jeankilbourne.com/lectures/

Lakshmi, C., & Selvam, V. (2016). Challenging stereotypes: A semiotic analysis of Indian advertisements. *Asian Journal of Research in Social Sciences and Humanities*, 6(11), 907–924.

Malik, S. (2014). Women's objectification by consumer culture. *International Journal of Gender and Women's Studies*, 2(4), 87–102.

McArthur, L. Z., & Resko, B. G. (1975). The portrayal of men and women in American television commercials. *Journal of Social Psychology*, *97*(2), 209–220.

Sarkar, S. (2015). Gender stereotyping in product promotion: A dominant tool of advertising in Indian media. *International Journal of Media, Journalism and Mass Communications*, *1*(2), 1–12.

Sexton, D. E., & Haberman, P. (1974). Women in magazine advertisements. *Journal of Advertising Research*, *14*(4), 41–46.

Venkatesan, M., & Losco, J. (1975). Women in magazine ads: 1959–1971. *Journal of Consumer Research*, *15*, 49–54.

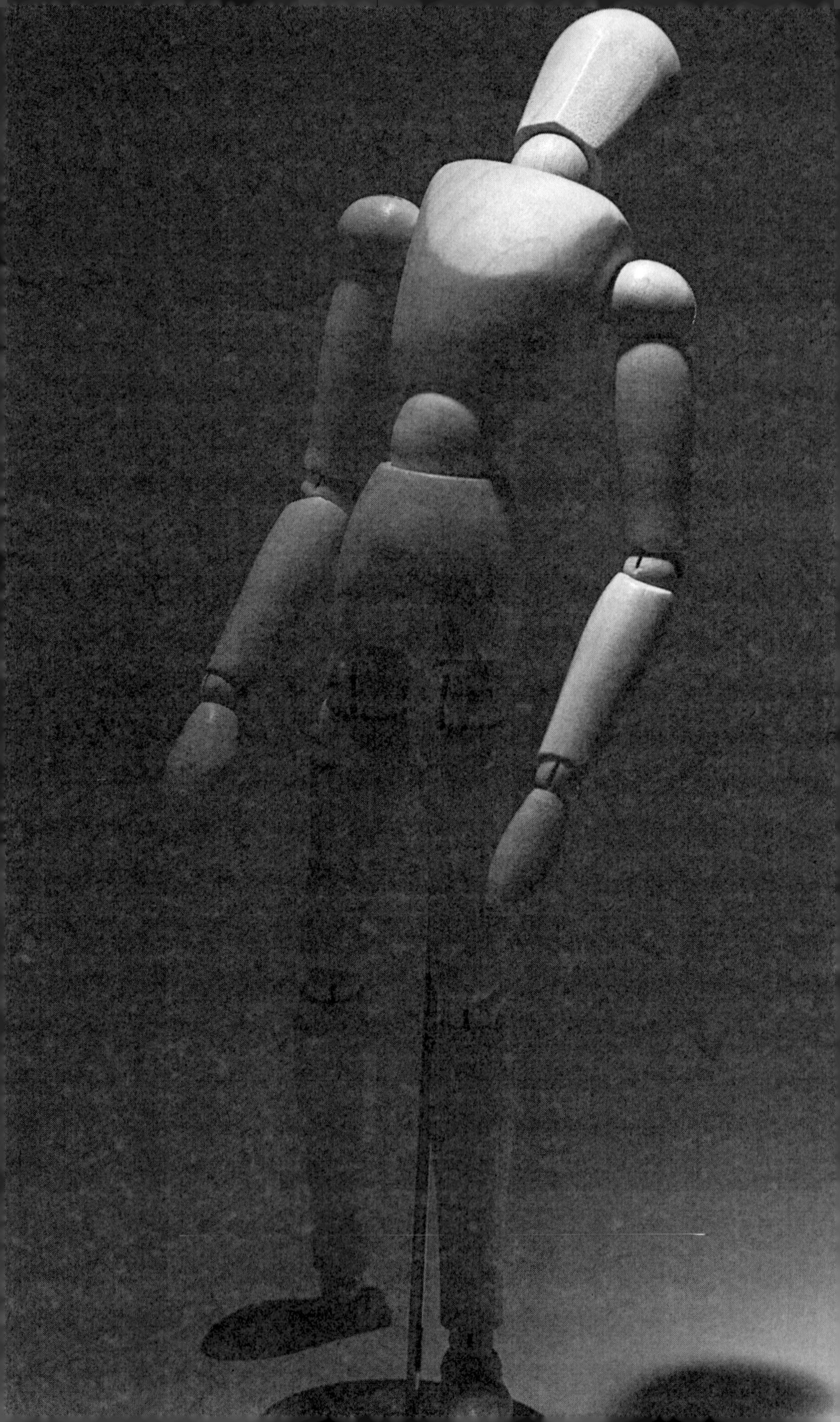

CHAPTER 4

SOME HOPE, SOME DESPAIR! A MEDLEY OF ADS

I am one who believes that one of the greatest dangers of advertising is not that of misleading people, but that of boring them to death.

Leo Burnett

Ads have this mysterious and uncanny attraction that an average media consumer cannot escape. Some ads regale us while others may bore us, but they do occupy our mind space. Advertising is believed to work sublimely. Some people feel that ad influence has to do with age. The younger one is, the more aspirational she/he is, making ads a reference point in their lives. Ads often draw extreme response, depending on where it is coming from.

Advertising is criticized for many things, including exaggerating claims, use of double entendre, misuse of children in ad narrative and surrogate advertising, but what has become an issue of open discord is the objectionable portrayal of women and stereotyping their roles. In the name of creative liberty and in an effort at reflecting a slice of life, women often find themselves as objects of voyeurism and male gaze.

In this chapter, we shall take a look at the ads randomly from various brand categories to get a feel on how they perform on the gender-sensitivity indicator. Later, a few ads would be deconstructed in detail.

Table 4.1 provides a glimpse of the brand categories and sub-categories within each brand category analysed for the gender narrative.

Table 4.1 Category-Wise Break-up of Ads

S. No.	Medium	Categories	No. of Sub-category	No. of Total Ads
1	All three (TVC, print, digital)	FMCGs	Beauty products	67
			Toiletries	47
			Detergent	47
			Aerated drinks	56
			Snacks	61
			Beverages	44
			Stationery	32
			Medicines	6
			Electrical appliance	4
			Cooking oil	8
2.	All three	Lifestyle	Apparel	99
			Contraceptive	60
			Accessories	33
			Shoes	37
			Jewellery	34
			Alcohol	50
			Tobacco	38
			Deodorant	34
			Furnishing/ sanitary	26
			Telecom	45
3.	All three	Auto	Cars	54
			Two wheelers	55
			Tyres	28
4.	All three	BFSI	Banks	48
			Insurance	40
			Mutual funds	29
5.	All three	Travel	Hotels	25
			Accessories	30
			Airlines	15
			Travel sites	6
			Apps	9

RANDOM GLIMPSES FROM ACROSS BRAND CATEGORIES

FMCG

Under the FMCG brand category, 10 sub-categories were analysed. In the sub-category of beauty products, 40 ads formed the sample population across three decades, representing different brands such as, Fair & Lovely (F&L), Dove, Lakmé, Ponds, Vivel, Nivea, etc. When we deconstruct this sub-category on the eight research indicators, at least two variables, stereotyping and objectification of women, can be found in various brands. Generalizing from the sample, the most common variable found throughout the sample was that of 'feminine touch' and 'ritualization of subordination'. The first variable, Goffman argues, indicates a form of gender display that depicts the women's body as delicate and a precious thing. He states that very often, in picture, a woman would be seen in a position where her fingers are barely touching or cradling an object, which needs to be differentiated from the utilitarian position of grasping and holding. This was something common in most of the ads in this sub-category. The second variable on ritualization of subordination is indicative of a display which places the women in a subordinate position. In this, two forms of gender display were most common, that is, 'expansive smile' and 'body or head cant'. This conveys childlike behaviour seeking approval from an authority.

Another interesting observation, if one takes a historical account of it, was when we took the three decades separately to analyse them comparatively, it was observed that the negative score (measured in terms of presence of one or more indicators explained in Goffman's typology before) of the ads, in general, for earlier decade was higher in comparison to the more recent ads. Further, the negative score of the first decade was very high, where variables such as 'family scene' and 'function ranking' were also common throughout. In one of them, for instance, the protagonist, Aishwarya Rai, comes to visit her home after marriage. She meets her sister and gives her advice on how to become fairer. The ads for this period and, to some extent, for the next decade as well reflected family bonding for beauty tips. Apart from this, the first two decades portrayed women along with men, where men were positioned superior to women. Take, for instance, the 1990s ad of F&L, where a married couple is shown throwing a party. Throughout the whole event, the woman protagonist is seen complaining about how her husband had not noticed her fair skin. Such a portrayal indicates how the woman's idea of ideal beauty is constructed along the lines of male gaze. The same kind of narrative continues in the Ponds ad, which features Priyanka Chopra and Saif Ali Khan, discussed in detail later in the chapter. In more recent ads, however, the variables of 'family scene' and 'function ranking' disappear or are so less that they seem insignificant. Further, the taglines have changed from those that stressed on fairness to that of radiance, as in the Karisma Kapoor ad for Ponds, where she was portrayed as a working woman. The narrative was built around her radiant beauty and not fair skin. This is almost similar for other ads as well in the genre. Some brands such as Dove and Pretty 24 have challenged the normative beauty standards, for example, the Dove campaign titled 'Let's Break the Rules of Beauty' or the Pretty 24 ads titled 'Rang nahi soch badlo' (Not colour, change your thinking!). Despite these new ways of portraying, it was still apparent that some form of gender display and stereotyping has been inevitable across all the three decades under analysis. The aspect of 'expansive smile' and 'touching self' by women in the ads has also been a continuous phenomenon.

In the sub-category of aerated drinks, 22 ads, representing three decades from the 1990s with brands such as Coco-Cola, Limca, Slice, Pepsi and Thums Up were deconstructed. Some of the famous taglines included 'Do pal tazgi ke', 'Aamsutra', 'Yehi hai right choice baby', 'Yeh dil mange more', 'Aaj kuch toofani karte hian', etc. In all these brands, some form of gender stereotyping was inevitable. The most common variable in the sample was that of 'ritualization of subordination' and display of expansive smile and body or head cant as common features. Take, for instance, one of the more recent ads by the Coca-Cola, where Deepika Padukone and her friends missed their bus and were getting late for their examination. She complained about her bad luck and said that if she failed, her dad would marry her off to somebody and she would end up peeling *matar* (peas) all her life, meaning, she would end up becoming a homemaker. Farhan Akhtar, an autorickshaw driver, who could later be seen trying to court her, offered the girls lift in his auto. As they rode the rickshaw, Farhan stared at her through the side mirror. Deepika displayed discomfort as reflected by her gestures that Goffman phrased it 'body or head cant', looking away with a bent head. Later, when they reached the college, Farhan was seen wooing her by telling her that he would never make her peel *matar*, to which Deepika responded with a big smile. This smile, as per Goffman's construct, could be read as a form of gender display that could be interpreted as her approval of other's action. In this case, it conveyed her approval of Farhan's way of courting or 'flirting' with her. The ad was not only inappropriate, using male gaze, but also stereotypical about how a woman would respond to the male overtures as said in the common parlance by boys, '*Hansi toh fasi*' (her smiling back means she has relented).

Two other variables of 'function ranking' and 'licensed withdrawal' were also observed somewhat consistently in this sub-category of brands within the FMCG category. Take, for instance, the 'Aamsutra' ad for the brand Slice, featuring Katrina Kaif, looking sensuous, she was lost in her fantasy world as she sipped the beverage sensuously, her gaze withdrawn from the setting. In a review of ads, Shaunak Roy commented, 'Katrina Kaif is trying to advertise Slice, a summer-time pickup. Mummy's summer rendition of home-made orange juice/squash is now virtually a sex-aided, re-packaged and re-envisaged offering of what I call 'mango sex': a concoction of luscious mango and imaginative sex' (Roy, 2013).

In the sub-category of coffee, 13 ads formed the sample from two brands, that is, Bru and Nescafe, representing three decades since the 1990s. Some of the taglines included 'It all starts with Nescafe', 'One Nescafe, many coffees', 'Not just any cold coffee', 'Bru se hoti hain khushiya shuru' (happiness begins with Bru), etc. In both the coffee brands, there are some forms of stereotyping, the most common being ritualization of subordination and function ranking. In most of the ads, whenever there were both a man and a woman in the frame, it was always the woman serving the man. In one of the earlier ads of Bru, a tired wife came home from work to a husband who was shown playing a game on his phone. The first thing that she did was to serve the man coffee. This indicated to, what Goffman would argue, a hierarchical distinction of gender position or role. Here, the role of the woman within the household was serving her man. In another ad of the same period, Amrita Rao was shown serving coffee to her father. This is not just the case for Bru alone but also for Nescafe, where Deepika Padukone is making coffee for Karan Johar and her male neighbour. Brand Bru, over a period, however, has attempted to challenge such gender-role stereotyping in some of its recent ads, where in one of the ads, the husband served coffee to his wife who came tired from office. Another observation on the parameter was that the women in the ads were always wearing an expansive smile. It was also not uncommon to show them lying on the floor or sofa. For instance, in one such ad, Priyanka Chopra was sipping her coffee while lying on a sofa. Yet another ad by Bru showed an expecting mother lying on her bed, while contemplating on the ways to tell her husband the news. Both the brands, in general, stereotyped women on a number of indicators.

Automobile

In the brand category of automobiles and, within this category, three sub-categories, namely cars, two wheelers and tyres were analysed on the gender narrative.

In sub-category of cars, a total of 23 ads across the three decades from the 1990s were analysed, represented by five different car brands, that is, Maruti, Mahindra, Ford, Volkswagen and Honda. Over the years, each of them has put out many ad campaigns with many interesting catchphrases such as 'Meri Maruti', 'Men are back', 'New definition for a new generation', 'Shaadi ke side effects', 'Let's go', etc. How do all of these brands reflect on the gender norms?

The most apparent negative indicators were functional ranking and ritualization of subordination. In most of the ads for cars, men seemed to be in command, literally in the 'driver's seat, either driving or instructing. Even when women were shown at the driver's seat, men often instructed them. Take, for instance, the Ford Figo ad titled 'Sorry', where a man narrated how to get a woman to say sorry first when she was angry. The man's wife, annoyed with him, was shown packing her suitcase with a plan to leave for her natal home. In the meantime, her husband went to the car and connected his cell phone with the car. Later, he helped her load her bag in the car, after which the wife drove away angrily. While she was driving, the man played a romantic song on his phone, which started to play in the car as well (the new feature of Ford Figo that the brand was using as its selling point). Hearing this, the woman took a U-turn and came back to say sorry to her husband who was waiting for her with a smile. So, despite the fact that she was driving, her mood and her action here were coordinated by the husband, making him the important player in the saga.

In the four-wheeler category, one can argue that, over the three decades, women in this category continue to play the role of either a prop by placing her alongside of a car to show their curviness or as a passive actor in the frame. The man is the one who plays the functional role of the instructor and superior; despite that a lot has changed in the society; there are many women who buy cars of their choice and also drive independently.

In the sub-category of two wheeler, a total of 26 ads were analysed, the sample represented by five different brands of two-wheeler bikes, including Hero, TVS, Bajaj, Yamaha and Honda. Before we begin, it is important to note that the sample comprised two kinds of two wheelers, namely bikes and scooty. In the category, the narrative was based on the assumption that bike was a masculine product and scooty, a feminine one. The larger theme was also very different between the motorbikes and scooters. While in the ads for bikes, the portrayal of women was more in terms of a supporting role, many a times as a prop, the portrayal of women for scooty was more empowering and oriented to the aspiration of women, especially the younger ones. It seems that such a difference in terms of portrayal is largely because of the stereotypical assumption made in terms of the target audience. In our analysis, two indicators dominated, namely function ranking and ritualization of subordination, in almost all the ads taken up for deconstruction. This indicates that most of the ads follow the normative gender structure, whereas in terms of function, a man is always the one instructing a woman, thereby placing the man's superiority over the woman. Take, for instance, the case of an earlier Bajaj ad, where a man is teaching his female friends how to ride a scooter. In another ad, a man is shown robbing a bank, while instructing the woman accomplice to fill the bag with money. This is particularly true for those ads for bikes rather than the scooty ads. When we look at the scooty ads of early 2000s, the portrayal of women at one time broke the stereotypes, but in the next breath, these were reinforced. For instance, in the scooty ad with Priyanka Chopra as the protagonist and an empowering tagline of 'Why should men have all the fun?', she takes her decision to go out in the evening, when her mother asks her where was she going and when would she be back, but the mother had different rules for her brother, reinforcing the age-old stereotypes that it is fine by men to be out of home anytime but not for women.

In the Bajaj ad titled 'Definitely male' in the early 2000s to a more recent Hero Xtreme ad titled 'Talking is such a waste of time', the gender narrative has been normative and stereotypical. The trend of positioning the woman as subordinate, inferior or as a mere prop has been a common occurrence.

In the sub-category of tyres, 16 TVCs were analysed, the sample representing four big tyre brands in the country, including CEAT, MRF, Bridgestone and JK. What has been observed on the indicators is some form of stereotyping in most ads. Women, in general, in the ads did not play a substantive role in any of the brand campaigns, albeit in some, they were shown as 'Idiots'. Here, we are talking about a popular campaign titled 'Idiot' from the makers of CEAT tyres. The campaign played on the theme of road safety and safe driving, with a satirical, tongue-in-cheek portrayal of ignorant and bad drivers on the road. Some of the ads here involved women and the portrayal seemed problematic at many levels. In one of the ads, two women were shown in a car, driving and chatting away, the older one trying to feed sweets to the other one on the driving seat, when she lost her control over the wheel and almost hit a man on the bike. None of the women were apologetic, but rather used the moment to shout at the man on the bike, for being an irresponsible driver. In another ad in the series, two women were shown on a street, presumably after a shopping binge. One of them, who had her kid accompanying her, did not realize when the child wandered her way without her noticing it. Later, when the women saw a commotion, they ran to find the child in the middle of the road, when a biker applied the break to save the child. Seeing that both the women ran towards the child and, while comforting her, shouted at the man for not being careful with his driving. In both of these ads, woman played an important role and were the focal point of ad narrative; however, their roles were depicted in a manner that showed them as 'idiots' (the theme of the campaign), who did not know the rules of driving or who found fault with others while being irresponsible themselves.

Bridgestone tyres' ads in the decade of 2011–2019 displayed women as consumers, but not necessarily in command. In one of the ads, it was her husband who was shown explaining to her, how to shop or reach her natal home, being the 'instructor' in Goffman's typology. There have been, however, some changes over the years, where some of the recent ads by CEAT have made some effort to break stereotypes about women. In one of the ads, the woman is the biker, which other brands rarely do. Further, in another CSR ad, they have addressed the issue of violence against women by showing their recent product, that is, a pepper spray on the handle of the scooty. Other than these few cases, the larger trend within this sub-category has not changed much. The inferior positioning of women vis-à-vis men as well as the self-positioning of inferiority by women remained to be the most common theme across all the ads from various brands within the category.

Lifestyle

In the category of lifestyle and sub-category of accessories, Tanishq, a TATA brand, has been the precursor to some of the out-of- ordinary themes in its ad campaigns. Both their 'Second marriage' and 'Office colleague' ads point towards the significant change in the Indian ad discourse, breaking the stereotypes about single mothers and status of women at work.

The ad regarding the remarriage of a single mother particularly dealt with multiple stereotypes, even though the remarriage of the single mother was the focal point of the ad. Apart from busting the myth that a single woman with a child can never find a life partner again, the ad shows how the campaign took on old taboos and stigmas and showed the positive side of the changing societal norms. The ad is discussed in detail later in the chapter.

In another ad, a young woman is told by her female superior to take off her earrings as 'It can distract clients', and she redeems herself by defying her superior and assuring her that the presentation would be fine with her earrings. Although the ad revolved around the image of the 'empowered modern woman of today', there were undertones of stereotypes and patriarchy in this ad. What comes in the face is the use of subtle patriarchal overtones to describe harsh work environment a woman worker could possibly face (even if the boss is of the same sex). For example, even though the senior female colleague is very impressed by her work, she still points a flaw in the woman's sartorial choices, which seems to indicate that the campaign perceives the position of a boss as that of an 'alpha male' and when occupied by a woman, she's acting like a woman in a man's world. What is also interesting to note is how the senior colleague (probably older in age) is shown in a sari and the young woman is shown in casual clothes, top and jeans. When we see the campaign as a whole, we get a feeling that the ad seems to attack the traditional patriarchal norms and how it clashes with present generation, even if it means pitting a woman against another.

However, on the other side, the redeeming thing about the ad narrative is its reflection on how the modern woman is empowered enough to not buckle under societal pressure and still stick to her beliefs and choices that define her.

In the category of Lifestyle, and within the Lifestyle in the sub category of Alcohol and Tobacco products, it has been seen, the companies taking a surrogate route in advertising to reach out to their target audience, after a legal ban on advertising of these products. In all, 13 surrogate ads from the alcohol sub-category were analysed, which included all the major brands like Seagram, Blenders Pride, AC Black, Hayworth, etc. Lisa Haydon and Priyanka Chopra appeared in one of the brands. In general, women were used as props, objects of desire; the patriarchal narrative could not escape from this sub-category.

In the tobacco category, take for instance the Chaini Khaini ad, where we see a man waiting at the airport, chewing on a khaini packet to pass time, when he starts fanaticizing about cine star Malaika Arora Khan dancing for him at the airport. Wearing a provocative dress, the woman is shown gyrating to the man's fantasies.

Ads of perfumes and deodorants brands from the lifestyle category have, often, blatantly objectified the woman form. For instance, the various ads for the brand Axe have often drawn dissension from the general public. In the 2000s, in the International campaigns 'The fallen angel' and 'The rap star and his crew', we see overt sexualization of the female form to highlight the strength of the deodorant. In comparison, the Axe India campaigns tend to use stereotypes and use women like props to emphasize on the power of perfume. In a celebrity endorsement, the campaign released, in 2010, cricketers Zaheer Khan and Virat Kohli, confident about the pull effect of the Axe deo, are counting the number of times a woman in the gym would turn towards them while exercising. In yet another Axe campaign, the ad narrative revolves around the theme of being smart enough to keep a small, pocket Axe to make any girl push the person next her in a theatre or train seat and bring the one with Axe next to her. (The girl after smelling the man actually pushes the man sitting next to her to make space for the one with a pocket Axe.) The ad may look funny, but makes a woman look shallow and easily lured.

When we looked at close to 1,200 ads across five brand categories and dozens of sub-categories under various categories, there was some hope and a lot of despair on the gender treatment as discussed above. Let us now take a few ads category-wise and deconstruct them thoroughly to understand the gender narrative.

AUTOMOBILE: TVS SCOOTY

'Go babelicious!' is the tagline of a television commercial. Try finding the word 'babelicious' in all dictionaries at your hand, but there would be no luck as there is no word like 'babelicious'. The word has been 'innovated' by a creative mind! What it aims at, you would soon unravel.

This TVS Scooty ad has a young, fashionable woman protagonist who is caught in a traffic jam. To make the most of the time lost

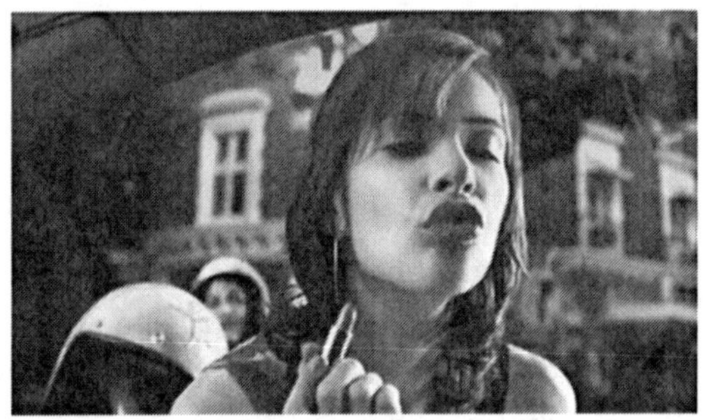

Source: https://www.campaignindia.in/article/tvs-scooty-pep-says-go-babelicious-in-new-tvcs/412681

in the jam, she gets off her two wheeler and reaches near the front side mirror of a stationary car (also stuck in the jam) to apply lipstick, attracting the attention of a young male driver, who seems to enjoy her being there, while a lady, presumably his wife, is sitting next to him. How this narrative fits the product category or the brand's features is anybody's guess. In the era of lifestyle ads, whether this narrative presents a slice of life is difficult to answer.

Commenting on the communication narrative to position the Scooty, S. Srinivas, General Manager Marketing of TVS Motor, said this to the advertising journal campaign,

> The constant endeavor of the Scooty brand team at TVS is to try and spot emerging style, fashion and lifestyle trends amongst young women that can keep Scooty as the boldest fashion statement on the roads and in the process give our consumers newer and fresher ways to express themselves as they continually redefine the meaning of feminity [*sic*].[1]

This is how the people behind the ad thought about femininity. Let us look at it from the societal perspective. Coming to the characterization of the woman in the ad, she is not just applying lipstick as many do; she is instead doing it with some sensuality. She is tall, fair, an embodiment of the ideal 'beauty'. She is sensually feminine with her gestures. The way she touches her hair, takes out her lipstick and applies it is a stereotypical feminine way. What this does is that it reinforces the idea that sensuality is femininity or, even worse, being sensual is seen as the embodiment of the ideal femininity. Another problem arises when one takes into account the man in the car and his reaction to it. What the ad does here is that it associates the woman's action as gratifying the male gaze. Although unconscious about the man in the beginning, her action is observed by the man, who is tempted to look at her. The girl also seems to enjoy the flirtatious moment, when she is seen pouting her lips in the direction of the man.

'Babelicious', as you would have guessed by now, is a combination of two words. Babe + delicious = Babelicious, something to be gobbled and enjoyed! If this were not commodification of the female form, then what else would be? Not only activists and woman rights proponents, even an average person (both men and women) would find the expression horrendous and highly gender insensitive!

The other ad in the series is equally whacky. This one has a young woman trying to pass through a traffic control barrier on an over-crowed road with vehicular traffic. She tries to plead with the traffic cop with her gestures and antics, to let her jump the queue and let go, which he does, attracting the annoyance of others held in the jam. Advertisers often claim to base their creatives on consumer insights. If this is their understanding of young girls, it certainly is demeaning to womenfolk, to say the least. Interestingly, however, the campaign did not receive much adverse reaction.

The creative minds, however, have a different take on this. Created by global ad agency McCann Erickson, Prasoon Joshi, Executive Chairman of McCann Worldgroup (he also heads the Film Censor Board, a government body), said, 'Any outstanding campaign is due to a great collaborative effort between the client and agency. Team TVS and McCann Erickson have a great relationship and understanding of the brand and that gets manifested in this campaign in a great fashion.'[2] Anil Thomas, Executive Creative Director, McCann Erickson, had this to say on the storytelling and the use of the expression 'bablecious':

> We saw an opportunity, with this collection, of going beyond the mobility factor, a look at the bold colours on offer and we wondered if we could position this collection as a fashion accessory. Yes, the bike helps you get there, but getting there looking absolutely babelicious does not hurt either! So what others might find as shocking, the babelicious girl finds perfectly innocent and natural—be it a behavior or the choice of bold striking colours for a scooter. Hence, the importance of spontaneity and effervescence in the characters who think its okay to create a ruckus so that she could get past a barricade or the simple act of wearing lipstick in middle of the road.[3]

A KFC ad for the Western audience with the same storyline (surprisingly!) was withdrawn by the fast-food joint when there was a huge furore on the social media for being gender insensitive and inappropriately portraying women (discussed in Chapter 1).

Tyre: MRF

This ad titled 'Lipstick' was released by MRF tyres in the year 2001. The ad features cine actor Vidya Balan seated in the back seat of a car trying to apply lip colour in two different situations; one with MRF tyre and one with another tyre. In terms of portrayal, she is shown as a working woman represented by the corporate suit she is wearing. When compared with other ads that time, the ad is empowering, in that she is not stereotyped as a homemaker or a dependent woman. There is, however, stereotyping of women in the sense as the ad reflects that women are concerned only about looking beautiful. The other stereotype is about dressing. Vidya Balan, who is seen as the quintessential Indian beauty who promoted sarees as fashionable, was made to wear Western clothes in an ad to present her as a working woman. Although in India, most working women dress up in traditional Indian attire of saree, but because the stereotype says that Indian traditional women usually don't apply make-up while in transit, the actress had to be shown as modern and uninhibited.

Incidentally, as brought in the previous chapter, automobile category is a big offender in presenting women stereotypically and objectifying them.

LIFESTYLE: DUREX CONDOM

This advertisement from the year 2017 features popular cine actor Ranveer Singh. A woman is seen in the ad, testing every nook and corner of the house with an overtly sensual body language. She is then tapping them up in preparation of what was to come. As the doorbell rings, she opens the door to find Ranveer Singh on the floor, trying to pick up condoms that had spilled out of his bag. There was another ad in the series with the same narrative but a reversal in role, with woman as the protagonist.

The brand, through a bold narrative, is making a strong statement that aims to remove the stigma around discussing sex. It also tries to create a healthy perception on sex by promoting the use of condom or buying a condom. Further, in terms of portrayal, the ad caters to a certain idea of a 'new-age woman'. In this ad, she is shown as being a part of an impending act and not as a passive player for the pleasure of the man. In another ad in the series, she is the one who is carrying the condom, which is an effort towards positioning woman as equal to man in terms of her desires and choices. It also tries to break the taboo on women buying or carrying condoms.

From the perspective of traditionalists and patriarchal norms, the ad may be construed as sacrilegious, reflecting a promiscuous woman who does not mind casual sex. The ad, though not inappropriate from the gender equity perspective, may still raise eyebrows among many.

Cigarettes and Alcohol: Imperial Blue—Men Will Be Men (Supermarket)

The campaign 'Men will be men' is a series of surrogate ads that Imperial Blue has been running for quite a long time. This particular ad is a part of the campaign released in the year 2015. In the ad, two men at a supermarket are seen eyeing at two women, who were busy shopping. Later, as they stand in the queue at the checkout counter, they find out that they had been ogling at each other's wife.

Such an ad narrative reinforces stereotype about men that men are men, flirtatious, stalkers, promiscuous, but that does not really matter, as 'men are men' after all. It also brushes off woman's' problem with male gaze and trivializes a serious social issue that women have been fighting against. Further, in terms of portrayal, there is women objectification in the ad as an object of male gaze.

LIFESTYLE

Apparel: Levi's

The ad titled 'Live Unbuttoned' was released in the year 2008, featuring popular cine actor Akshay Kumar. In the ad, Akshay Kumar and a woman are shown getting intimate with each other as she unbuttons his jeans. That's when the director yells 'cut' and the two get some make-up done. The woman then approaches Akshay and says to him, 'Next time, I'll unbutton all the way.'

As far as the portrayal of women in the ad is concerned, there is a fundamental problem of objectification. Akshay is shown caressing his bare body. Woman is shown behind Akshay, holding him from the back. Although it may seem that both reflect sensuality, but there is a subtle positioning of the woman as the object of sexual pleasure of the male protagonist. Further, although the brand has argued that the theme of the ad caters to the young audience, it is important to note that the nature of the ad is such that it caters to the young male audience and not the youth per se.

As a part of its campaign, the brand participated in the Lakmé Fashion Show 2009, where a shirtless Akshay Kumar does not allow a model to unbutton his pants but comes down to the audience gallery where his wife Twinkle Khanna was seated and asked her to unbutton him, which she did.

Source: http://archive.indianexpress.com/news/prosecute-akshay-kumar-twinkle-khanna-in-obscenity-case-high-court-to-cops/1148644/

Note: A case of indecency was filed against them in the Bombay High Court in 2009 by social activist Anil Nair. Mumbai police arrested Twinkle (Akshay Kumar was not in station then) but let her out on bail.[4]

Deodorant: Wild Stone

The ad 'Rain', released in the year 2009, features a Bengali homemaker in saree running out of her room to the balcony as it starts to rain. While she struggles to save the clothes, her neighbour is watching her. Smelling the scent of his deodorant, she is shown sensually dancing in the rain, oblivious of everything else around her. While all this goes on, her mother-in-law calls her from inside her house. The gender narrative is on the expected lines; the ad blatantly sexualizes the woman. The narrative objectifies the woman and makes her the object of male gaze. Interestingly, the protagonist is not a young girl but a married homemaker, shown quirky, ending up as gullible and easily distracted by the sensual scent of a man next door.

Mint, writing on steamy commercials that use sex as a strategy, argued that many agencies use sex as a strategy with a purpose for a better recall value of such ads. Commenting on the Wild Stone ad, the story quoted R. R. Garnayak, CEO, Asian Shopping Club, a Kolkata-based agency that handles the Wild Stone account, who said, 'Our consumer is between the age group of 15–30 and the imagery in the advertisement was created keeping in mind what will appeal to them the most.' Citing another example of a similar kind of ad narrative, Amul Macho, a male underwear brand that had an uproarious response for being in bad taste from many women groups followed by complaints to ASCI, the paper quoted Sandeep Seksaria, Director, JG Hosiery, who seemed thrilled at the response the ad generated, 'After we launched the commercial in May, our sales have gone up 35%,' he said (Mehra & Parker, 2007).

ACCESSORIES: JEWELLERY

Tanishq: Second Marriage

The ad is about the second marriage of a single mother. What it has shown is path breaking, in that it has dared to question the norms of an ideal marriage and family. It speaks of a large number of people in the country who are seen as deviant and outcast because of being single, especially when it comes to women. In contrast to such a belief and practice, the ad has shown second marriage can also be an occasion for celebration. In this case, the protagonist is not only a single woman, but she also has a young daughter. To top it all, she is also dark, a triple whammy in a country where the matrimonial ads often ask for 'very fair' bride. In the Tanishq ad, the parents of both the bride and the bridegroom are also in the frame, happy and blessing them, again breaking of a stereotype. It touches an emotional chord when one sees the easy camaraderie between the little girl and her new father. Light-heartedly, one can say that Tanishq found an opportunity to sell its precious jewellery the second time to the bride to be, but then, why not!

This ad brought quite a buzz in the media for being progressive and gender sensitive. The ad did not attempt to create a world of make-believe. Second marriages are happening amidst joy and celebrations today. The ad, therefore, depicted a 'slice of life'. Created by Lowe Lintas that has also incidentally created the controversial 'F&L' campaign (discussed later), the Tanshiq campaign on second marriage came as a breather. The ad can be rated as inclusive and gender sensitive.

FMCG

Aerated Drink: Limca

The ad 'Do Pal Taazgi' was released in the year 2011. In the ad, a man and a woman walk past each other, but the man stops halfway, captivated by the woman in the frame. He then follows her around as she is shown sipping Limca while also teasing him playfully.

A fundamental problem with this ad is that a man is following a woman which, in a normal situation, would be a case of stalking. The ad romanticizes such a situation that would make many women uncomfortable. Further, the woman is shown as being okay with a stranger following her, thereby, reinforcing the common conclusion that people come up with when there is a case of eve-teasing and public harassment, that the woman only invited it.

The ad is problematic in reinforcing the stereotypical perception about women.

PERSONAL CARE PRODUCTS

F&L: The Airhostess Ad

This ad was released in the year 2003 but pulled off the air due to objections from many women groups in the country and lodging of cases in various consumer courts. The ad features a father who is shown constantly complaining and lamenting, if only he had a son, despite the fact that the daughter was the only earning member in the family. The daughter is disheartened at the kind of job she had and her dark skin. When she looks at an ad for an airhostess job, she uses the F&L cream, which instantly makes her fair, landing her a higher paying job, making her father proud.

The fundamental problem with the portrayal of woman here is that there is this idealization of fairness. Such an idea about beauty in India is demeaning and demoralizing to a large number of women, especially young girls. Further, the ad does not only idealize fairness but equates it with success, which becomes a double whammy.

The ad is inappropriate as it discriminates women not only on skin colour but also relates success to fair skin.

Buckled under public pressure, ASCI stepped in, and not only had the ad withdrawn but also it added a provision in its code on what the advertisers needed to keep in view in the narrative on fairness creams and the colour of skin, reflected in Chapter 3.

Ponds: Priyanka Chopra and Saif Ali Khan

The ad titled 'White Beauty' was released in the year 2008. The ad is actually a five-part long ad about the love story between the protagonists Priyanka Chopra and Saif Ali Khan, popular cine actors. It begins with both of them parting at an airport as Saif leaves for another country. Priyanka waits for him eagerly but later finds out that a more successful Saif is now with another woman. She is sad and lonely and finds solace in the new Ponds beauty cream. When Saif finds out that she is fair and, thereby, more 'beautiful', he returns to her.

There are so many things that are problematic here, but fundamentally, what is objectionable is the patriarchal narrative throughout the series. Beauty in the ads is defined by fairness, which is a big issue in India. It does not stop there; the ad reinstates that fairness is an issue not only for women but for men as well. Therefore, when Priyanka aspires for a certain kind of ideal 'beauty', she is doing so to please and attract Saif and not for her own sake. In that way, a woman is not defined by her own aspirations but rather by the man's standards and, therefore, seeks approval of the man.

Dove

The Dove ad 'Let's Break the Rules of Beauty' was released in the year 2016, as a part of the brand's marketing strategy which has been termed as 'femvertising', wherein the theme was to create a positive body image of women. In the ad, a woman's voice narrates how surprising it is that in a country of 631 million women, there is still one face of beauty. It then rapidly shows different types of women, in terms of colour, age and culture.

In terms of portraying women, there is not much to be critical about it. It is true that most beauty products portray an ideal kind of beauty for women, which is fair and spotless. In such a context, ads like this become a message of empowerment. The brand, however, misplaced itself, when it came out with a limited edition of bottles of varying shapes to celebrate various body types, slim and obese. It was criticized for being unflattering as it ended up ridiculing women, thus enhancing women's insecurities.

One also needs to remember that deep down, the brand does play with women's insecurities about themselves. So, even if there are one or a thousand ideal types of beauty, it is still problematic, in that the brand exploits on women's deepest insecurities about themselves by asking them to strive for some form of ideal desirability, whether that is one or multiple.

Stationery: Rotomac Pen

The ad was released in the year 1995 with the tag line 'Likhte likhte love ho jaye' (you can fall in love while writing). The ad features Raveena Tandon at a shoot, performing on a song. At the end, fans are chasing her for her autograph as she gets into the car. She pulls out a Rotomac Pen from her blouse. In some scenes, she is shown sensually dancing. The ad capitalizes on the celebrity status of Raveena by associating her with the brand, while showing things that are not really functional with the product. What is fundamentally problematic with the portrayal is the use of sensuality, which in no way goes well with the product and especially when it is young children chasing her for her autograph. What the storyline does is associate a sensual Raveena with the brand, without really showing the functionality of the brand itself.

In a personal interview, the concerned account servicing head shared that the brief to the agency from the client was that the protagonist would be popular cine actor of that time (Raveena Tandon) and she had to be seen pulling out the pen from her blouse, asking the agency to build a narrative around that. This made it clear in no uncertain term the ubiquitous role played by the client, in general, in the final narrative.

Slice: Katrina Kaif (Aamsutra)

In the 2011 Slice ad, a mango juice advertisement, cine actor Katrina Kaif essays the role. The ad is a part of the series of campaign titled 'Aamsutra', and this particular ad has the theme

'Sabr ka phal meetha hota hai' (patience pays!) In the ad, Katrina is shown sitting sensually in a meadow as she seductively picks up a mango and waits for it to ripen.

In terms of gender sensitivity, the ad is problematic mainly in terms of the product category and the use of seduction and sensuality as a strategy. Katrina Kaif, as a celebrity, embodies a certain standard of the Indian ideal beauty and is labelled many times as a sex symbol. Her role here then becomes important, and with that, her portrayal here, being seduced by an inanimate object, is quite problematic, which has no connect with the brand or the product functionality.

A product from the global company PepsiCo, the ads for its Aamsutra brand with Katrina Kaif as the protagonist, often, have been erotic. Interestingly, the various juice brands from the PepsiCo stable elsewhere use functionality and not sexual undertones in positioning the brand, except in India. Competitor Maaza, with a slightly bigger market share in India, stands in stark contrast to the Slice ads. Avant-garde filmmaker Sudhir Mishra said about the Aamsutra ad in an entertainment programme that how such ads were cleared from the Censor Board. Interestingly, there is no law that requires pre-censoring of ads in India.

TRAVEL AND LEISURE

Luggage–VIP

The ad from the year 2012 has in the storyline two men sitting at the airport, when a woman walks past them. As she does so, there is an announcement that the flight going to Paris has a sexy model travelling in it and the seat next to her is vacant. Hearing that, both the men get off their feet and are seen racing for that seat.

The objectification of women is quite apparent in the ad. The woman in the ad is referred as 'sexy'. She is then portrayed as a 'prize' that the two men compete for, thus objectifying her. The ad plays a very common scenario of the society, drawn from the perspective of male fantasy of encountering what is idealized as 'sexy' woman.

LUXURY, HOSPITALITY: TAJ– 'SHE IS TAJ'

The ad created by ad agency Rediffusion was released in the 1990s. Very sleekly directed, the camera in the ad follows a woman in a classical attire, a saree, who is walking sensually around various interiors of the Taj Hotel, displaying its opulence. Mystery surrounds her as the camera shoots her from a distance and never focuses on her face. There are also different texts shown as she walks around. The text one time is 'She welcomes Presidents and Kings, but she welcomes you as warmly. She works with tycoons and chairmen .... She treats you like family. She is the Taj. She welcomes you to her hotels, resorts, and palaces across India.'

Straight off, the analogy of hotel with woman is characteristically stereotypical—care and warmth associated with women is quite commonplace. The ad narrative uses these stereotypes to brand itself on good hospitality by associating the hotel with a woman and by using the pronoun 'she' for the hotel. Though stereotypical, the storyline and the visual treatment enhances the brand value.

SOAPS AND DETERGENTS: ARIEL–WHY IS LAUNDRY A WOMAN'S JOB?

The first ad in this campaign was released in the year 2016, which depicts two senior women discussing about each other's daughters-in-law. They say that women in this generation were so different from theirs, as they earned so less, but their *bahus* now earn more than their sons. As they are discussing these issues, they hear the son asking his wife if she had washed his clothes.

The ad raises a very important question about inequality of gender roles in a patriarchal structure. Women are portrayed being financially independent, but despite that, the home scene remains the same. It can be read as one of the cutting-edge attempts, raising the issue of gender equality in changing times. Media reported that the brand invited response from men and received about half a million replies, some heart-rending, others funny (Shetty, 2015).

BFSI

Insurance: LIC– Need for Insurance

The ad, released in the year 2006, shows a widow giving a send-off to her daughter after her marriage. In the next frame, she is shown near the picture of her dead husband with moistened eyes, when she is asked by a voice-over on how she has managed to carry off all the responsibilities even after her husband's death. To which, she replies that she was able to carry out her responsibility because her deceased husband fulfilled his responsibility before he died.

Now, there is a positive aspect to this narrative, where a widow is not shown as weak, sad and helpless. She is shown as a capable mother who could still fulfil all of her duties as a mother even after her husband's death. However, one aspect that cannot be ignored is how a hint of patriarchy is subtly present in it. The narrative is such that the woman as a widow is capable of fulfilling her duties but only because of her 'responsible' deceased husband. So, the man is still the protector and provider, and all credit still goes to him, despite him being not present anymore. The voice-over in the ad is also of man, establishing who is in command, and the tagline 'Zindagi ke saath bhi aur zindagi ke baad bhi' (in life as in death) only reinforces patriarchy.

In conclusion, it can be posited that despite a very visible critical discourse on gender discrimination and insensitivity, which has only increased with a hyper social media, ads, in general, continue to be stereotypical on the one hand and inappropriate and irreverent on the other, disrespecting, to put it mildly, half the human race. The redeeming thing, however, is that people are now becoming vocal about it. It is hoped that in time to come, there would be a paradigm change in the ad discourse, but only if we do not remain passive as people and use our right to question such advertisements. The real change would be discernible when men also feel repulsed at such narratives as women do!

Jumma chumma de de.
Choli ke peeche kya hai?
Sexy, sexy, sexy, mujhe log bole.
You are my chammak challo.
Tu cheez badi hai mast mast.
Aajaa meri gaadi main baith jaa.
Tu hai meri fantasy.
Munni badnaam hui, darling tere liye.
Women are not item numbers. They are not chikni chamelis.
They are definitely not fevicol.
They have not been put on this planet
for your supreme entertainment or pleasure.
A woman is not an adjective.
If you cannot respect a woman,
you are nothing.
Respect women. Full stop.

Source: The Times of India. https://www.change.org/p/times-of-india-stop-objectifying-women

An ad from the *Times of India* to end the chapter on a good note!

NOTES

1 Read more at: https://www.campaignindia.in/article/tvs-scooty-pep-says-go-babelicious-in-new-tvcs/412681

2 Read more at: https://www.campaignindia.in/article/tvs-scooty-pep-says-go-babelicious-in-new-tvcs/412681

3 Read more at: https://www.campaignindia.in/article/tvs-scooty-pep-says-go-babelicious-in-new-tvcs/412681

4 See India Today (2013) and Ali & Dubey (2009); the story reflects that Twinkle Khanna was arrested and let out on a personal bond of ₹950. The arrest was made invoking the indecent portrayal by a social worker who complained about both indulging in obscene behaviour in public.

REFERENCES

Ali, S. A., & Dubey, B. (2009, 10 April). Akshay's unbuttoning act: Twinkle arrested, released. *The Times of India*. https://timesofindia.indiatimes.com/india/Akshays-unbuttoning-act-Twinkle-arrested-released/articleshow/4382598.cms

India Today. (2013, 29 July). Prosecute Akshay Kumar, Twinkle in obscenity case: HC to cops. https://www.indiatoday.in/movies/bollywood/story/prosecute-akshay-kumar-twinkle-in-obscenity-case-in-a-fashion-show–2009-hc-to-cops–172043–2013–07–29.

Mehra, P., & Parker, L. A. (2007, 22 June). Heat over 'sexy' commercials turns ad agencies on. *Livemint*. https://www.livemint.com/Consumer/TY2pecByqmiiajbYy2S3uO/Heat-over-sexy-commercials-turns-ad-agencies-on.html

Roy, S. (2013, 23 December). *Does sex in advertising sell?* Introspectmarketing. https://introspectmarketing.wordpress.com/2013/12/23/does-sex-in-advertising-sell/

Shetty, A. (2015, 31 March). Is laundry only a woman's job? These epic reactions from men will leave you stunned. https://www.india.com/viral/is-laundry-only-a-womans-job-these-epic-reactions-from-men-will-leave-you-stunned–330690/

CHAPTER 5

STRAIGHT FROM THE SOURCE!

The most powerful element in advertising is the truth.

Bill Bernbach

Indian ad industry is pegged at over ₹70,000 crore or about US$12 billion (2019). Advertising is an aspirational profession, especially for the youth. That over 300 universities and institutions of higher learning in India offer courses in mass communication and many among them in advertising is reflective of the fact that advertising is a popular vocation. Young persons, especially from the cities, are attracted to the profession of advertising for its perceived glamour and creativity.

While there are thousands of agencies, there are 964 accredited to the Indian Newspaper Society (INS). The location of ad

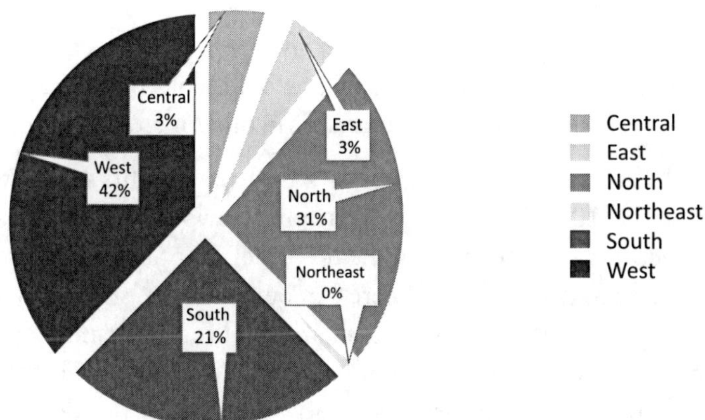

Source: Author, based on data from INS, 2018.

agencies makes for an interesting study, as the following graphs would reflect.[1] This would suggest the sourcing of manpower, in general, from these locations.

When we look at the specific location of these accredited agencies, the following graph emerges.

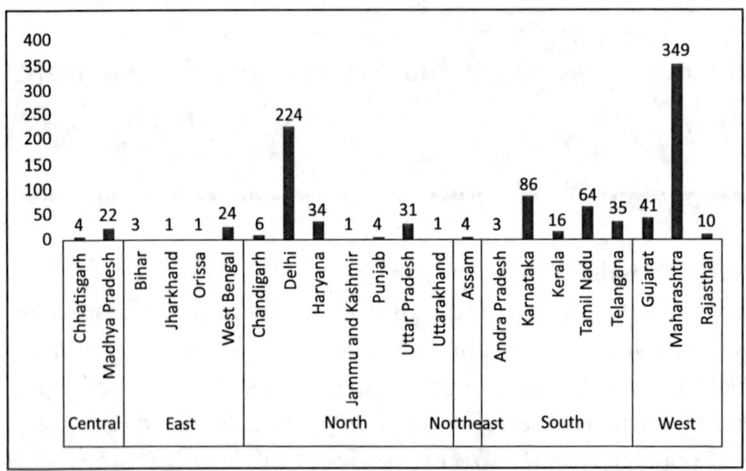

Source: Author, based on data from INS, 2018.

So, we see that Mumbai (Maharashtra) and Delhi/National Capital Region (NCR) take away the maximum bandwidth of advertising agencies' locations in the country. As most of the ad business is concentrated among the six international conglomerates (reflected in Box 5.1), wherever the agencies are located, it is not of much import as these agencies would work on a pan-India approach, assisted by smaller branches in other metros and towns.

The discussion in this chapter is based on insights harvested out of the 10 FGDs and in-depth interviews (IDIs) with over 30 practitioners from among the top echelons of the ad industry in India.[2] So, what you read here can be said to be 'straight from the horse's mouth', giving readers an insight into the making of campaigns, how the creative minds work, create gender narrative around brands and, most importantly, who finally decides what would appear in a brand campaign. Let's address these insights.

Box 5.1 Advertising Agencies with Global Affiliations

Wire and Plastic Products (WPP; UK) owns a number of advertising, public relations and market research networks, including IMRB, Millward Brown, Grey, Burson-Marsteller, Hill+Knowlton, J. Walter Thompson (JWT), Ogilvy & Mather, TNS, Young & Rubicam and Cohn & Wolfe (over US$19 billion worth).

Omnicom, the second largest advertising and corporate communications company employs more than 74,000 employees in about 100 countries worldwide (US$15.3 billion worth).

Interpublic (US) consists of three major networks: McCann Worldgroup, Lowe and Partners, and Futbol Club Barcelona (FCB). Its media agencies are bundled under the IPG Mediabrands entity. It also owns a number of specialty agencies, including public relations, sports marketing, talent representation and healthcare (US$7.5 billion worth).

Publicis (French) has operations in over 202 cities in 105 countries, including a strategic alliance with Dentsu. In 2013, Publicis announced plans to merge with Omnicom to form Publicis Omnicom Group (US$9.6 billion worth)

Dentsu is currently the 5th largest advertising agency network in the world in terms of worldwide revenues (US$6.00 billion worth).

Source: Adapted from agencies sources and https://www.worldatlas.com/articles/the-largest-advertising-companies-in-the-world.html

Role of the client: What came across unambiguously from all the FGDs from both the global and home-spun agencies is the ubiquitous role of the client on what would appear in the ad, including the choice of celebrity, based on his personal understanding of their appeal, which does not necessarily mean how suitable he/she may be in enhancing the brand value. In case of a difference of opinion between the agency and client's choice of celebrity, it is always the client whose choice prevails, as it came out clearly in the research.

Ignorance of laws and policies on indecent portrayal: Surprisingly, none of the participants from among over 80 persons across 10 FGDs had any clue on the existence of any law in India that had to do with the prohibition of indecent representation of women in advertising. An aided recall in various FGDs also did not elicit any response. It came out in the various interactions that there is no orientation for young professionals when they join the ad profession on gender, policies or laws governing the sector. Most respondents across FGDs knew about the existence of the ASCI, but the engagement with its professional code also seemed to be inconsequential. Most respondents said that the ASCI Code came into discussion only when there was a complaint against some ad from their agency or a known brand. Some felt that ASCI's provisions were important to follow when these were mandatory provisions, especially in case of financial advertising.

Absence of written gender policies: There are no written rules on gender, but conventions and stereotypes are referred to build up the narrative. For instance, if a working woman is to be shown as the protagonist, she would often be reflected in a business suit, though the fact is that a staggering majority of Indian women who go to work wear traditional Indian attire like a saree. Similarly, if the ad is meant for an energy drink, it would be an urban setting with a young mother dressed in a tracksuit and not in saree.

Brand categories likely to objectify the woman form: Condoms, deodorants, innerwear, beauty and surrogate products like alcohol and tobacco brands are more likely to inappropriately portray women, felt most respondents. The other categories may not objectify woman, per se, but project her in a traditional manner for immediate connect with the target audience. In other words, women would be projected like the caring mother, wife and daughter-in-law as expected in patriarchy. This was not considered by most FGD participants as stereotyping women but only reflecting a 'social reality', thus underscoring the point that stereotyping, in a way, would help the brand in striking a chord with the target audience.

In an all-women FGD in Kolkata, representing small agencies, the participants believed that stereotyping of women happened all the time, but keeping in view the changing times, newer stereotypes were being created like the concept of 'super mom' and a 'super confident' woman, thus creating more expectations from women from families and society. They held advertising squarely responsible for this new phenomenon, which, in their opinion, was not good.

Respondents from the global agencies, in general, talked about various filters within their agencies that ensured that nothing derogatory would pass for public viewing. This, however, is difficult to take at the face value, if most of the ads across all categories coming from the global agencies are any indication. One could also argue that their understanding of what, in their view, was 'indecent' and 'inappropriate' portrayal may be quite different from what public's perceptions about these terms, in general, are.

Creative teams feel no connect: Most ad professionals are aware of the criticism that advertising draws, especially on the social media, but do not accept that they could be held responsible for gender insensitivity. The defence, often, is that advertising, in its 'slice of life' narrative, only reflected a social reality. They talked of the perceptible change in the ad discourse in some recent campaigns like the Tanishq's second marriage and Mia brand's working woman, Myntra's same-sex relationship, Vicks' transgender mother, Ariel's 'Share the Load' or Airtel's 'Boss or Wife'. It is interesting to find that when good advertising is created, it gets a nod for being progressive, even from competitors, as the interface with ad professional across agencies reflected.

Missing women in the ad sector: Many young women who join various courses in mass communication work in the advertising sector, but their number dwindles over a period of time. While there is no authentic data on the man:woman ratio in the Indian advertising industry, the industry sources put it 70:30. A visit to various ad agencies during the field survey reiterated this fact as one could see less women in the FGDs. Most respondents, especially among the branch managers and HR professionals, ascribed this to the 'long working hours' and 'lower capacity to handle stress' among many others on why women did not sustain for long.

WHAT PROFESSIONALS ARE THINKING: INSIGHTS FROM IDIS

Thirty-four IDIs were conducted with very senior ad professionals from among large, global, medium and small agencies across some states that also included IDIs with chairs of advertising professional bodies, namely the Advertising Agencies Association of India (AAAI) and ASCI.

Highlights from IDIs

Of the several complaints received by the ASCI on misleading claims, only about 5 per cent complaints were on the women portrayal, as shared by the ASCI chairman. Among the many initiatives, the ASCI has come up with an app named 'ascionline' that enables complainants to click the ad against which the complaint has to be made and share with ASCI for acting as per its procedure. 'Not many people may know that ASCI can be approached for violation of the code on the digital platform,' said the then ASCI Chairman, D. Shivakumar. He shared that ASCI was planning to educate the consumers on this. ASCI, he informed, is on board with the Ministry of Women and Child Development (WCD) on the proposed amendment in the Indecent Representation of Women (Prohibition) Act, 1986.

The AAAI Chair, Ashish Bhasin (2018), shared that, among many things, the AAAI sends advisory to members to ensure diversity in recruitment, but gender sensitivity in the portrayal of women in the ad space, he said, was not really a top-of-the-mind issue with the AAAI. The AAAI, unlike ASCI, said Bhasin, did not have a policing role!

P. V. Narayanamoorthy, who once headed Carat, said that advertising was very insensitive to gender in general. Showing a man cooking in the kitchen or washing clothes as one finds now in some ads was not a reflection of gender sensitivity, he rued. A lot more, he said, was needed by the ad industry to reflect the changes in the society and not just pay a lip service.

Ashish Chakravarty, Executive Director and Head of Creative in India with McCann Erickson, on the dwindling ratio of women in the ad sector, said that it was indeed an area of concern. He shared that, once, his group went to a client for a brief on a beauty product and there was not a single woman with them, which looked awkward even to the client, especially when they had to work on a woman-centric brand.

Sunil Gupta, who headed JWT once, said on commodification, 'Agencies are bound by their clients, who are notoriously and needlessly conservative, so even if one goes with a new idea, most are stillborn. It's a vicious circle.'

Vivek Srivastava, managing director of the Korean agency Innocean Worldwide, felt that advertising has turned out to be more sensitive than mainstream entertainment avenues towards the portrayal of women. 'I think in the garb of the so-called political correctness,' he said, 'the portrayals are being made too simplistic and robbing women of the new age attitude, their own swagger and independent identity.'

Colvyn Harris, former CEO South Asia, JWT, referring to the Kingfisher calendar depicting scantily dressed women, commented that surrogate advertising relating to liquor promotion, including ads with celebrity endorsement, had the potential to indecently portray women. When the interviewer cited the case of the Ford Figo car ad that his agency had created which received a lot of dissension for its gender insensitivity, he defended his agency's position saying that the posters that were posted online were not a part of the campaign but regretted that they landed there.[3]

Celebrated ad man, social commentator, once president of McCann Erickson and now CEO of Futurebrands, Santosh Desai said of women's portrayal, 'advertising tends not to run afoul of indecent representation as much as inappropriate and stereotypes. Those are the kind of things that advertising conflicts with much more,' giving a reference of the Amul Macho ad, 'Yeh Toh Bada Toing Hai'. In this ad, the woman was not indecently dressed, but her body language was such that it was considered inappropriate and indecent, reasoned Desai. This ad incidentally was withdrawn after a huge public outrage. On asking whether the issue of indecent portrayal needed policy intervention, Desai said, 'The thing is that when the government speaks of such things, I am terrified. The government should not be given the task of gender sensitisation because they have no clue, what it is.'

The only woman CEO of a global agency Contract Advertising, at the time of field survey in 2018, Raji Ramaswamy said of objectifying women in advertising thus:

> It's neither progressive nor ahead of the curve. Equality, empowerment, strength, overcoming barriers and adversity are far more attractive ways to build a brand and create communication and conversations that appeal to the consumer, yet there are instances and cases where commodifying is the way a marketer wishes to communicate and a publisher or media wishes to connect in the name of reality or being cool and fashionable. It's regressive and short sighted and does not in any enhance the way a woman is perceived in the society.[4]

Lowe Lintas, the agency that has created both the F&L campaign that drew a lot of opposition and the Tanishq's second marriage campaign, which won them a lot of applaud, the CEO Raj Gupta had this to say, 'We helped Fair & lovely to get out of the old narrative of fairness and beauty as a way to succeed to a more progressive story of women empowerment and equality.' On the innovative Tanishq campaign, he said,

> We never conceived Tanishq only as a jewellery brand .... We cannot keep telling the society, 'hey change the way you treat women.' We decided to tell people, this is how women think today. We became the voice of working women through Mia, a Tanishq sub brand. They (women) do not let negative situations, small talk, and gossip wherever they go, affect them. They just get their best at work.[5]

He then referred to other campaigns that his agency had created, namely 'Touch the Pickle' to fight the taboo on menstruation and an advocacy campaign 'Power of 49' (49% women voters), who needed to be taken seriously by lawmakers.

Citing an example of insensitive ads, a creative head of global agency, FCB Ulka, referred to the 'Jack & Jones' campaign, which she thought was very sexist and misogynist. Cine actor Ranveer Singh, the protagonist, also received a lot of flak for it. The billboard ad had a woman flung over Singh's shoulders with the caption 'Don't hold back. Take your work home.' She shared that there was a growing awareness about the need for gender sensitivity among ad professionals, but one did not see it reflected in the campaigns as much, for reasons not unknown. She referred to a client who insisted on including only a boy and not a girl for an energy drink, when the creatives presented to him by her agency had the girl child. The client, she said, unfortunately believed that the boy's imagery would resonate more with the target audience as compared to the girls. There is no money for guessing that the will of the client prevailed, a case of 'he who pays the piper calls the tune!'

Regrettably, an executive director of an agency had this to say on the objectification of women, 'Yes, commodification and stereotyping of women is rampant, but advertising mirrors reality. If there is commodification of women in society, and it helps advertisers and marketers to connect faster with their target audiences by using stereotyping, so be it! It is a means to an end.[6]'

On the near absence of gender-sensitive guidelines in the agencies, a national planning director of a global agency said that while his agency had no 'gender-specific guidelines', they followed a 'creative scale' to evaluate the work. 'The first number on the scale, he explained, was #1, which signified "Damaging" work to client, to consumer, to society at large. Work that was gender insensitive would squarely, he said, be graded #1 and not be allowed to be released.'

Research that was once an essential part of the advertising industry is no longer considered important because of tight budgets, rued a woman branch head of a global agency. Campaigns, in general, she shared, were no more scientifically pre-tested unless the client invested in research. On hindsight, she felt this could be responsible in some way in creating inappropriate narratives about women as what finally appeared in an ad was often not backed by research.

DISCUSSION

Advertising, the backbone of marketing, is more than visible by what it does for the brands, rather than what it stands for. Advertising and the stereotypical and inappropriate portrayal of women have become almost synonymous in public perception. What the content creators see as the reflection of social reality in the ad narrative is, in fact, what they create, based on their understanding of the social milieu and, more importantly, keeping in view that brand's requirement. Advertising sector seems to have created a world of 'make-believe' in which they operate and construct the 'desired reality', keeping in view the 'desired response'. As highly paid professionals in a glam world, critics believe that there is an overt sense of pretentiousness and pomposity among ad professionals on what they contribute towards brand building. Everyone may not agree with this position. Maurice Lévy, well-known ad man, who one time was the chairman and CEO of Publicis Groupe, writes in a foreword to the book *Born in 1842. A History of Advertising*,

> I love this profession for many and varied reasons and for the experiences it brings by the dozen. I love it because advertising is an exercise in modesty. I know this will come as shock to some people, but advertising on behalf of a brand means having the discretion to speak on its behalf yet not to steal its place in the limelight. (Pincas & Loiseau, 2006)

Interesting argument!

The agencies, in general, do not have any written policies or gender sensitivity parameters that would help the creative teams to measure insensitivity in the ad narrative. The content creators per se seem to go by their gut feel and what in their view is the 'social reflection'.

The portrayal of women in stereotypical and inappropriate manner is not really a top-of-the-mind issue with the ad professionals. They, however, seem to be aware that there is a growing criticism against advertising in the public domain, especially on the social media platforms.

Advertising people, in general, are very gifted when it comes to their capability of creating powerful narrative and imagery. When their magic works in the brand sphere, it can equally also work in breaking the social stereotypes. This can be achieved only when both the corporate sector as clients and the ad industry as content creator understand and absorb the social shift and the changing role of women in the sociocultural sphere, which needs to be reflected in the ad narrative.

For long, Indian scholars referred to research studies and theoretical construct coming from the Western world. The last couple of decades, however, have witnessed a good body of empirical data emerging from the Indian academia and professional organizations that largely reinforce the prevalence of objectification of women in advertising. The data thus generated can help policy-makers and the ad industry in bringing about the much-required change.

In conclusion, it is hoped that the growing concern of the civil society on the objectionable portrayal of women in media, including advertising and the articulation of dissension by a growing community of influencers, especially on the social media platform, would be heard loud and clear by the ad sector. The ASCI and the AAAI, it is expected, would work towards the sensitization of the ad professionals and, at the same time, encourage the public to file complaints against ads that they feel are distasteful and prurient. The ad agencies on their part would test their creatives on gender-sensitivity indicators before releasing them in the media. Gender-sensitive work by some brands hopefully would continue to influence others. Sustenance of such campaigns at the end would define the seriousness on the part of the ad industry.

NOTES

1 Adapted from information collated from *Indian Newspaper Society Press Handbook 2018–2019*, Volumes I & II.

2 As a part of an ICSSR seminal research that enquired into the portrayal of women in advertisements in 2018–2019, one of the authors conducted 10 FGDs with creative teams comprising in all over 80 persons from among global and Indian agencies and 34 IDIs with the senior management

professionals. For both FGDs and IDIs, the agencies covered in the five cities, namely Delhi/NCR, Mumbai, Kolkata and Lucknow included large global agencies such as JWT, Contract, Dentsu, Bates, Madison, FCB India, Innocean Worldwide, MullenLowe Lintas, McCann Erickson, Ulka, Carat and Soho Square. Among the medium and small agencies including OOH, the sample covered Adfactors Advertising, Adinfinitum, Voyagers, Isha Advertising, In Circle, Advantage India, Synergy Result—Advertising and Marketing, ABM Communications and Garuda Advertising.

3 JWT is a part of the global conglomerate WPP. This is what it said after the controversy, in a statement emailed to The Huffington Post: 'We deeply regret the publishing of posters that were distasteful and contrary to the standards of professionalism and decency within WPP Group,' the statement said. 'These were never intended for paid publication and should never have been created, let alone uploaded to the internet. This was the result of individuals acting without proper oversight and appropriate actions have been taken within the agency where they work to deal with the situation.' See https://www.huffingtonpost.in/2013/03/24/ford-india-figo-ad-bound-and-gagged-women_n_2941297.html s

4 Based on a personal interview with Ms Raji Ramaswamy at her office in Mumbai on 30 August 2018. Formal reply sent by her via e-mail to the author on 31 August 2018.

5 Based on reply to a questionnaire received by the author via e-mail.

6 Based on reply to a questionnaire received by the author via e-mail.

REFERENCE

Pincas, S., & Loiseau, M. (2006). *Born in 1842. A History of Advertising* (pp. 11–16). Mundocom.

CHAPTER 6

THE ARRIVAL OF METROSEXUAL MAN IN THE INDIAN AD NARRATIVE

Of course, fashions come and go but metrosexuality isn't a fashion—it's an epoch. It represents a fundamental shift in what men are allowed to be and to want. Men are now permitted to be 'passive'—inviting our gaze.

Mark Simpson

The 1990s saw a new expression in the urban lexis, the 'Metrosexual man', supposedly coined by Mark Simpson in 1994 in his article, 'Here Come the Mirror Men: Why the Future is Metrosexual'. Simpson defined a typical one as

> a young man with money to spend, living in or within easy reach of a metropolis—because that's where all the best shops, clubs, gyms and hairdressers are. He might be officially gay, straight or bisexual, but this is utterly immaterial because he has clearly taken himself as his own love object and pleasure as his sexual preference. Particular professions, such as modelling, waiting tables, media, pop music and, nowadays, sport, seem to attract them but, truth be told, like male vanity products and herpes, they're pretty much everywhere. (Simpson, 1994)

Commenting on the phenomenon, Warren St. John in *New York Times* wrote:

> Paradoxically, the term metrosexual, which is now being embraced by marketers, was coined in the mid-90's to mock everything marketers stand for. The gay writer Mark Simpson used the word to satirize what he saw as consumerism's toll on traditional masculinity. Men didn't go to shopping malls, buy glossy magazines or load up on grooming products, Mr. Simpson argued, so consumer culture promoted the idea of a sensitive guy—who went to malls, bought magazines and spent freely to improve his personal appearance. (St. John, 2003)

DEFINING METROSEXUAL

Since the time the term metrosexual appeared in Simpson's article, there have been articulation of what real 'metrosexual' means from among various sources. Below, we shall take a look at a few of them.

Askmen.com (Brennan, 2007):

> A modern, usually single man in touch with himself and his feminine side; grooms and buffs his head and body, which he drapes in fashionable clothing both at work or before hitting an evening hotspot; has discretionary income to stay up to date with the latest hairstyles, the newest threads, and the right shaped shoes; confuses some guys when it comes to his sexuality; makes these same guys jealous of his success with the ladies—for many metros, to interact with women is to flirt; impresses the women who enjoy his company with the details that make the man; Such as: his appreciation for literature, cinema, or other

arts; his flair for cooking; his savoir faire in choosing the perfect wine and music; his eye for interior design; is a city boy or, if living a commute away from downtown, is still urbane, if not rightly urban; enjoys reading men's magazines ....

Eurometer International (2006):

Metrosexual, essentially the heterosexual male with an unashamed interest in shopping, fashion, fitness and personal grooming. In one way Metrosexual is the development of an aspect of the macho man often referred to as the 'peacock male', where the determinedly masculine male aggressively shows off his fine plumage to attract females and intimidate rival males. However, the Metrosexual is a more sophisticated variant, with the preening but without the aggression and with an implied acceptance of alternative lifestyles.

Online Oxford Dictionary (*Oxford English Dictionary Online*, n.d.):

A heterosexual urban man who enjoys shopping, fashion and similar interests traditionally associated with women or homosexual men.

Cambridge Dictionary (n.d.):

A man who is attracted to women sexually, but who is also interested in fashion and his appearance.

Chris Bates, Director of Bloke, a part of the research agency 2CV that gathers consumer insights around 'the average guy', had this to say on the metrosexual men: 'Masculinity has been redefined. Men are taking more of an interest in themselves, in home design, cooking and other areas that have traditionally been seen as female' (Costa, 2010).

David Beckham is believed to have rewritten masculinity for all times to come. Ad practitioner Marian Salzman, in one of her articles, articulates his role interestingly.

> Beckham, 29, is an icon of modern masculinity at a time gender roles are changing faster than runway styles. He has been known to don sarongs and even his wife's panties, the better to set of his pink nail polish. It ain't easy being the metrosexual pinup boy, but Beckham doesn't flinch different from the term. With seemingly a different hairstyle each week, he has gone from skinhead to fauxhawk to dreads to a ponytail—he keeps hair salons worldwide flooded with followers eager to mimic his style. (Salzman, 2014)

Ellis Cashmore, a British professor of culture, media and sports, underscores the role of Beckham on the cultural history thus:

> In the late 1990s, when he first surfaced, only Beckham could get away with it .... Today, cultural history is unimaginable without Beckham—because he helped change that history. He slew the image of the unrelentingly macho sport hero and emerged heroically as the world's first all-purpose celebrity athlete. A symbol of a new masculinity. (Cashmore, 2013)

There are umpteen examples that show metrosexual man in the art and culture landscape. Johnny Depp wore thick mascara in the film *Pirates of the Caribbean*; Grammy Award winner Justin Bieber has a nail polish collection under brand Nicole by OPI. Fashion house Maybelline's Big Shot Mascara campaign released in 2017 had a male model supporting eye make-up on a bearded face (*New Indian Express*, 2017).

From the stereotypical 'pink' for girls and 'blue' for boys, the stereotype has been challenged by many brands. Wearing pink and peach colour shirts became the fashion statements by men, especially from the 2000s. The LGBTQ movement that gathered momentum some two decades ago, further received impetus, when the Supreme Court unanimously ruled in September 2018 that section 377 was unconstitutional as it violated the right of the LGBTQ community to 'equal citizenship and equal protection of laws', thus explicitly overturning its 2013 judgement. The fashion industry has over the years experimented with colors considered effeminate for men, seen by many as a sign of inclusivity.

Over a period of time, the term 'metrosexual' has now come to be used for men who are urban, economically independent, fashion conscious and believe in personal grooming, not minding visiting a beauty parlour, not just for haircut but also for pedicure, manicure and, you heard in right, facial.

Priyanka Golikeri, taking a look at the beauty and grooming brands' interest in the metrosexual men, comments that every brand was trying to chase the 'Instagram-savvy males in the 20–40 year age bracket for whom grooming provides the ultimate rejuvenation'. For instance, Chanel, in 2019, had introduced a complete make-up portfolio for men called Boy de Chanel, which has varying shades of foundation, eyebrow pencil, lip balm and what have you. High-end fashion house Fenty has not only 40 shades of foundation for men but also tutorials on beauty and grooming. L'Oréal and Estee Lauder haven't lagged behind in grooming men. The personal care market for men is pegged at US$166 billion by 2022 by Allied Market Research. The product range includes skincare, beauty, wellness and also innerwear and loungewear (Golikeri, 2019).

Sudha Venkataswamy (2013) talks about transcending gender by fairness creams in India. 'The convergence of class hierarchy, colonial history and social prejudice are central to the firmly entrenched notion of 'superiority' being synonymous with 'fairness' and mediated by advertisements.'

Table 6.1 Major Fairness Creams for Men in India

S. No.	Company	Brand	Year of Launch
1	House of Emami	Fair & Handsome	2005
2	Hindustan Unilever	F&L Menz Active	2006
3	Elder Health Care	Fair One	2007
4	Garnier India	Garnier Men Power Light	2009
5	Hindustan Unilever	F&L Max Fairness for Men	2010
6	Hindustan Unilever	Vaseline Men	2010

Source: Venkataswamy, 2013, pp. 129.

There was a lot of competition among FMCG companies to woo men with fairness after Emami launched its cream for men in 2005, as Table 6.1 reflects.

EXPANDING MARKET FOR METROSEXUAL MEN

As per market trends, Indian men are experimenting with a wide range of grooming products, if the figure of 177 products in the category in a year between 2018 and 2019 is any indication. In terms of the market for male-grooming products, North India leads, followed by western parts of the country (Ambwani, 2019).

More and more beauty parlours are turning to be 'unisex', where men can be found getting their hair streaked or going for skincare treatments. If display of masochism and masculinity, bare-bodied men, flaunting their six-pack and eight-pack abs is one reality, man displaying emotion, crying in public, doing 'womanly' jobs at home is seen as yet another one that reflects the traits of the modern man who does not believe that man is the provider and woman's role is procreation. They also question the age-old adage 'Mard ko dard nahi hota' (Man does not feel pain!).

The personal grooming industry for men was pegged at ₹16,800 crores in 2018 in a study conducted by industry body ASSOCHAM. The study projected it to go up to ₹35,000 crores in 2021, a jump of more than 100 per cent (ASSOCHAM, 2018). The study points out that of the total beauty salon business, at least 40–45 per cent comes from the menfolk. In terms of buying, it is bath and shower products, hair care, skincare, deodorants and shaving brands ASSOCHAM, 2018). In yet another projection based on TechSci Research, the Indian market for male grooming is projected at US$3.3 billion by 2022 (ASSOCHAM, 2018).

In their research paper, Archana Sharma et al. quote a study by 'Media Research Users Council'(MRUC) that found more than 30 per cent boys in a hostel in Andhra Pradesh who used girls' fairness cream (Sharma, 2019). Craving for a fair skin is a well-known fact in India among women, but getting to know that men were also not averse to look fair, using the fairness cream clandestinely, gave an idea to the House of Emami to launch a brand that men would not mind using with pride. In 2005, when the narratives of several brands were already catering to the metrosexual men, the company came out with 'Fair & Handsome', choosing, unmistakably, Shah Rukh Khan to endorse the brand, who is known to be the 'king of romance' and metrosexuality in the Bollywood parlance (Exchange 4 Media, 2019).

The actor in the same year, 2005, was roped in by beauty soap Lux, commemorating its platinum jubilee. The ad had shock value for some, seeing Shah Rukh in a bathtub strewn with rose petals with many Bollywood actresses who had endorsed the brand in the past standing around the tub, sealing and defining for all times the arrival of the metrosexual man on the Indian ad scene. 'Aapka favourite LUX star kaun hai? Dream girl Hema, beautiful Juhi, stylish Kareena ya sensuous Sridevi?' He asked, then went on to say, not displeasing anyone, 'Meri choice charon' (My choice is all the four). When they wanted a superstar for their platinum celebration, he told them with a grin 'Mein hoon na' (I am there!).[1]

WHAT KIND OF MAN WOMEN LIKE?

There are varying views, opinions and jokes on what kind of men attract women. It could be the sensitive, risk-taking, accomplished, intelligent, the list could be very long. This is trivialized when men in the popular discourse complain that when gods cannot fathom a woman's mind, how can mortal men do. The daily newspaper *Hindustan Times* reported news about an interesting study that appeared in the *Daily Star* carried out by party planner Hen Heaven on the matchmaking app Tinder, bringing in key insights on what kind of men women liked to partner with. It was found that metrosexual men had 39 per cent matches while the macho, gym-type men received just about 7 per cent matches (*Hindustan Times*, 2014).

Ad practitioner Ashish Mishra gives a sociological take on the reversal of attitudes of men becoming softer and women more assertive when he says, 'In a cyclical behavior of humans and societies, men and women both are showing signs of reverting to their rightful and biologically compatible positions, with of course, a few mutations.'[2] He refers to a few campaigns that reflected the trend in communication. For instance, the Kinetic Flyte, a two wheeler launched by Kinetic Motors for women as primary buyers, ran a communication campaign with the tagline 'Girls are not girly.' When the narrative on the 'arrival' of the metrosexual man was gaining ground, pink became the colour of men's fashion. Cosmetic company that has for long used the tagline of 'Because we're worth it' for its women brands, came out with men-centric products called Men Expert using the tagline, 'Because men are worth it too.' This, 'condescending tagline of the cosmetics brand,' commented Mishra, 'was the tipping point. Or perhaps it was the self-sneering collective burden of accommodating the sissiness of pink, and the cultivated façade of "extra sensitivity" that finally embarrassed the metrosexual man.'[3] Some campaign later, masculinity again seemed to be the flavour when the 'Men are back' tagline from Maruti and 'Bikers don't cry' campaign from the Fastrack, a Titan subsidiary dealing in lifestyle accessories, appeared.

Some brands, however, are still experimenting metrosexual narrative, like Axe that traditionally has objectified women and used a stereotypical approach for long. Their campaign, a part of its 'Find your Magic' positioning titled 'Is It Ok for Guys?' talks about the insecurities and anxieties of men and their struggle with the notion of masculinity. Similarly, diaper brand Pampers brought in the role of a father in the upbringing of a child (Nair, 2017).

Ad professionals, in general, believe that advertising generally mirrors the on-ground reality. For instance, if there is more reflection of gym scenes to sell energy drinks, it is because going to gym has become a fad among the urban population.

Ratna Bhushan and Byas Anand for their article in the *Economic Times* 'Metrosexual Men Are Rocking Ad World' in 2005 interviewed industry stalwarts to unlock the phenomenon. They believed the opinions were divided on whether meterosexuality would work for Indian audience, but that was in 2005, when Arvind Sharma of Leo Burnett was of the view that the concept of metrosexuality may work, but only for niche brands. In a presentation at Cannes, he stated that the concept lacked mass appeal and was a bit of oddity (Bhushan & Anand, 2005).

A study of metrosexual men in Punjab by Kaur and Bawa (2018) throws some interesting findings and insights. With a sample of 680 males in the age group of 18–50, some of the characteristics of metrosexual men as per the research included 'public display of affection', 'matching of different garments', 'choosing products that would create first good impression', among others.

Suman Mishra, in her paper, has examined ad content in four top-selling Indian editions of transnational men's lifestyle magazines, including *Men's Health India, GQ India, FHM India* and *Maxim India,* to enquire how the ad narrative constructs masculinity for upper-class urban Indian men. Through content analysis of advertisements, the study found a larger presence of international brands and Caucasian models than domestic Indian brands and Indian models (Mishra, 2017).

Matthew Hall, in his seminal work for his PhD in 2014, has used descriptive analysis as a method to study the phenomenon of the metrosexual man by undertaking four studies—one, by examining metrosexuality in the media and readers' responses to that; two, by 'constructing metrosexuality and masculinities in an online forum by also adding 'more specific dimensions of self-identified metrosexuals'; three, 'I am Metro, NOT gay!' have men's accounts of 'make-up use on You Tube' that takes a step further focusing on a self-identified metrosexual's online video of his everyday make-up regime and, four, staying with facial cosmetics, the study 'we want to look our best without appearing flamboyant'—the study, in short examines how men manage, using typically feminized items and how the marketers deploy them (Hall, 2014).

BOLLYWOOD A REFERENCE POINT?

One cannot but draw references from Bollywood on the advent of the bare-bodied men and, later, the soft and effeminate protagonists. Partha Bhattacharjee and Priyanka Tripathi, in their paper 'Silhouetting the Shifting Perspective of Bollywood from "Machismo" to "Metrosexuality"', draw some astute references to make their point (Bhattacharjee & Tripathi, 2017). Although the original 'he-man' was Dharmendra, who bared his body in *Phool Aur Patthar* in the 1960s, later Rishi Kapoor, by no means masculine, did the same in 1973 in *Bobby*, but post 2000, quite a few did it including Salman Khan, who, in a true sense, defined masculinity. Fitness craze was started by Sanjay Dutt, who inspired many within Bollywood and a whole generation of youth, but Hrithik Roshan became the epitome of fitness, when he was seen flaunting his six-pack physique in his debut film *Kaho Naa Pyaar Hai* in 2000.

The real treat for viewers on metrosexuality came when male protagonists were doing various things that normally were not seen as man-like behaviour. Saif Ali Khan in *Salaam Namaste* was seen wearing chef's cap, Arjun Kapoor was running the household while the lady was busy in her profession (Arjun Kapoor–Kareena Kapoor starrer *Ki & Ka*). The paper refers from the film the lyrics of a song that define the metrosexuality of the protagonist thus:

Munda can shop,

Munda can chop

Kehnde bargaing mein hai ye top

Munda hega smart, master of the art

Iske to seene mein kudiyon wala heart

(the boy can shop, chop, bargain; he is smart, master of the art; he has the heart of a girl) (Bhattacharjee & Tripathi, 2017).

Ranveer Singh went many steps further when he donned a lehenga in a fashion show promoting his and Deepika Padukone's film *Bajirao Mastani* in 2015 (Bhattacharjee & Tripathi, 2017).

THE FUTURE OF METROSEXUAL MAN IN THE AD NARRATIVE

As discussed previously, in the Indian landscape, while on the one hand there are definite signs of metrosexual narrative, but others have shifted to the 'tough boy' approach as the Maruti and Fastrack ads discussed before point out. We shall take a look at some more ads to critique the way the ad industry is dealing with the phenomenon.

The Nivea ad for body deodorant for man has supermodel Arjun Rampal portraying a character who has a certain upper-class air in his persona. The ad has a young father with a toddler who seems to be irritated with his body odour. Rampal appears to say

'When odour comes from your body, why use deo on the clothes?' and the camera pans to the man who is splashing deodorant over his shirt.

'Nivea men. It starts with you,' the tagline for the Nivea face wash for men has Arjun Rampal who, with an air of confidence, is showing going from one place to another with admiring women following him everywhere.

In another ad, he is dealing with the issue of fairness cream. 'Everyone wants to be a few shades fairer. Why this, when the real problem is dark spots?' he asks looking in the camera.

In the Nivea Men All in One face wash ad, Arjun Rampal as protagonist questions 'You think that men's face care is as complicated as women's face care, or as time consuming or even as painful?' The camera, then pans to a man in the salon with cucumber slices over his eyes, undergoing the process of waxing of the nose for removal of blackheads, which seemed painful, looking at his facial expression. The protagonist suggests Nivea Men All in One face wash to reduce dark sports, acne and excess oil. At the end, while he is walking on a street, a girl driving her car gets distracted by his charm only to hit a car. In the ad, Rampal is not shown using it but as an influencer.[4]

Garnier, a brand owned by French company L'Oréal, has for long used Aishwarya Rai for women-centric brands. For its face wash for men, the protagonists chosen were not the soft or effeminate, metrosexual kind of men, but macho and fitness freaks, such as John Abraham and Tiger Shroff, both known for their body fitness and six- and eight-pack abbs. 'Matcha detox for deep cleansing' is what Abraham suggests to Tiger, when they face air pollution choosing skateboards to a closed vehicle. 'Now don't just wash, detox,' adds Tiger Shroff. Here, we see the tough man is back, who needs to detox his skin, which is again a masculine expression (Shelani & Ruparel, 2019).

First in the line of launching a fairness cream 'Fair & Handsome' for men, the House of Emami expectedly used the quintessential metrosexual Bollywood superstar Shah Rukh Khan. However, as other competitors entered the fray, taking a different positioning on the grooming products by using strong, macho protagonists, Emami also did not lag behind. For its Fair & Handsome facewash, it used both Hrithik Roshan and Vidyut Jammwal, both with perfect bodies, one known for his dancing prowess, besides action roles, and the other with a tough body and also known for his action sequences. 'Just ek flash; chehra fresh and fair' was the tagline of the ad that emphasized that one may be very tough but can't escape dirt and pollution.[5]

Unilever was the first global company to bring in the concept of fairness cream for women in India in 1975, for which it earned the ire of many stakeholders, but this did not stop many competitors to join the brand war to tap a large potential for such a product, owning to craze for fair skin in the Indian society. Unilever also ventured into fairness cream for men as a late entrant in 2007, when there already were about half a dozen players. For its F&L Men Fairness Face Wash, it used Sidharth Malhotra, a cine actor, not in the league of Shah Rukh Khan or Hrithik Roshan, but quite presentable and younger in age to find resonance with the youth. In this ad, also like the competing brands, it is an action sequence of a shoot, in which the protagonist is using his strength and heroism fighting in the open with half a dozen men, when he is exposed to dirt and pollution, the answer for which, of course, is the brand endorsed.[6]

When we analyse a cross section of ads in this genre, we find that the market for grooming products for men is already there and has a great potential to expand; however, the strategy by and large has been positioning men as men, tough and strong, but, at the same time, conscious about looking fresh and good by fighting the extraneous elements like dust, dirt, pollution and grime. In most of the narratives, there were women looking and following such men admiringly! On a lighter vein, if this trend continues, men may not complain about the woman gaze, but the discourse on male gaze by women advocates may mellow down!

NOTES

1 To watch the ad, see https://www.youtube.com/watch?v=_lf7_AcsIqI

2 Ashish Mishra is vice president, strategic planning, Mudra Group. Source: Campaign India. See https://www.campaignindia.in/article/metrosexual-gobbled-by-the-urban-lion/408443

3 See https://www.campaignindia.in/article/metrosexual-gobbled-by-the-urban-lion/408443

4 Ads can be watched at this link: https://www.google.com/search?q=rampal+in+nivea+ad&oq=&aqs=chrome.0.69i59i450l8.12125822j0j15&sourceid=chrome&ie=UTF-8

5 You can watch the ad here: https://www.dailymotion.com/video/x3nbnmo

6 You can watch the ad here: https://www.facebook.com/sidharthmalhotra1985/videos/fair-lovely-mens-facewash-ad-starring-sidharth-malhotra-pooja/553573438134749/

REFERENCES

Ambwani, M. (2019, 16 October). Indian male grooming segment is now worth rs 5000 crore in urban India. https://www.thehindubusinessline.com/economy/indian-male-grooming-segment-is-now-worth-rs-5000-crore-in-urban-india/article29698078.ece

ASSOCHAM. (2018). *Male grooming product market to grow at 45% CAGR: ASSOCHAM*. https://www.assocham.org/newsdetail.php?id=6697#:~:text=Male%20grooming%20product%20market%20to%20grow%20at%2045%25%20CAGR%3A%20ASSOCHAM&text=The%20male%20grooming%20industry%20is,%25%2C%20adds%20the%20ASSOCHAM%20report

Bhattacharjee, P., & Tripathi, P. (2017). Silhouetting the shifting perspective of Bollywood from 'machismo' to 'metrosexuality.

Journal of English Language and Literature, *8*(1). https://www.researchgate.net/publication/318980158

Bhushan, R., & Anand, B. (2005, 3 October). Metrosexual men are rocking ad world. *The Economic Times*. https://economictimes.indiatimes.com/metrosexual-men-are-rocking-ad-world/articleshow/1249993.cms?from=mdr

Brennan, J. (2007). *Are you a metrosexual?* AskMen.com. https://www.askmen.com/daily/austin_100/102_fashion_style.html

Cambridge Dictionary. (n.d.). Metrosexual. https://dictionary.cambridge.org/dictionary/english/metrosexual

Cashmore, E. (2013, 17 May). *David Beckham: Rise of the metrosexual*. CNN. https://edition.cnn.com/2013/05/17/opinion/beckham-metro-symbol

Costa, M. (2010, 15 September). What men want from a brand relationship. *Marketing Week*. https://www.marketingweek.com/what-men-want-from-a-brand-relationship/

Euromonitor International. (2006, 6 November). Metrosexuality The male shopping giant awakes. http://marketresearchworld.net/content/view/1056/77/

Exchange 4 Media. (2019, 8 August). Women get competition in fairness department from men, thanks to Emami. https://www.exchange4media.com/marketing-news/women-get-competition-in-fairness-department-from-menthanks-to-emami-18074.html

Golikeri, P. (2019, 16 August). *Grooming products chasing the metrosexual man*. DNA. https://www.dnaindia.com/business/report-grooming-products-chasing-the-metrosexual-man-2782145

Hall, M. (2014). 'It's a metrosexual thing': A discourse analytical examination of masculinities. https://www.researchgate.net/publication/260423950_%27It%27s_a_metrosexual_thing%27_A_discourse_analytical_examination_of_masculinities

Hindustan Times. (2014, 4 December). It turns out women find metrosexual guys more desirable. https://www.hindustantimes.com/sex-and-relationships/it-turns-out-women-find-metrosexual-guys-most-desirable/story-iAFMTipa0ssGhVtnReexQP.html#:~:text=It%20turns%20out%20that%20women,groomed%2C%20says%20a%20new%20study.&text=45%20PM%20IST-,It%20turns%20out%20that%20women%20are%20most%20attracted%20to%20metrosexual,groomed%2C%20says%20a%20new%20study

Kaur, J. P., & Bawa, J. (2018, January–February). Public display of perfection in metrosexual men: An approach to redefining masculinity. *Global Journal of Commerce and Management Perspective*, 7(1), 15–19. ISSN: 2319–7285.

Mishra, S. (2017). Looking westwards: Men in transnational men's magazine advertising in India. *Global Media and Communication*, *13*(3), 249–266.

Nair, R. (2017, 5 June). Boys do cry: Advertising and its portrayal of men. https://bestmediainfo.com/2017/06/boys-do-cry-advertising-and-its-portrayal-of-men/

Oxford English Dictionary Online. (n.d.). https://www.lexico.com/definition/metrosexual

Rajagopal, K. (2018, September 6). Sc decriminalises homosexuality, says history owes lgbtq community an apology. *The Hindu*. https://www.thehindu.com/news/national/sc-de-criminalises-homosexuality-says-history-owes-lgbtq-community-an-apology/article24881549.ece

Salzman, M. (2014, 26 February). The man brand. *Forbes*. https://www.forbes.com/sites/mariansalzman/2014/02/26/the-man-brand/?sh=3c01879870b1

Sharma, A., Sagar, M., Tushar, P., & Gupta, H. K. (2019). Emami men's fairness cream: Creating a new product category. *Journal of Case Research*, *10*(2), 21–32. https://xub.edu.in/jcr/cases/Case02-Dec2019.pdf

Shelani, F., & Ruparel, N. (2019). Masculinity in metrosexuality expressed in Indian television advertisement for men's personal care products. *Oakbrook Business Review*, *4*(2), 25–31. http://oakbrook.ac.in/wp-content/uploads/2019/01/4.-Paper-3-Falguni-Shelani-Dr.-Neelima-Ruparel.pdf

Simpson, M. (1994). Here come the mirror men: why the Future is metrosexual. https://www.marksimpson.com/herecome-the-mirror-men/

St. John, W. (2003, 22 June). Metrosexuals come out. *The New York Times*. https://www.nytimes.com/2003/06/22/style/metrosexuals-come-out.html

The New Indian Express. (2017, 21 July). 'Beauty conscious' Indian men boost skincare market. https://www.newindianexpress.com/lifestyle/fashion/2017/jul/21/beauty-conscious-indian-men-boost-skincare-market-1631674.html

Venkataswamy, S. (2013, July). Transcending gender: Advertising fairness cream for Indian men. *Media Asia*, *40*(2), 128–138. https://www.tandfonline.com/doi/abs/10.1080/01296612.2013.11689961

CHAPTER 7

GENDER MAINSTREAMING IN MEDIA SCHOOLS AND WORKPLACES

We've begun to raise daughters more like sons ... but few have the courage to raise our sons more like our daughters.

Gloria Steinem

Environment has a great impact on our learning and, more importantly, how we look at things. Home is said to be the cradle of civilization. Children often become what they learn from their elders at home. In traditional societies, girls at a young age are made to believe that they are different from their brothers when it comes to their treatment and the choices they can make. Whether this makes home the cradle of civilization is a moot point! Girls enter schools and then colleges to find their male batchmates often carry an air of superiority and behave in a manner that they have learnt in their homes. The work environment is no different despite whatever the human resource people may want you to believe about equality, diversity and safe work environment. There is an imminent need for gender mainstreaming in the media schools from where most professionals are resourced for the ad sector and the workplace itself.

WHAT IS GENDER MAINSTREAMING?

Bringing gender into focus is mainstreaming the issue. Gender mainstreaming involves ensuring that gender perspectives and attention to the goal of gender equality are central to all activities—policy development, research, advocacy/dialogue, legislation, resource allocation and planning, implementation and monitoring of programmes and projects (United Nations, 2002).

In this chapter, we shall look at two aspects, the state of women working in the ad industry and whether gender is part of teaching and learning at the media schools in the Indian universities and institutions of higher learning.

HUMAN RESOURCE: A BLIND SPOT IN THE AD SECTOR

Human resource is a blind spot in the advertising sector. There is no official data on the total number of people working in the ad sector and the men:women ratio. Industry insiders put it at 70:30. The INS that brings out detailed volume each year on the accredited advertising agencies also does not record this important aspect of the industry. Ad agencies rarely advertise for their vacant positions. Some of the known methods are recruiting young people from well-known media schools, by reference or 'poaching' the best talent from competing agencies.

If we look at the new labour law with four labour codes waiting to be implemented in 2021, while it promises 'gender equality' but it is silent on equality at the time of recruitment, equal wages, promotions, on-job training, women's special needs like issues concerning night shifts, late shifts, sexual harassment at workplace, gender-based violence, maternity benefits, etc. The labour law specifically mentions about news media and working journalists, but there is no mention either of the advertising industry or the people working in the sector in the labour codes. The AAAI that represents agencies was not a part of the consultative process when the Parliamentary Standing Committee on labour reached out to various stakeholders to get their views on the bill.

The following reflects the goal of AAAI.

> Advertising Agencies Association of India (AAAI) is the official, national organisation of advertising agencies, formed in 1945, to promote their interests. The Association promotes professionalism, through its founding principles, which uphold sound business practices between Advertisers and Advertising Agencies and the various media. AAAI today is truly representative, with a very large number of small, medium and large-sized agencies as its members, who together account for almost 80% of the advertising business placed in the country. It is thus recognised as the apex body of and the spokesperson for the Advertising industry at all forums—Advertisers and Media owners and their associations and Government.

Source: https://www.aaaindia.org/

STATE OF WOMEN IN THE AD SECTOR

An important area that remains under-researched is the state of working women in India. Talking specifically about the advertising industry, which has crazy working hours, client pressures and, to top it, finding the right trigger for the brand's ad narrative, women often find themselves at a disadvantage. Many young women join the ad industry and some reach a reasonably senior position, but advertising industry remains a male bastion. Is the environment gender sensitive in the ad industry? Does the industry have women-centric policies in place? The answer, without mincing words, is 'No'. A lot of young women who join media schools make it to the ad industry, but owing to many factors, not many last there for long.

GENDER-INSENSITIVITY LOOMS LARGE IN THE AD SECTOR

Advertising sector that is commonly known for its uninhibited and non-conformist approach is unfair to women workers, if the field survey and stories in the media are to go by. Dilshad Irani and Mukta Lad's article 'Here's Why Women Leave Ad Agencies' is a sad commentary on the state of women in the ad sector. The story which has quotes from some well-known women from top-notch global agencies points out to a highly insensitive environment where a few women are able to survive. The story points out, quoting women about their male colleagues who

> Openly and audibly rue the lack of 'eye-candy' to ogle at in office or marvel at their screen savers of female strippers, leadership follows the principle of benign neglect. And in the absence of a robust HR structure, with no powers beyond hiring and negotiating salaries, women subjected to this variety of harassment are left with just two options: be a 'tattle tale' or forget about it. (Irani & Lad, 2015)

The story shares that one saw diversity in the 1980s, but not in the decades that followed. Women do join the ad sector, but, over a period, they do not continue. One of reasons ascribed in the story includes motherhood. 'We lose some of our best people when they transition from working girl to working women,' quotes the story, 'we lost them to uterus,' is yet another quote from a senior professional included in the story. 'For an industry celebrated for its open-mindedness in the workplace and progressive attitude,' write the authors, 'that's alarming indeed'. (But then again, advertising is the biggest purveyor of gender stereotypes.) Aditi Bhattacharya, one of the senior creative professionals, said that life in the ad sector was a microcosm of the world outside. If the society was gender insensitive, how could the advertising sector be any different (Irani & Lad, 2015)?

To take the argument further, when there is gender insensitivity in the profession itself, it is hard to find sensitivity in the narrative from the very same mindsets. Dozens of women reiterated the same sentiment during the fieldwork done for the United Nations Educational, Scientific and Cultural Organization and

Sex Workers' Rights Advocacy Network (UNESCO–SWAN) research in 2018. Most women, when asked what could bring about the change, felt stringent law, punitive action and sensitization of menfolk was the way out.

WOMEN-CENTRIC LAW FOR WORKING WOMEN

The year 2013 was a watershed moment when the Parliament passed the Sexual Harassment of Women at Workplace (Prevention, Prohibition and Redressal) Act. This was followed by a public information campaign. Organizations that employed 10 or more women, the Act posited, had to set up Internal Complaints Committee (ICC) to address the issues of sexual harassment of women.

Defining sexual harassment:

> Unwelcome acts or behaviour (whether directly or by implication) namely, physical contact and advances, a demand or request for sexual favours, making sexually coloured remarks, showing pornography, any other unwelcome physical, verbal or non-verbal conduct of sexual nature (Sec 2(n) of the Act).

Source: https://legislative.gov.in/sites/default/files/A2013–14.pdf

The ICSSR field survey reflected that all big agencies including the global ones have set up ICC as per the law. A visit to some agencies also reflected big posters displayed at prominent places within the premises on 'Zero Tolerance on Sexual Harassment'. One global agency shared that every employee has to undergo the prevention of sexual harassment test (POSH) and pass it with distinction; else, the test has to be repeated again and again till one fully understand the law. Interestingly, however, not a single agency surveyed said there were any cases of sexual harassment, except one, which also did not refer the case to the

ICC but 'solved the problem to the satisfaction of the concerned employee'. When asked why the agency did not follow the laid procedure in the case, the reply did not come as surprise, which was 'to avoid unnecessary public attention'.

When the #MeToo movement exploded in India in the later part of 2018, the bluff was called when many well-known names surfaced from large agencies as more and more women took to the social media to share their experiences of sexual harassment. As reported by the advertising portal Media4exchange, a group of senior women from the ad sector under the aegis of The Collective, wrote an open letter and proposed the setting up of an independent body for the ad sector to address the issues of sexual harassment.

Here is the text of the letter signed by The Collective.[1]

> Dear Women of Indian Advertising, Design & Media,
>
> We have spent the last few days in pain.
>
> After reading horrifying accounts of harassment in our industry, we've questioned ourselves and each other. We've felt sad, angry and violated at the same time.
>
> Any form of harassment is not okay. Period. Nobody should be able to use their power of authority or gender to discriminate, abuse or harass anyone. As an industry we cannot move forward till the time we can make it a safe space for everybody.
>
> We are aware thar each of our companies has policies and practices in place. However, we do feel it will only help to have a platform that is agency/network agnostic, easily accessible, backed by women leaders, with a singular focus on addressing harassment across the Indian Advertising, Design & Media industry, at both network and independent agencies. We need to work towards it as an industry.

We realize our leadership positions come with immense responsibility and therefore can help trigger a change, start a conversation and help bring the talk on the table.

We appreciate the courage of those of you who have come forward.

We also call upon men in leadership positions to help us do this so that both women and men see a bright future here.

We love this business as much as you do and we will continue working to make our industry better and responsible, where we can hold our work and our standards high.

We stand with you.

Signed: The Collective

Many senior ad professionals, including agency heads, branch heads, creative heads, both men and women, in personal IDIs gave interesting responses on how the Me Too movement may change or not change the ad-sector environment. Here are a few responses: 'It has made it loud and clear that what you consider a normal behaviour might not be that .... Naming and shaming will happen and it might not go unnoticed ... their voices will not be curbed as millions voices will join them in their fight'; 'The overall behaviour towards women has vastly improved in recent times. Men are generally exercising restraint knowing well that women are better served legally'; 'The "lad culture" which has characterized the advertising industry for long, unfortunately, often results in women being harassed verbally and physically. The Me Too has shone a light on the unacceptable behaviour and, hopefully, this will create a lasting change in behaviour'; 'It (Me Too movement) has made the men wearier and has given the vulnerable a voice ... there is a growing realization that if you raise your voice, you are not alone'; 'It (Me Too) began on a meaningful note but deteriorated into a sensation spreading mechanism with half lies and motivated slander … however it has made people more aware of the rights of women at workplace. It will act as a deterrent to the habitual predators'; '#MeToo has come as a massive wake-up call for the advertising industry, in general, by shining a light on decades worth of predatory behaviour that many men thought they were perfectly entitled to', 'we've seen some heads roll already …. The usual easy banter and camaraderie in agencies will disappear, sadly.'[2]

In the follow up, men and women, hopefully, are better informed of the law and the rights of women against sexual harassment at workplace. One has not heard of any action plan from 'The Collective'. The Ad Club, in collaboration with the AAAI, as reported in the media, decided to spearhead a communication programme to address the issue of 'violence against women in society'. This meant inviting creative minds to make entries in the Goafest 2020 on the theme, 'to design a high-impact behaviour change campaigns to aid the fight against violence towards women'. It was announced that the winning campaign would be given the newly instituted special award 'The Red Abby' (Best Media Info, 2020). Goafest scheduled in April 2020 had to be cancelled due to the outbreak of COVID-19 pandemic. The organizers announced that this would be taken in 2021 as reported by the media (India Campaign, 2020).

A seminal study of nine South Asian countries done, taken in tandem under the aegis of UNESCO and SWAN in 2018–2019, covering both the portrayal issues and the state of women working in the media including advertising, bears this out across all these countries. Based on the research data received from all the nine countries, the following trends emerge as shown in Figure 7.1.

1. *Gender-insensitive content*: In the advertisement content of almost all the nine South Asian countries, one finds stereotypes about women. In Bangladesh, advertising content is

Figure 7.1 Female Participation in Advertising Industry in South Asia

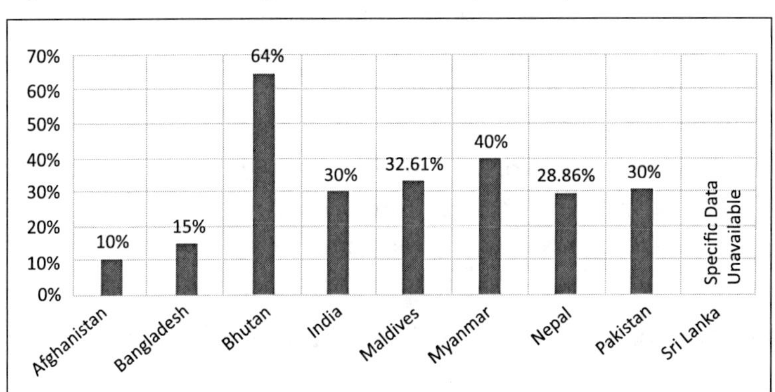

regarded as 'skewed against women'. In Nepal, the ad content, as pointed out in the country report, is seen as 'stereotypical' but not necessarily 'derogatory towards women'. In India, although the trend is changing to portray women in liberal and bold roles, women in advertisements are, in general, portrayed as passive, low in intellect and social hierarchy. Some brand categories, relating to beauty products, deodorants, condoms and apparel often sexually objectify women. Stereotypes are also common in Myanmar, Pakistan, Maldives, Afghanistan and Sri Lankan ads.

2. *Essentialist content*: Essentialist content here implies that the advertising content continues to portray women in essentialist roles, that is, roles determined based on set gender attributes, as per essentialist understanding. This trend is specifically observed within the advertising industry of Maldives, Pakistan and Sri Lanka, where women are often portrayed in jobs as nurses, secretaries or in lower-rung office jobs, which are regarded suitable to women because of their 'natural attributes'. Women also continue to be portrayed within traditional and typical domestic roles. In Sri Lanka, even young girls are projected in a similar manner, helping their mothers in the household chores.

3. *Content promoting body shaming*: While this is a common trend across most of the South Asian countries, it was particularly pointed out in the country report from Bhutan, where being slim is considered an attribute of beauty. Some research studies in Bhutan reflect that body shaming in Bhutanese advertising contents has a major influence on young girls and women in the country, which the country report said was affecting them in a negative manner.[3]

MEDIA: A NON-ACCREDITED PROFESSION

People who join the ad sector, often, come from big cities with a decent educational background, but they do not necessarily have any exposure to gender discourse and issues surrounding women. The course curricula across various streams, in general, are not gendered. To top it, media is not even an accredited profession in India. This means that for entering the media profession, one does not need a degree in mass communication, journalism, advertising or public relations. In the past, one has seen some discourse in the public domain on the state of journalism and mass communication education in India (CMS and UKIERI, 2015) but there, probably, has been none on advertising teaching and training, which is an important subset of mass communication.

TEACHING MASS COMMUNICATION IN INDIA

There are over 300 universities and institutions imparting teaching and professional training in mass communication including advertising, as per Table 7.1.

UNGENDERED ADVERTISING SYLLABI AT MASS COMMUNICATION SCHOOLS

An ICSSR study, undertaken in 2018–2019, deconstructing the course curricula in mass communication in general and advertising in particular, found that, in general, the course curricula were

Table 7.1 Mass Communication Teaching in India

Institute/University/College	No.
Number of central universities	25
State universities	81
Private universities	29
Distance learning	54
Private institutes	48
Colleges affiliated to university	46
Deemed university	10
Media owned institute	11
Total	310

Source: http://cmsindia.org/sites/default/files/Aug_Monograph_Vision-&-Communication_for-web.pdf

not gendered and inclusive across public and private universities and institutions of higher learning in India.[4]

Advertising Component in Mass Communication Studies

There are over 650 universities, about 35,000 colleges and over 13,000 stand-alone institutions in India, out of which over 300 universities and institutions in both public and private domains teach media and mass communication courses and prepare over 20,000 students each year for the industry. All the various courses, namely journalism, mass communication, digital media, corporate communication, public relations, etc., incorporate some component on advertising. There are also exclusive courses in advertising at both undergraduate and postgraduate (PG) levels in a number of universities. The mass communication courses are available in major metros, mini metros and various districts, where both central and state universities and private institutions are located.

Advertising Curriculum in Business Schools

Advertising is a part of marketing; therefore, business schools, while teaching marketing as a core subject, also include advertising in their curriculum. Just to provide a bird's-eye view, in 2015–2016, B Schools offered 520,000 seats in MBA courses, compared to 360,000 in 2011–2012.[5] At a rough estimate, over 20,000 mass communication students and a couple of lakhs of MBA students get exposure in advertising curriculum each year.

Content Analysis of Curricula

The examination of 64 different courses, taught in 31 different universities and institutions around the country revealed a common problem that stands out unambiguously, that is, the near absence of gendered syllabi. The University Grants Commission (UGC) prepared syllabus, also, is not gendered and inclusive. In other words, the syllabi in most cases are neither inclusive nor gender sensitive across a majority of universities and institutes of higher learning, both in the public and private domains. Of the different courses examined, only nine courses in eight different universities have gender as a course of study within the mass communication course curriculum. Here, it is included either as an exclusive paper or as a separate elective or compulsory paper and, in some cases, as a sub-unit of some other courses. For instance, the IIMC has it in the curricula of their PG diploma course on advertising and public relations as 'Development, Gender Issues and Women Empowerment'. Reading from how the course is titled, there seems to be an association of different concepts such as gender with that of development and empowerment. This speaks of the contemporary discourse within the larger academia, where there is a conscious effort to bring together the conceptual framework of theory and practice together. The Delhi School of Journalism has a section titled 'Gender in Media' as part of its five-year integrated course on journalism. Sharda University offers a paper on 'Media and Diversity: Race, Gender, Religion, Ethnic and Class' as a part of the MA course in journalism and mass communication. Sikkim Manipal University has a paper on 'Ethics in Advertising' as a part of its MBA course in marketing.

In contrast to this, some universities have incorporated gender in the course curriculum more in terms of theoretical engagement. For instance, the St. Xavier's College, Kolkata, offers a BA course in mass communication and videography, where gender is a part of a paper titled 'Paradigm and Practices'. Here, the engagement seems to be more in terms of theory, because the theory of feminism is one part of the course along with other theories. Another such case is of the Khwaja Moinuddin Chishti Urdu Arabi Farsi University, Lucknow, where under the BA course in journalism and mass communication, a paper titled 'Gender Studies' forms part of the curriculum. The master's programme at the Indraprastha University in Delhi has a module on gender studies that includes feminist theory of cinema and various codes of ethics by professional bodies including ASCI. The difference in the structuring of these courses may be because of the level at which the courses are introduced. Therefore, for those courses at the undergraduate level, the choice is more towards a theoretical engagement for an introductory course. In contrast to this, at the master's level of higher study, the focus is on the mode of engagement through the intersectionality of gender as a concept and its practical relevance along with a theory. At this level, the assumption is that some basic introduction about gender as a concept has already been taught at the undergraduate level, and that the need for an understanding that is grounded in the application of these concepts is needed at the master's level. This may, however, not always work in the favour of students, as many students at the master's level come from varying stream of science and arts and not necessarily from mass communication.

Other than this handful of courses that offer gender as a part of their courses, a majority of the course curricula examined reflected a complete absence of gender content. This, in a way, is indicative of the larger structural problem of the discipline, where gender and the critical engagement of a long feminist scholarship do not form part of the discipline. This absence is even more astonishing if it is contextualized in relation to other disciplines of social sciences such as sociology, where engagement with issues concerning women in India began a few decades ago, sometime around the 1980s. This although was late in comparison to the West, where feminist critique has been part of the larger academia for a while. It is, now, almost a given in most courses of social sciences, say sociology, that gender is a component that cannot be ignored and, therefore, forms part of each course. This change has a close relation with the institutionalization of women studies and gender studies as a separate discipline in many of the Indian universities. Further, all of these changes had a dialectical relation with the larger social current, where a strong uprising among the general mass of Indian society on the issue of gender equality is slowly gaining momentum in the public and the private sphere, which thereby influences the academic thinking as well. This can be observed from the rise in the number of political assertions made by women and men all over the country against factors that create inequality and unsafe environment for women, which are rooted in the gender-insensitive social norms. These social movements, in turn, have shaped the nature of research in social sciences and have resulted in the emergence of new perspectives and ways of understanding gender in various dimensions.

Interestingly, despite the absence of gender in course curricula, portrayal of women in advertising is quite a popular area of research among students and faculty. In the UNESCO–SWAN study referred before, the state of gender content in mass communication courses, except for in Bangladesh, is either insignificant or dismal, as reflected in the Figure 7.2 and Table 7.2.

Based on data and parameters derived from empirical research, the matrix in Table 7.2 has been constructed to estimate how gender sensitive each South Asian country's media and mass

Figure 7.2 Women Participation in Media Education in South Asia[6]

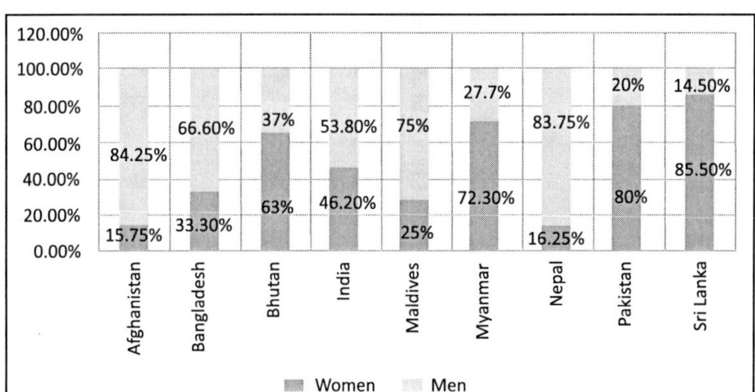

Table 7.2 Matrix for Gender Sensitivity in Media and Mass Communication Courses in South Asia

Missing	0%
Insignificant	1%–20%
Average	20%–50%
Good	50%–65%
Very good	65% 75%
Excellent	75% +

communication course curricula is. The results are seen in Table 7.3. Five countries—Afghanistan, Bhutan, Myanmar, Nepal and Pakistan—fall within the category of 'missing', signifying an absolute lack of inclusivity (of gender studies) or gender sensitivity in the media and mass communication course curricula. Three countries, including India, Maldives and especially Sri Lanka, have reported some elements of gender-sensitive media curriculum, but the focus is weak and limited to a small percentage of the total number of faculties/institutions, less than 20 per cent, and so, all three fall within the category 'insignificant'. Only Bangladesh

Table 7.3 Extent of Gender Sensitivity in Media Curricula in South Asia

Afghanistan	Bangladesh	Bhutan	India	Maldives	Myanmar	Nepal	Pakistan	Sri Lanka
Missing	Very good	Missing	Insignificant	Insignificant	Missing	Missing	Missing	Insignificant

reported a significant percentage (73%) of departments offering journalism and mass communication programmes which include specific focus on gender studies. Bangladesh falls in the category of 'very good'. The situation across all the known countries is as reflected below.

WHY GENDER IN MASS COMMUNICATION COURSES IS A MUST!

Mass communication through news, entertainment and commercial messages advertising through a variety of vehicles including newspapers, radio, television and digital space reaches out to a large section of people in the world. The Internet has cut across the artificial boundaries of geography, language and culture. With this kind of pervasiveness, it holds a huge power in influencing the minds of the people in an unimaginable manner. While the digital space has a large amount of user-generated content that has brought its own challenges, the classic media like newspapers, radio, television and films with professional content creators who work as journalists, screenplay writers, advertising writers, directors, photographers, art directors and photo journalists bring millions of stories and images, thus facilitating an average person to make a sense of the world around her/him through this stimuli. Not all that comes to us is an objective reflection of reality. There is a possibility of inherent bias in the news stories, exaggerations in the commercial messages and creation of a 'world of make-believe' in the entertainment programmes. Therefore, it is important that the people behind such writing and creations be sensitized to various issues, as it affects the minds and behaviour of the people who partake the media messages. Media, they say, is also a good barometer of how a society treats its people.

Promotional media, including advertising, provides glimpses of popular culture at a given time. Women who comprise half the world population have not received the space and the treatment that they deserve in mass media, both in its narrative and in job situation. If under-representation of women in the media space is a reality, in whatever space they get, women often have been portrayed stereotypically and as sex objects, on the other. The content, both in words and imagery, bears this out across cultures.

UNESCO, in its publication *Gender-Sensitive Indicators for Media: Framework of Indicators to Gauge Gender Sensitivity in Media Operations and Content* (2012), has come out with certain parameters for gauging gender content in the media, including advertising. In its subset on advertising, it also indicates the users that include: (a) media organizations, (b) unions, associations, clubs and organizations of journalists, other media professionals, media self-regulatory bodies, (c) citizens' media groups and other NGOs and (d) journalism schools and universities, communication schools, training institutes and NGOs

Critical Area of Concern: Gender Portrayal in Advertisements

In the strategic objective on the fair portrayal of women and men in commercial messages in the media, following 'Indicators' have been recommended:

1. Proportions of women and men in advertisements (voices and images)
2. Proportions of women and men as ad voice-overs (voice of authority)
3. Proportions of women and men appearing assertive rather than passive in advertisements (voices and images)
4. Proportions of women and men featured in ads as expert/advisor, informed/intelligent/conscious/cautious consumer, uninformed/gullible/pliant consumer, decorative prop
5. Occupations of women and men in ads

6. External or societal orientation of women and men in ads (e.g., work related, home related, family/relationship related, etc.)
7. Appearance (including closing and posture) of women and men in ads that are presented as primary, and other characteristics only secondary or absent
8. Proportions of women and men in ads for various product categories that stereotype or naturalize gender roles (e.g., household goods associated with cooking and cleaning, food, beverages [alcoholic/non-alcoholic], grooming and hygiene products, products for children, electronic goods, automobiles, sports equipment/accessories, etc.)
9. Proportions of women and men in ads for different categories of services/activities which stereotype or naturalize gender roles (e.g., travel and leisure, hospitality, education, health, childcare, telecommunications, banking and investment, real estate, sports events)
10. Depiction of sexuality in ads (e.g., relevant or not)

On the means of verifying gender-based stereotypes in commercial messages in media, following 'Indicators' are recommended:

1. Percentage of ads depicting subtle stereotypes (which emphasize traditional 'feminine'/'masculine' characteristics and male/female roles, making them appear normal and inevitable)
2. Percentage of ads that include multidimensional representation/portrayal of men and women (indicating creative efforts to challenge/counter gender-based stereotypes and other forms of sexist representation.[7]

RECOMMENDATIONS ON MAINSTREAMING GENDER IN MEDIA SCHOOLS

As brought out in the chapter, thousands of youngsters who pass out from media schools often lack exposure to any gender discourse. After they pass out, they become content writers and creative minds in the news, entertainment and advertising sector. Therefore, there is a strong need to mainstream gender at both the places, namely media schools and workplaces. Often in universities, various schools work in isolation of each other and do not take a multidisciplinary approach to teaching.

Some of the universities in India have a separate degree courses on gender studies, women or sexuality. Interestingly, in courses relating to women studies, there is often a paper or component on 'gender and mass media', which looks at the gender perspectives, besides the 'influence of media, patriarchy in operation, use of feminist methods for critiquing media representation' (Pondicherry University [Centre for Women's Studies, n.d.]).

In an MA programme in gender studies, there is a full paper on gender, culture and media, which includes 'media and stereotyping, gender discourse, perspectives on feminism: Western and non-Western (Jamia Millia Islamia)'; in yet another MA programme in women studies, there is full paper on gender and media, which, besides news media's construct of gender, also has a full module on gender in the 'paid' media space like advertising: 'critical analysis of gender in magazines and newspapers, advertising and the image of women, women's magazines, politics of paid news' (Goa University). The courses in sociology in most cases also have exclusive paper on gender and media. These courses have academics who are experts in their area of scholarship. The universities that have both mass communication departments and sociology or women studies departments would not suffer a faculty resource crunch if this area of study were to be included in the mass communication syllabi. Therefore, the UGC, universities and stand-alone institutions that offer courses in mass communication can consider including gender studies in mass communication, in general. The various niche areas like advertising, public relations, digital media, integrated marketing communication can also consider including a compulsory paper in gender studies/gender and media with a view to sensitize the future communication professionals on gender and related issues. Here also, the faculty can easily be sourced from the departments of sociology and women studies. The Ministry of Human Resource Development (HRD) and the UGC can consider making it mandatory for all the universities and institutions in both public and private domains to have gender-sensitive curriculum in various courses in media and mass communication. In Chapter 12 on policy interventions, a template on the proposed gender course has been included.

NOTES

1 The following women from the industry signed the letter, which was placed in the public domain: Tista Sen, Regional Creative Director, JWT; Kainaz Karmakar, Chief Creative Officer, Ogilvy West; Swati Bhattacharya, Chief Creative Officer, FCB Ulka; Deepa Geethakrishnan, National Creative Director, Lowe Lintas; Delna Sethna, Chief Creative Officer, Law & Kenneth Saatchi & Saatchi; Ashwini Deshpande, Co-founder Director, Elephant Design; Malvika Mehra, Founder & Creative Director, Tomorrow Creative Lab; Preeti Vyas, Chairwoman & Chief Creative Officer, Vyas Giannetti Creative; Shagun Seda, ECD, DDB Mudra; Pallavi Chakravarti, ECD, Taproot Dentsu; Lulu Raghavan, Managing Director, Landor and Alpana Parida, Managing Director, DY Works. See https://www.exchange4media.com/marketing-news/metoo-ad-women-collective-moots-independent-body-to-investigate-allegations-92462.html

2 Thirty-two professionals from among the top echelons including agency heads, branch heads, HR heads and creative heads, global and India, were interviewed for the purpose in 2018 by the author and her team members as a part of the ICSSR research.

3 See https://www.swaninterface.net/report-on-the-status-of-women-in-media-in-south-asia-march-2020/; the author

did the research for India and was also regional research coordinator for all South Asian countries. The website carries both the volumes of the reports, which can be referred to for a detailed understanding.

4 See Jethwaney & Gualnam (2019) Detailed study can be accessed at http://isid.org.in/wp-content/uploads/2020/08/JJ01062019.pdf

5 See http://www.assocham.org/newsdetail.php?id=565

6 Data presented in figures are for the period 2015 to 2019. Please refer to the country-specific discussion in this chapter and the country research reports presented in Volume II, available at https://www.swaninterface.net/report-on-the-status-of-women-in-media-in-south-asia-march-2020/

7 Full report available at http://www.unesco.org/new/en/communication-and-information/resources/publications-and-communication-materials/publications/full-list/gender-sensitive-indicators-for-media-framework-of-indicators-to-gauge-gender-sensitivity-in-media-operations-and-content/

REFERENCES

Best Media Info. (2020, 29 January). The Advertising Club, the Advertising Agencies Association of India launch communication programme at Goafest 2020. https://bestmediainfo.com/2020/01/the-advertising-club-the-advertising-agencies-association-of-india-launch-communication-programme-at-goafest-2020/

Centre for Women's Studies. (n.d.). Syllabus. http://www.pondiuni.edu.in/sites/default/files/downloads/pgdiploma-womemstudies.pdf

CMS & UKIERI. (2015). *Symposium on vision for media and communication education in India*. http://cmsindia.org/sites/default/files/Aug_Monograph_Vision-&-Communication_for-web.pdf

India Campaign. (2020, 6 April). *Goa Fest 2020: Abby Awards for 2020 Cancelled.* https://www.campaignindia.in/article/goafest-2020-abby-awards-for-2020-cancelled/459322

Irani, D., & Lad, M. (2015, 20 May). Here's why women leave ad agencies. *The Economic Times.* https://economictimes.indiatimes.com/heres-why-women-leave-ad-agencies/articleshow/47341904.cms?from<hig>=</hig>mdr

Jethwaney, J., & Gualnam, T. (2019, January–June). Appraisal of gender content in the advertising syllabi of mass communication course: A case for gendered and inclusive curricula. *International Journal of Communication Development*, *9*(3 & 4), 1–18.

United Nations. (2002). *Gender mainstreaming: An overview.* https://www.un.org/womenwatch/osagi/pdf/e65237.pdf

CHAPTER 8

GENDER SENSITIVE LAWS: A GLOBAL CONCERN

Advertising is legalized lying.

H. G. Wells

One often hears that India is the most regulated country in the world, albeit with a judicial system that is one of the most sluggish. The other reality is that, as a society, we for long have been rather passive and forgiving, but thanks to an overactive and a hyperactive social media, things are changing, both for good and not-so-good reasons. Among many themes that find resonance in social science research, civil society discourse and social media platforms is also the issue relating to the representation of women in media and narrative surrounding women in the commercial space including advertising and entertainment.

Women who comprise nearly half the world's population have contributed equally, if not more, to the social, economic and cultural life of the world, but despite that, gender equity is still a far cry, both in their personal and public sphere. The coming of mass media and its tremendous spread in the last 100 years or so, which could have become a level playing field for women, has rather been unfavourable to them, both in terms of space and representation as many empirical studies from various societies reflect in no certain terms.

Advertising is criticized for many things, but what has turned into a public debate and emerged as an area of discord is the inappropriate portrayal of women in advertising, cutting across cultures and geographical boundaries. Realizing the impactful role of advertising, even the Vatican is believed to have conveyed that advertising should be based on three moral principles, namely 'truthfulness', 'the dignity of the human person' and 'social responsibility' (Murphy, 1998).

The redeeming thing is that, in the last couple of decades, governments and civil society organizations in many countries and, to some extent, the ad industry are getting sensitized to the need for breaking the status quo on the inappropriate gender narrative in media including advertising. In this chapter, we shall take a look at the regulatory environment in India and some other countries and also the state of self-regulation.

A specific law on the Indecent Representation of Women was passed in 1986 by the Indian Parliament after a protracted struggle and efforts on the part of many women advocacy groups to bring legislation in this regard. Let us take a look at what it promises and expects the content creators to follow.

INDECENT REPRESENTATION OF WOMEN (PROHIBITION) ACT, 1986

Tabled in Rajya Sabha in 1986 in response to the demands made by various women groups, the aim of the bill then was to ensure that the portrayal of women in media through advertisements, writings, publications and illustrations was not such that could be termed 'indecent'.

What Does the Law Say?

The Indecent Representation of Women (Prohibition) Act, 1986 (no. 60 of 1986), to 'prohibit indecent representation of women through advertisements or in publications, writings, paintings, figures or in any other manner and for matters connected therewith or incidental thereto' (Government of India [GoI], n.d.).

The act defines: 'indecent representation of women' as

> the depiction in any manner of the figure of a woman; her form or body or any part thereof in such way as to have the effect of being indecent, or derogatory to, or denigrating women, or is likely to deprave, corrupt or injure the public morality or morals. (GoI, n.d.)

The 'advertisement' refers to notice, circular, label, wrapper or other document and also includes any visible representation made by means of any light, sound, smoke or gas. 'Indecent representation of women' implies depiction in any manner of the figure of a woman, her body or any part thereof in a way as to have the effect of being indecent or derogatory to, or denigrating women, or is likely to deprave, corrupt or injure the public morality or morals.

The Act suggests that no person will produce, sell, let to hire, distribute, circulate or send by post any book, pamphlet, paper, slide, film, writing, drawing, painting, photograph, representation or figure which contains indecent representation of women in any form. The Act, however, does not apply to the following.

1. Publications proved to be justified as being for the public good on the ground that such book, pamphlet, paper, slide, film, writing, drawing, painting, photograph, representation or figure is in the interest of science, literature, art or learning or other objects of general concern.
2. Kept or used bona fide for religious purposes. (It also includes sculptures and paintings on monuments, archaeological sites and temples.)
3. Any film in respect of which the provisions of Part II of the Cinematograph Act, 1952 (37 of 1952), will be applicable.

In 2012, an amendment was introduced to the law, which aimed at covering the law to all forms of media, particularly those that emerged with the new technology. The proposed amendment, however, did not take place and the amended bill lapsed. In 2018, the Ministry of WCD again proposed some more amendments, but the bill again lapsed.

In the new proposed amendments, the ministry has expanded on the original definition of indecent representation of women as a 'depiction of women as a sexual object, which appeals to the prurient interest'.

In a press release issued by the Ministry of WCD in June 2018, the ministry has conveyed the following changes in the law.

The reformulated Bill proposes following amendments in the parent Act:

- Amendment in definition of term **advertisement** to include **digital form or electronic form or hoardings, or through SMS, MMS etc.**
- Amendment in definition of distribution to include publication, license or uploading using computer resource, or communication device or in
- Insertion of a new definition to define the term **publish**
- Amendment in section 4 to include that No person shall **publish or distribute or cause to be published or cause to be distributed by any means any material** which contains indecent representation of women in any form:
- Penalty similar to that provided under the Information Technology Act, 2000
- Creation of a Centralized Authority under the aegis of National Commission of Women (NCW). This Authority will be headed by Member Secretary, NCW, having representatives from Advertising Standards

Council of India, Press Council of India, Ministry of Information and Broadcasting and one member having experience of working on women issues.

- This Centralized Authority will be authorized to receive complaints or grievances regarding any programme or advertisement broadcasted or publication and investigate/examine all matters relating to the indecent representation of women. (GoI, 2018)

Media reported that provision for penalty would be in line with the Information Technology Act (IT Act), 2000 'for the first offence was increased to imprisonment of three years and a fine between ₹50,000 and ₹1 lakh. Earlier the punishment was two years and a fine of ₹2,000' (*Indian Express*, 2021).

It does not come as a surprise that women issues are not of priority interest to lawmakers as two successive governments let the bill lapse in 2012 and 2018, that is, both the United Progressive Alliance and National Democratic Alliance (NDA) governments during the 15th and 16th Lok Sabha terms. A lot has changed in media and technology since the Act came into being in 1986. A huge surge in the digital media and computer manipulation techniques have made women more vulnerable and at the receiving end of misogynists and voyeuristic individuals that are aplenty, especially on social media platforms. Therefore, the existing law requires urgent amendment, expecting that the concerned ministry would take it up during the 17th Lok Sabha term (2019–2024).

INTERNATIONAL LAWS ON GENDER-SENSITIVE ADVERTISEMENTS

Advertising is a global phenomenon. With marketplaces turning flat, thanks to globalization and e-commerce, one finds advertising narrative also cutting across geographical boundaries, raising issues of propriety of Western style of advertising discourse in traditional societies. In order to understand the various policies and laws on representation of women in advertising, an analysis of practices in select countries has been made to get a perspective.

In the United Kingdom (UK), the advertising industry is regulated under the Advertising Standards Authority (ASA), which is a self-regulatory body. The ASA's role is to make sure that ads across the UK abide by the given rules of advertising codes. Ads in the UK come under two systems, self-regulation and co-regulation. Under self-regulation system, the ad industry writes its own rules through a committee called the Committee of Advertising Practice, which consists of members from within the industry, such as advertisers, media owners and advertising agencies.[1] The UK has seen its fair share of controversial ads and marketing practices that are insensitive to women. Take, for instance, the case of Dove packing controversy, wherein the company sold its product in different body shapes to promote a certain body-positive image. This, however, backfired and the critics rallied against its ban as, for many, it did not provide a healthy body image but instead helped reinforce the existing normative values.[2] Such discourse over a long period of campaign and movement led to the formulation of the most recent prohibition on ads that reinforce gender-based stereotypes.

The United States of America (USA), said to be the fountainhead of advertising, does not have any specific law on woman representation in advertising, despite that it was in the USA where the feminist movement in the 1960s accused advertising of creating stereotypes about women in the commercial space. In the USA, the Federal Trade Commission (FTC) that governs the advertising industry is primarily responsible for enforcing the Federal Consumer Protection Law, including the FTC Act that protects the consumers from 'unfair and deceptive acts or practices'. There is also the state attorney general and local district attorney who can enforce the state and local consumer protection law.[3] What is interesting to note is that the codes and rules under the FTC do not have anything on the issue of gender-sensitive portrayal. There is a small section that prohibits sexually explicit ads, but what would be construed 'sexually explicit' is not defined. This may be the reason why there are some very explicit ads full of sexual innuendos in the USA. Take, for instance, Carl's Jr. Burger ads, where all of their ads display women with some references to the body or sex of the woman. In one of their ads, a nude woman is walking around in public while men stare at her and different vegetables are used to hide her body parts. At the end of it, she poses in a bikini and takes a bite of the burger.[4] The persistence of such ads over the years—despite criticism from the public—maybe because of the lack of proper regulatory provisions that could address the issue. What is even more surprising here is that despite its long tradition of women's movement and much critical feminist writing, the USA does not have a proper regulatory body in government or industry on this.

NORDIC COUNTRIES

In 2016, under the presidency of Finland, the Nordic Council of Ministers initiated a project for gender equality, submitting its 152-page report in 2017. The report states the undeniable role that media plays in constructing or deconstructing our understanding of gender and related issues. Within the larger sphere of media, the report argued that advertising played a pivotal role in shaping people's ideas of self, values and general outlook of the world. Therefore, it was pertinent to combat gender discriminative advertising, to progress toward a more gender-equal society. Giving a bit of historical background, the report acknowledged the important role that the feminist movement in the 1960s played in pushing for various legislations towards creating a gender-equal society, including the need for regulation in the advertising industry, which was also an offshoot of that movement (Kosunen et al., 2017).

Over the course of many years, the European Parliament, the Council of Europe and the Parliamentary Assembly of the Council of Europe have passed resolutions on how advertising affects equality between women and men, and how deeply stereotypes presented via advertising can be rooted. Along with these, there are different international laws, regulations and guidelines that led to the formulation of different laws in the Nordic countries. The Convention on the Elimination of All Forms of Discrimination against Women, 1981 (CEDAW), is one such treaty that helped in the formulation of country-specific laws across the world. According to Article 5 of the CEDAW, parties must take appropriate measures, including legislation,

> To modify the social and cultural patterns of conduct of men and women, with a view to achieving the elimination of prejudices and other practices which are based on the idea of the inferiority or the superiority of either of the sexes or on stereotyped roles for men and women.[5]

The UN Beijing Platform for Action, 1995, although not a legal platform, provides a commitment from its signatories. It calls for action against gender stereotypes in public and private life and has a separate objective (J2) concerning the promotion of a balanced and non-stereotyped portrayal of women in the media.[6] The International Chamber of Commerce Advertising Code serves as a basis for self-regulatory systems around the world. Article 4 'Social Responsibility' of the Code states: 'Marketing communications should respect human dignity and should not incite or condone any form of discrimination, including that based upon race, national origin, religion, gender, age, disability or sexual orientation.'[7] In Europe, the variations in the scope and content of national codes and pressure from the European Commission led to the establishment of the European Advertising Standards Alliance.[8]

Sweden is the only country with a self-regulatory body that looks into the issue of gender-based discrimination in advertisements (Kosunen, et al., 2017). What is interesting is that all these countries have different ways of regulating the practice. For example,

Denmark, Norway and Finland regulate the advertisements under the Consumer Protection Law or the marketing legislation, while Iceland regulates it under the equality legislation. However, among those that have legislation on it, Denmark and Finland do not clearly define what gender discrimination exactly means and entails. It is only Norway and Iceland that have a specific and elaborate definition of what gender discrimination means.

EUROPEAN COUNTRIES

The issue of advertising regulation is a mix of legislation and self-regulation in Europe. Most of the countries, however, opt for self-regulation by the industry. The European Commission's *Strategic Engagement for Gender Equality 2016–2019* lists dismantling gender stereotypes and promoting non-discriminatory gender roles as few of its priority areas. While in the media sector, the 2010 Audiovisual Media Services Directive prohibits any discrimination based on gender and sex (European Parliament, 2018).

To cite a few examples, in Germany, the Constitution and general competition law regulates the contents of advertisements. The law clearly states that women's personality rights and the concept of human dignity can reasonably limit freedom of expression. The German competition law contains the standards for regulating advertising, including recognizing certain types of discriminatory advertising that degrade persons or groups based on gender. In 2016, the Berlin government agreed to ban advertising that sexualized women on billboards rented out by the city.

In France, a recent study by Conseil Supérieur de l'audiovisuel (High Authority for Audio-visual Media), based on an analysis of 2,055 television advertisements on 24 select channels, revealed gender stereotypes and obscenity in large measure. Speaking from a legal standpoint, the 1986 Law no. 86–1067 on the Freedom of Communication Act contains provisions in respect of human dignity, diversity and women's rights (EPRA, 2017).

AUSTRALIA

A country that enjoys a relatively higher degree of media freedom, the scope of regulations on media is relatively narrow. The Advertising Standards Board provides a free public service of complaint resolution and comprises 20 independent members of the community. The Group of Independent Reviewers is an entity of people selected for their expertise in relevant fields who review appeals against decisions of the Standards Bureau. The Advertising Claims Board is a jury for complaints from competitors. Advertising Standards Bureau is Australia's self-regulatory organization that administers complaints resolutions, which is a part of Australia's national system of advertising self-regulation. It has a secretariat of seven people who report to the Bureau (Governance) Board comprising six industry members (Ramanathan, 2011).[9]

ASIA

In Malaysia, the Communications and Multimedia Act 1998 contains governing standards and practices in the communications and multimedia industry. About the portrayal of women, the code specifically bans the depiction of both men and women as sexual objects. The code also has a provision referring to 'crude references', which explains crude references to sexual activity or display of sexual organs.[10]

In comparison, in Singapore, the Ministry of Communications and Information , the Infocomm Media Development Authority and the Infocomm Development Authority of Singapore support self-regulation. They together foster co-industry regulations. Advertising self-regulation, in general, is still not considered very effective, as media regulations are subservient to the Singaporean government regulations.[11] However, when it comes to South Asian countries, India is the only country that has self-regulations and legislation in place for regulating advertisement content. In Pakistan, the control over media has shaped multiple changes over a period. In Bangladesh, as majority of the population lives in rural areas, there are no advertising regulations in the country.[12] In Nepal, the Advertisement (Regulation) Act came into force for the first time in 2019. Among other provisions, the Act, in general, prohibits 'advertisements that affect one's religion, gender, caste, financial status or language.'[13]

OVERALL ANALYSIS

An analysis of practices in many continents across the globe makes it amply apparent that the issue of gender-sensitive laws in the sphere of advertising is a global concern. Different countries have taken different approaches to address the problem of insensitive representation of women in media; some have opted for just legislation, while others have put their faith in the autonomous regulation of the industry by itself. There are also those who think that cooperation between the State and the industry is required for achieving gender-sensitive advertising. In terms of region, the European countries have been very active in putting in place such regulation on the industry, be it in terms of legislation, self-regulation or both. The USA has been lagging behind in this regard, as it does not have a body that keeps a check on the issue. In Asia, from the countries examined, only India has a law in place. The government is also active in sending advisory to the industry and industry bodies from time to time, especially when there is public uproar on certain ads. The common problem among all the countries under reference is the issue of balancing the need to regulate the industry but, at the same time, to also not infringe on the freedom of expression. The argument, especially for the Nordic countries, has been that while gender-sensitive portrayal is important for protecting a woman's dignity, it is not a provision constitutionally enshrined, whereas the right to freedom of expression is a fundamental right, that is enshrined in the Constitution, thereby legitimizing arguments against any effort for regulation in the industry (Kosunen et al., 2017). Creative people in India expressed similar concerns during a field survey of the ICSSR study when questions of regulations were put up. Many saw such an effort from the government as a process of censoring the creative expression and thereby limiting their capability of expressing freely.

Yet another issue of debate is when self-regulation is not seen as viable, especially in the Southeast Asian countries like Malaysia and Singapore. The media sector, especially the advertising sector, in both the countries is subservient to the government regulations. In contrast, European countries like Sweden see self-regulation as the only way to keep the industry in check, mainly in continuance of the previous debate on the freedom of expression. With such a body around that has no interference from the government, there advise would not be seen as censorship but a self-management protocol to keep a check on the industry keeping in view the dynamic nature of society. The report by the Nordic Council (2017) expressed some limitations on the self-regulation system. The report stated that such a system without power would fail to bring about any substantive change because there is no provision for any stringent punishment suggested for the offenders. Most of the European nations (Norway, Finland, Denmark, Iceland and the UK) have followed the system of both legislation and self-regulation. Such a process is believed to have created an environment for discussion among different stakeholders; mainly those fighting against gender inequality and the proponents of free speech and expression.

Laws and ethics are two sides of the same coin. The issue of self-regulations and codes of ethics and professional conduct in India and some countries would be discussed in the next chapter.

NOTES

1 Advertising Standard Authority of United Kingdom: https://www.asa.org.uk/about-asa-and-cap/about-regulation/about-the-asa-and-cap.html

2 Dove pulls ad viewed as racially insensitive. https://www.marketingdive.com/news/dove-pulls-ad-viewed-as-racially-insensitive/506793/

3 Federal Trade Commission, USA. https://www.ftc.gov/policy

4 New Carl's Jr. Super Bowl ad depicts 'naked' woman, sparks outrage—ABC7 San Francisco. https://abc7news.com/super-bowl-best-commercials-ads-carls-jr/486706/

5 Convention on the elimination of all forms of discrimination against women. https://www.un.org/womenwatch/daw/cedaw/

6 Beijing Declaration. https://www.un.org/womenwatch/daw/beijing/platform/declar.htm

7 ICC Advertising and Marketing Communications Code. ICC—International Chamber of Commerce. https://iccwbo.org/publication/icc-advertising-and-marketing-communications-code/ (iccwbo.org)

8 Welcome to EASA. easa-alliance.org

9 Ad Standards (April 2018). https://www.accc.gov.au/system/files/Ad%20Standards%20%28April%202018%29.pdf

10 The Malaysian communication and multimedia code available at https://www.mcmc.gov.my/skmmgovmy/files/attachments/ContentCode.pdf (mcmc.gov.my)

11 Sankaran Ramanathan, Advertising self-regulation in Asia and Australasia. Available at https://icas.global/wp-content/uploads/2011_04_Ad_SR_Asia_Australia.pdf

12 *Bangladesh Journal of Legal Studies*. Comparative Advertising in Bangladesh and Global Perspective | Bangladesh Journal of Legal Studies. https://bdjls.org/comparative-advertising-in-bangladesh/#:~:text=Consumers%20and%20business%

20institutions%20in,between%20them%20and%20the%20consumers.&text=Unlike%20other%20countries%2C%20we%20do,for%20comparative%20advertising%20in%20Bangladesh. (bdjls.org)

13 Pioneer Law-Advertisement (Regulation) Act, 2019. http://www.pioneerlaw.com/news/advertisement-regulation-act-2019

REFERENCES

EPRA. (2017). The image of women in television advertising: Report by the French CSA. https://www.epra.org/news_items/the-image-of-women-in-television-advertising-report-by-the-french-csa

European Parliament. (2018). *At a glance*. http://www.europarl.europa.eu/RegData/etudes/ATAG/2018/614730/EPRS_ATA(2018)614730_EN.pdf

GoI. (2018). *WCD proposes amendments to widen the scope of Indecent Representation of Women (Prohibition) Act (IRWA), 1986*. Ministry of Women & Child Development, GoI. https://pib.gov.in/PressReleasePage.aspx?PRID=1534316

GoI. (n.d.). *Indecent representation of women*. Ministry of Women and Child Development, GoI. https://wcd.nic.in/act/indecent-representation-women

Kosunen, N., Asikainen, A-R., Gústafsdóttir, G., Haggrén, H., & Lång, K. (2017). *Regulation of gender-discriminatory advertising in the Nordic countries*. Nordic Council of Ministers.

Murphy, P. (1998). Ethics in advertising: review, analysis, and suggestions. Journal of Public Policy and Marketing, 17(2), 316–319. https://doi.org/10.1177/074391569801700215

Ramanathan, S. (2011). *Advertising self-regulation in asia and australia*. Asian Federation of Advertising Associations and

International Advertising Association—Asia Pacific. https://icas.global/wp-content/uploads/2011_04_Ad_SR_Asia_Australia.pdf

The Indian Express. (2021, 17 March). PC Chacko joins NCP, to campaign for left in Kerala elections. https://indianexpress.com/article/india/maneka-gandhi-to-push-amendment-on-indecent-representation-of-women-bill-heres-what-it-states-5206320/

CHAPTER 9

DO SELF-REGULATION CODES IN ADVERTISING HAVE ENOUGH TEETH?

Every profession is governed both by laws and ethics. Ethical considerations often are incorporated in the professional codes of conduct propounded by various industry associations. The profession of advertising is affected by many laws but more specifically the Consumer Protection Act and the Indecent Representation of Women (Prohibition) Act. The ASCI, a self-regulatory body of the advertising industry, has an elaborate professional code that the ad agencies are expected to follow. Under pressure and public outcry, ASCI has added issues relating to fairness creams and skin colour in its code in recent times, which will be discussed later in the chapter. Before that, let us look at the issue in the larger perspective of how and whether advertising and ethics can go together.

ADVERTISING AND ETHICS: A PARADOX TOGETHER?

To an ardent critic, advertising and ethics do not go together. Advertising, a commercial activity, is seen as false, flimsy, propagandist and immoral, which, the antagonists feel, should rather be dispensed with in lieu of price discounts to consumers. For the proponents, advertising is an important marketing activity that enables individuals to make informed choices about various brands. Ethics in advertising, they believe, is the purpose and function of advertising.

How does one define 'ethical advertising'? Analysts believe that ethical advertising is all about knowing the truth about a product and respecting that truth. In the USA, the FTC has an interesting definition of ethical advertising: Ad must be truthful, not misleading and, when appropriate, backed by scientific evidence. FTC

> files actions in federal district court for immediate and permanent orders to stop scams; prevent fraudsters from perpetrating scams in the future; freeze their assets; and get compensation for victims. When consumers see or hear an advertisement, whether it's on the Internet, radio or television, or anywhere else, federal law says that ad must be truthful, not misleading, and, when appropriate, backed by scientific evidence. (Federal Trade Commission, n.d.)

ASCI's code exhorts advertisements to be 'truthful and honest to consumers and competitors; within the bounds of generally accepted standards of public decency and propriety; against harmful products and situations and fair in competition'.[1]

The difference between FTC and ASCI is that the former is a regulatory body, and the latter is a self-regulatory body. Therefore, FTC is able to assert and take action on unethical advertising, which ASCI may not be able to, but over a period of time, it has asserted its role and made provisions in its code that have found resonance both with the government and the media channels (more about this later in the chapter).

A number of empirical studies reveal that people like to buy things and do business with companies that are ethical. Names of three Indian companies, namely Infosys, Tata Steel and Wipro appear in the list of the world's most ethical companies in the ranking of the Ethisphere's 2021 Ethics Index, a collection of publicly traded companies recognized as recipients of this year's World's Most Ethical Companies designation (Business Wire, 2021).

Large companies that advertise their brands and have nurtured their reputation over a period of time are often wary of adverse media coverage against their brands. The proliferation of social media has only made companies more conscious of the need to be on the guard. Of and on, one finds companies adopting social issues and talking about them in the media to project an image of being ethical and responsible corporate citizens. Some companies adopt certain ethical guidelines as a part of their core values and talk about it. For instance, there is this interesting example of a cosmetic company, The Body Shop, which has positioned its advertising narrative on how the company believes in ethical treatment of animals and, hence, does not use them for testing their cosmetics. The company believes not only in this fundamental but also advocates for others to follow. In 2018, it ran a signature campaign to gather support for reaching out to the UN to put a complete ban on the use of animals by cosmetic industries. Its signature campaign included the message:

> How long will it take to end animal testing in cosmetics? We're heading to the UN before the end of 2018 with our petition. With Cruelty Free International, we'll be working hard to reach an agreement. International decision-making can take time, but your signatures prove people want action now. We are already seeing more and more countries, like Canada, Brazil and Australia, move towards ending animal testing in cosmetics. We expect this momentum to continue. That means it's really important to create a unified framework, so that all countries have the same laws to finally end it for good. (Body Shop, n.d.)

It then explains how the company tests its cosmetics as reflected in the following box.

SO HOW DO WE TEST OUR PRODUCTS?

Our products undergo extensive testing to ensure they're safe and effective but still cruelty-free. We use three main testing methods involving computer data, laboratory-created tissues and people:

1. In-silico (computer-based) analysis uses readily available, existing data to help us to assess the suitability of similar materials through extrapolation.
2. Laboratory-produced EpiSkin is grown from human skin cells. It allows us to conduct safety checks on cells that react in virtually the same way as human skin, without harming any people or animals.
3. Finally, to ensure good tolerance on people, we will often test our products using patch testing. This involves placing a very small amount of product on a person's skin to ensure that it is safe and effective, usually at the final stage of testing a new formula.
4. We will also carry out controlled user trials where people test our products for both skin compatibility and cosmetic effectiveness, under the supervision of medical experts when required.

All cosmetics companies can adopt these kinds of cruelty-free testing methods. That's what we're fighting for worldwide with our Forever Against Animal Testing campaign. (Body Shop, n.d.)

There may be many more examples of such companies. On the other side, there are a dime a dozen companies that may not necessarily believe in what they profess. Many a time, companies say what is politically correct to avoid being on the wrong side of the narrative at that time.

Insensitive gender talk, unfortunately, has been the bane of advertising for as long as one can remember. Some of the unethical ads in the last few years that caught the public imagination and dissension include the 2012 Reebok ad 'Cheat on Your Girlfriend, Not on Your Workout'; the 2010 ice cream brand Antonio Federici's ad 'Submit to Temptation' that mixed sexual and religious undertones reflecting a nun with a macho man in the frame. In the past, also, the company used a pregnant nun enjoying the ice cream in its ad. The People for the Ethical Treatment of Animals (PETA) ad in 2009 'Save the Whales' was truly in bad taste. The large billboards had the back of an obese woman in a bikini. After a huge public outrage, PETA pulled out the ad. 'This Mother's Day, Get Back to the Job that Really Matters' was the ad of Mr. Clean, a detergent brand that had the young generation up in arms on the social media against this overtly sexist and stereotypical ad, inferring that washing was a woman's job (Bedros, 2016; Group Four, 2015).[2]

Advertising is known for making exaggerated claims and surreal storylines to make a point, but it may not necessarily be with a view to mislead the consumer who is smart enough to differentiate between puffery and reality. For instance, Fevicol ads are out of the ordinary and dramatic but convey the message of strength and long lasting quality of the brand. Another example is the Bisleri bottled water ad 'Piyo Bisleri' (2019–2020), where two camels looking for clean water end up drinking from the Bisleri bottles to their satisfaction. The concept is surreal but conveys the point that even camels know what good water is all about. About two decades back, a Biselri ad got in the eye of the storm when its ad released in 2001 with the tagline 'Pure and safe' changed to 'Play safe', targeting the youth with a double entendre. Play safe as positioning statement for water was perfect, but the imagery of a woman, man and the beach suggested that 'play safe' was being hinted at 'safe sex', which could have been an independent social issue undertaken by the brand. Here, the idea obviously was to attract eyeballs. The ad was soon pulled out after a public outcry (Pathak, 2015). There are scores of ads that have used sex and sensationalism to attract male gaze, some of which have been discussed in various chapters. Let us now look closely at the codes of conduct of professional bodies.

PROFESSIONAL CODES OF CONDUCT

ASCI's Code for Self-regulation

The ASCI, set up in 1985, representing the advertising industry, clients and civil society, is the country's apex self-regulatory body for the advertisement content. The ASCI Code 'is a commitment to honest Advertising and to fair competition in the market-place. It stands for the protection of the legitimate interests of consumers and all concerned with Advertising—Advertisers, Media, Advertising Agencies and others who help in the creation or placement of advertisements.'[3]

In its Code in Chapter II, the ASCI exhorts advertisers thus: 'advertisement should contain nothing indecent, vulgar, especially in depiction of women, or nothing repulsive which is likely in the light of generally prevailing standards of decency and propriety, to cause grave and widespread offence.'[4]

The provisions, as we see, are quite general in nature and do not have any indicators for advertisers to follow.

Critics believe that the ASCI needs more teeth to be more assertive and useful. The general criticism against the self-regulatory body is that the industry does not take it seriously as it lacks teeth. In a dispatch, the *Economic Times*, reminiscing about the 1990s Tuff shoes ad that had super models Madhu Sapre and Milind Soman wearing nothing but shoes and, later, the Amul Macho ad that had to be withdrawn for its explicitly sexual undertones, the story talked about the Tata Docomo ad, which had a maid pinching a phone and a doctor leaving the mobile in the stomach of a patient he had operated, which left the community of doctors and maids fuming with anger. The story compared ASCI with

Great Britain's ASA, an independent regulator across all media including digital that often dealt with genuine complaints severely, if its record of handling complains was anything to go by (Bapna, 2011).

AFAQS, an advertising online portal, reported that ASCI, in recent times, was asserting itself, especially on obscene and vulgar ads. The story shared that ASCI had launched a new initiative, called the suspension pending investigation (SPI), which would mean that ASCI could ask the advertiser to immediately withdraw an ad perceived to breach its code until the Consumer Complaints Council (CCC) takes a final decision on it. The initiative, which is an amendment of its articles of association, would empower the regulatory body to crack the whip on the 'gravely obscene, indecent, vulgar ads which are not in public interest'. The SPI could be invoked on a suo moto basis, which means the concerned ad would be stopped from being displayed or telecast within the same day it appeared (Afaqs, 2013).

Of late, one has seen the government taking ASCI on board for various issues concerning advertising, including on the amendments to the Indecent Representation of Women (Prohibition) Act, 1986 (Kinhal, 2018).

Prasar Bharati's Code for Commercial Advertisers

Besides ASCI's code, public broadcaster Prasar Bharati that has All India Radio (AIR) and Doordarshan under its aegis lays down that the 'Responsibility for the observance of these rules rests squarely upon the Advertiser and the Advertising Agency.' It exhorts all those engaged in advertising to 'familiarize themselves with legislation affecting advertising in this country,' listing out 16 Acts, codes, etc., indicating the list is 'indicative and not exhaustive'. The list among others has the following important citations:

- The Indecent Representation of Women (Prohibition) Act (1986)
- Consumer Protection Act, 1986 (the Act since has been repealed with the passing of the Consumer Protection Act, 2019)

- AIR Code for advertisers
- ASCI's Code of Conduct
- AAAI's Standards of Practice.

The provision relating to portrayal reads:

> Indecent, vulgar, suggestive, repulsive or offensive themes or treatment shall be avoided in all advertisements. This also applies to such advertisements which themselves are not objectionable as defined above, but which advertise objectionable books, photographs or other matter and thereby lead to their sale and circulation. (GoI, n.d.)

The Code exhorts advertisers to refer to Annexure 1 that has ASCI's Code and Annexure III of AAAI's Standards of Practice as a part of its code for advertisers. There are no specific indicators on portrayal or on gender sensitivity per se in the public broadcasters' code. By putting in the annexure both ASCI's Code and AAAI's Standard Practices, it is an indication that the government takes ASCI's code seriously.

Informing the Members of Parliament, the former I&B Minister Venkaiah Naidu, in 2016, said that between 2013 and 2016 there were no cases of obscene and vulgar advertisements on the public service broadcaster Doordarshan. The minister shared that there, however, were 21 cases in 2013, 5 cases in 2014, and 11 cases of obscene ads on some private channels, which were all pulled off on the basis of the Cable Television Networks Rules, 1994, enshrined under the Cable Television Networks (Regulation) Act, 1995. He also shared that, in some cases, apology on the ticker was telecast by the erring channels (Indian Television, 2016).

This is a very interesting development as it creates a liability on not only the advertisers but also the media vehicles that carry such ads, invoking the Cable Television Networks Act referred earlier.

Broadcasting Content Complaints Council's (BCCC) Content Guidelines for Non-news Channels

The BCCC code has an elaborate code for television channels that are 'non-news', which includes indicators on what constitutes 'suitable' for various age groups, but it does not talk of advertising at all, except adding in its code that all complaints relating to advertisements would be regulated by the ASCI, as per the Cable TV Networks (Regulation) Act (Indian Broadcasting Foundation, n.d.).

Press Council of India, a watchdog body, looking after the interests of the newspapers, has included a provision on commercial advertising (Serial Number 17) in its code that reads:

Obscenity and vulgarity to be eschewed

i) Newspapers/journalists shall not publish anything which is obscene, vulgar or offensive to public good taste.

ii) Newspapers shall not display advertisements which are vulgar or which, through depiction of a woman in nude or lewd posture, provoke lecherous attention of males as if she herself was a commercial commodity for sale.

iii) Whether a picture is obscene or not, is to be judged in relation to three tests; namely

   a) Is it vulgar and indecent?

   b) Is it a piece of mere pornography?

   c) Is its publication meant merely to make money by titillating the sex feelings of adolescents and among whom it is intended to circulate? In other words, does it constitute an unwholesome exploitation for commercial gain. (Press Council of India, 2010)

GENDER-SPECIFIC INITIATIVES BY ASCI

In the absence of any specific indicators on gender sensitivity and portrayal issues, there is not much for advertisers to follow specifically. However, bowing to public pressure and outrage against some fairness cream ads, the ASCI has included amendments in its code since 2014 to include the following:

> Preamble: While all Fairness products are licensed for manufacture and sale by the relevant state Food & Drug Administrations (FDA) under the Drugs & Cosmetics Act, there is a strong concern in certain sections of society that advertising of fairness products tends to communicate and perpetuate the notion that dark skin is inferior and undesirable. ASCI Code's Chapter III 1(b) already states that advertisements should not deride race, caste, color, creed or nationality. Yet given how widespread the advertising for fairness and skin lightening products is and the concerns of different stakeholders in society, ASCI, therefore felt a need to frame specific guidelines for this product category.[5]

To quote from its guidelines:

> The following guidelines are to be used when creating and assessing advertisements in this category.
>
> 1. Advertising should not communicate any discrimination because of skin colour. These advertisements should not reinforce negative social stereotyping based on skin colour. Specifically, advertising should not directly or implicitly show people with darker skin, in a way, which is widely seen as, unattractive, unhappy, depressed or concerned. These advertisements should not portray people with darker skin, in a way, which is widely seen as, at a disadvantage of any kind, or

inferior, or unsuccessful in any aspect of life, particularly in relation to being attractive to the opposite sex, matrimony, job placement, promotions and other prospects.

2. In the pre-usage depiction of product, special care should be taken to ensure that the expression of the model/s in the real and graphical representation should not be negative in a way, which is widely seen as unattractive, unhappy, depressed or concerned.

3. Advertising should not associate darker or lighter colour skin with any particular socio-economic strata, caste, community, religion, profession or ethnicity.

4. Advertising should not perpetuate gender-based discrimination because of skin colour. (ASCI, n.d.)

With gender issue coming centre stage in the public sphere, one has, of late, seen ASCI trying to take some more specific initiatives.

UN Women's gender-based programme called Unstereotype Alliance, that brings together industry leaders, decision-makers and creative minds globally to end harmful gender stereotypes in advertising, has looped in ASCI as its 'founding ally' in March 2021, as reported in the media. The story also mentioned about ASCI making an announcement on the microblogging platform Twitter on this development: 'After announcing a nationwide GenderNext study, ASCI is pleased to announce that we are now a founding ally of the UN women's programme, the UNstereotype Alliance'. (Tiwari, 2021)

As informed in the tweet, ASCI's research study GenderNext has been undertaken 'to understand the contribution of advertising over the years in creating and perpetuating gender stereotypes'. The study is expected to 'help Indian brands and advertising agencies shape gender narratives in advertising positively' (Sharma, 2021). Quoting the Secretary General of ASCI, Manisha Kapoor, the media reported,

> Women have been a matter of debate for many years. From time to time, these are issues which are of interest to both advertisers and society because advertising impacts the gender discourse, and gender discourse impacts advertising. They contribute to how the other develops but advertisers definitely have the responsibility through their brands of making sure that their own depictions are responsible, that they are fair, that they are progressive, and they're very positive. (Sharma, 2021)

The study, she shared, would be looking at five segments: 'decoding of advertising, consumer immersion, ad agencies/ people who create ads, gender policy makers and draw insights from Bharat Darshan, a proprietary study done by Futurebrands over a decade, and across more than 200 towns' (Sharma, 2021).

STAKEHOLDER MEET AT THE MINISTRY OF I&B

It is pertinent to share here that the Ministry of I&B, in November 2019 at the behest of the present author, had organized a stakeholder meeting at Shastri Bhawan, the headquarters of the ministry, inviting representatives of various media and advertising associations including ASCI, when the findings of the ICSSR research that had concluded the existence of blatant stereotyping of women in Indian advertising were presented. This was followed by presenting a policy brief to the concerned including the Ministry of I&B and the Ministry of WCD (Jethwaney, 2019). The policy brief has been reflected in Chapter 12 that, in brief, has made specific suggestions for various stakeholders to bring about the change.

Steps such as these, taken by various stakeholders to address the issue, are a positive development to take the gender debate to its logical conclusion for the ad sector.

COMPLAINTS MECHANISM AT ASCI

Anyone who feels concerned about any ad can make an online complaint to ASCI. The self-regulatory body receives scores of complaints every year, which it puts in the public domain with details about the nature of complaints and the action taken. It also facilitates personal hearing from the agency and the marketer in the first place, when it impresses upon the concerned advertiser to withdraw or edit the ad, which normally they do because they would be worried about public opinion going against them. In case some advertiser does not agree to the proposed amendments or withdrawal of the ad, ASCI then resorts to cautioning the media vehicles that carry such an ad, on its judgement against the erring advertiser.

In general, it is the competitors who lodge complaints on exaggerated claims against the rival brand to ASCI, but interestingly, complaints on the portrayal, though not very high, do get registered. In an email interview (October 2018 as a part of the ICSSR research), the then ASCI head, Mr D. Shivakumar, replying to the question on the percentage of complaints about indecent portrayal of women in advertising, said, 'Of the 2600+ advertisements looked into by the Consumer Complaints Council (CCC), approximately only 5 per cent of the advertisements were complained against for potential violation of the ASCI code with respect to indecent portrayal of women.'

The ASCI disposes off the complaints regularly. Let us look at some of the ads withdrawn from the category of 'objectionable' representation during March–April 2020, quoted from the ASCI website.

ASCI exercised the 'Suspension Pending Investigation' (SPI) option against an extremely offensive advertisement of an online video app. The contents of the advertisement were extremely obscene and vulgar. The advertiser issued an apology and internally banned all similar video content

> on their platform. Among various complaints examined by the CCC, complaints against advertisement of a well-known brand was upheld as the depiction of a woman protagonist slapping the male protagonist was considered as normalizing violence. Complaint against a famous skincare product claiming to provide 'HD glow' to the face was considered to be misleading as the advertiser had used image enhancement effects. While the advertisement did not make any reference to 'fairness' as a product benefit, the mention of the brand name being a trademark was missing in the advertisement. (Best Media Info, 2020)

ASCI did neither reflect who the complainant was nor the brand names or the ad agencies' coordinates while posting the above report on the disposal of the complaint.

MEASURES FOR ATTITUDE CHANGE

In order to bring about the required change in the attitude of creative professionals and advertisers, per se, it is important that ASCI and AAAI consider organizing periodical workshops on gender discourse and laws in collaboration with the academia and gender experts. They may find it challenging but not difficult to achieve, as it is the need of the hour. The professional bodies also need to engage more with ad agencies and advertisers in making them agree to certain gender-sensitivity norms that the ads need to go through before they are released in the media. The research has reflected the ubiquitous role played by the advertisers in deciding on the ad narrative. Therefore, any discussion for change has to take companies that are large advertisers in the loop. Instead of regulations coming from the government, self-regulation would go a long way in bringing about an inclusive and gender-sensitive ad discourse in India.

In conclusion, it can be posited that laws and ethics are two sides of the same coin; what is illegal cannot be ethical and vice versa. Steps, even if small, taken by various stakeholders, a vigilant society and an empathetic and objective media would go a long way in making the point that enough is, indeed, enough. Advertising that aims at changing the mindset of the people, for once, has to change its own mindset on its gender discourse in brand advertising.

NOTES

1 See https://www.ascionline.org/index.php/ascicodes.html

2 See https://www.entrepreneur.com/slideshow/280504#4

3 See note 1.

4 See www.ascionline.org

5 See note 4.

REFERENCES

Afaqs. (2013, 3 April). ASCI gets itself some extra teeth. https://www.afaqs.com/news/advertising/37145_asci-gets-itself-some-extra-teeth

ASCI. (n.d.). *The code for self-regulation of advertising content in India*. Downloads/code_book_revised_as_on_26th_oct_2016.pdf

Bapna, A. (2011, 14 September). ASCI needs more teeth to deal with cheeky campaigns like Tata Docomo's 'No Getting Away.' *The Economic Times*. https://economictimes.indiatimes.com/asci-needs-more-teeth-to-deal-with-cheeky-campaigns-like-tata-docomos-no-getting-away/articleshow/9969835.cms?from=mdr

Bedros, M. (2016, 24 February). *Gender analysis of Mr. Clean advertisement*. Marilina's Chronicles. https://marilinabedros.wordpress.com/2016/02/24/gender-analysis-of-mr-clean-advertisement/

Best Media Info. (2020, 24 June). ASCI looks into 533 objectionable ads in March–April, 2020; 115 ads withdrawn by advertisers. https://bestmediainfo.com/2020/06/asci-looks-into-533-objectionable-ads-in-march-april-2020-115-ads-withdrawn-by-advertisers/

Business Wire. (2021, 23 February). Ethisphere announces the 2021 world's most ethical companies. https://www.businesswire.com/news/home/20210223005189/en/Ethisphere-Announces-the-2021-World%E2%80%99s-Most-Ethical-Companies

Federal Trade Commission. (n.d.). Truth in advertising. https://www.ftc.gov/news-events/media-resources/truth-advertising

GoI. (n.d.). *Code for commercial advertising*. Prasar Bharati. https://prasarbharati.gov.in/code-for-commercial-advertising/#1531079405701-0401cfb4-2592

Group Four. (2015, 2 December). Creative project: The sexualization of religion in advertising. https://medium.com/@rlg233_group4/creative-project-the-sexualization-of-religion-in-advertising-108e4be8b280#:~:text=The%20message%20%E2%80%9Csubmit%20to%20temptation,such%20thing%20as%20bad%20publicity%E2%80%9D

Indian Broadcasting Foundation. (n.d.). Programme classification system. In *Broadcasting Content Complaints Council: Content self-regulatory guidelines for non-news channels* (pp. 19). https://www.ibfindia.com/sites/default/files/IBF%27s%20Self%20Regulatory%20Guidelines%20%28updated%20version%29.pdf

Indian Television. (2016, 30 July). *No cases of obscenity in ads on DD; 41 in last 42 months in private channels: Naidu*. https://www.indiantelevision.com/television/tv-channels/terrestrial/no-cases-of-obsccenity-in-ads-on-dd-41-in-last-42-months-in-private-channels-naidu-160730

Jethwaney, J. (2019, October). *Portrayal of women in Indian advertising: A case for policy intervention* [Policy Brief No. 4]. Institute for Studies in Industrial Development. http://isid.org.in/policy-brief/

Kinhal, D. (2018, 7 June). *WCD ministry's proposed amendments to IRWA Act limited, leave much to be desired; are they too little too late?* Firstpost. https://www.firstpost.com/india/wcd-ministrys-proposed-amendments-to-irwa-act-limited-leave-much-to-be-desired-are-they-too-little-too-late-4500585.html

Pathak, J. (2015). Portrayal of lasciviousness: An analysis of Indian TV ad. *IOSR Journal of Humanities and Social Science*, *20*(4), 20–28. http://www.iosrjournals.org/iosr-jhss/papers/Vol20-issue4/Version-6/C020462028.pdf

Press Council of India. (2010). *Norms of journalistic conduct* (pp. 18–19). https://presscouncil.nic.in/OldWebsite/NORMS-2010.pdf

Sharma, K. (2021, 31 March). All about ASCI's latest gender next report and what women of the ad world are expecting the industry body to address. https://www.businessinsider.in/advertising/brands/article/all-about-ascis-latest-gender-next-report-and-what-women-of-the-ad-world-are-expecting-the-industry-body-to-address/articleshow/81763758.cms

The Body Shop. (n.d.). Forever against animal testing. https://www.thebodyshop.in/against-animal-testing

Tiwari, S. (2021, 28 March). ASCI joins US women's gender programme Unstereotype Alliance. *Livemint*. https://www.livemint.com/news/india/asci-joins-un-women-s-gender-programme-unstereotype-alliance-11616911824391.html

CHAPTER 10

CURRENT DISCOURSE ON GENDER IN THE ECOSYSTEM AND ITS IMPLICATIONS

A good ad should be like a good sermon: It must not only comfort the afflicted, it also must afflict the comfortable.

Bernice Fitz-Gibbon

The state of women, if the World Bank review of 2018 is any indicator, leaves much to be desired. About 2.7 billion women are still restricted from having the same choice of jobs as men. Women still face widespread barriers, entrenched in laws that keep them out of jobs and prevent them from owning a business. The World Bank's *Women, Business and the Law* report finds that 104 economies prevent women from working in certain jobs; 59 economies lack laws on sexual harassment in the workplace, and, in 18 economies, husbands can legally prevent their wives from working. The report assesses gender legal equality in 189 economies based on 7 indicators, with scores ranging from 0 to 100 (Barne & Wadhwa, 2018).

It is an irony that the quantum of laws and policies, often, is an indication of the vulnerability of the particular group for whom these are made in a society. India has passed many laws to safeguard the interests of women and, also, aimed at ensuring gender justice. It is, often, the ignorance about the laws, in general, and the social conditioning of women in a rigorous patriarchal milieu that a large number of them remain untouched by what the laws could have done in their lives. Some of the laws concerning women are:

- The Immoral Traffic (Prevention) Act, 1956
- The Dowry Prohibition Act, 1961 (28 of 1961; amended in 1986)
- The Indecent Representation of Women (Prohibition) Act, 1986
- The Commission of Sati (Prevention) Act, 1987 (Act no. 3 of 1988)
- Protection of Women from Domestic Violence Act, 2005
- The Sexual Harassment of Women at Workplace (Prevention, Prohibition and Redressal) Act, 2013
- The Criminal Law (Amendment) Act, 2013
- The 2005 amendment to Section 6 of the Hindu Succession Act, 1956, now grants daughters equal rights in the family property
- Section 498A of the Indian Penal Code (IPC), which defines the offence of matrimonial cruelty, was inserted into the IPC by an amendment in 1983.

SOME DISCERNIBLE VOICES

With the growing number of voices against media projecting, reinforcing and creating new stereotypes about women who comprise half the human race, organizations are feeling a pressure to address the issue of gender inequality in the brand narrative. The Geena Davis Institute on Gender in Media in partnership with JWT, one of the largest global ad agencies, conducted 'The Truth About Gender Bias in Ads in 2017', using machine learning to analyse gender representation, screen time and speaking time across more than 2,000 English-language ads between 2006 and 2016. Nothing seems to have changed in the last one decade or, for that matter, in so many decades, the study found out. Men still got more space, time and voice on-screen vis-à-vis women. Research revealed that men who appeared on-screen four times as often as women did and spoke seven times as much were nearly three times as likely to be presented as funny and were usually engaged in outdoor activities, driving or sports. Women, as expected, showed up most often in domestic settings, across ads from across cultures. The spots featured women averaging in their 20s but men in their late 30s, gave women one-third the volume of dialogue of men (with a vocabulary dominated by monosyllabic words) and portrayed women as clearly intelligent 61 per cent of the time versus 89 per cent for men. The basic takeaway from this study was that 'women are getting younger, and they're getting dumber' (Beery, 2017). Improving women's representation in film is a long-term task, but the advertising industry could effect change sooner. Madeline Di Nonno of the Geena Davis Institute pointed out that while advertising was often created on short timelines, films took a period of two years or longer to complete. Even TV took longer, she said, but when one looked at the mass volume of production of advertising, the ad sector was in a better position to take advantage of cultural trends far easier than scripted television and film (Beery, 2017).

In a dispatch, 'Desi Ads Follow Gender Stereotypes: UN Study', Ambika Pandit shared that in UNICEF's new research that it did with the Geena Davis Institute, 'Gender bias & Inclusion in Advertising in India', based on deconstruction of more than 1,000 most-viewed ads, found 'consistent gender differences in sexualization'. UNICEF and the International Advertising Association would be 'working with members to launch campaigns to deconstruct harmful stereotypes' (Pandit, 2021).

In an initiative from the White House in 2016, the Association of National Advertisers (ANA) and Alliance for Family Entertainment (AFE) have begun a major movement to improve gender roles as reflected in advertising and media programming, aimed at reducing stereotyping and sexism. The movement known as

#SeeHer called on national marketers to 'portray women and girls more accurately' in their marketing and advertising messages. Specifically, the goal of this initiative was 'to improve the accurate portrayal of women and girls in advertising and programming by 20 per cent by 2020, the 100th anniversary of women gaining the right to vote in the U.S.' (Wolfe, 2017).

ANA–AFE reached out to its advertising testing partner, Advertising Benchmark Index, to help them develop a series of metrics for measuring gender roles for both women and girls. The metric is designed to become the gender equality measure for advertising (GEI™). Twenty-five thousand ads were measured across media, namely print, electronic and digital, to begin with, to measure them on the measuring tool to find both conscious and unconscious bias (Wolfe, 2017).

As global advertising conglomerates orchestrate most of the advertising in India, it is hoped that the changes underway in the West, as discussed before, would find resonance in the Indian ad space also.

The industry's self-regulatory body ASCI mandate says that

> ASCI & its Consumer Complaints Council (CCC) deal with complaints received from consumers and Industry against advertisements which are considered as 'False, Misleading, Indecent, Illegal, leading to Unsafe Practices, or Unfair to Competition', and in contravention of the ASCI code for Self-regulation in advertising .... Under its National Advertisement Monitoring Service (NAMS), ASCI proactively monitor over 80% of new print and all new TV advertisements released in the country every month, for contravention of Chapter I of the ASCI code. (ASCI, n.d.)

A review of the thousands of complaints received over many years, however, reflects that the ratio of complaints against 'indecent' or sexist portrayal is very negligible. One of the exceptions witnessed in recent times was the huge public outrage against Unilever's F&L ad, which showed a girl getting a job in an airline after she became fair. The advertisement faced criticism with cases being filed in the consumer court and complaints made to the ASCI. Thus, in 2014, the ASCI, under public pressure and adverse opinion, drafted new guidelines and proposed, among other things, that ads should not show darker-skinned people as 'unhappy, depressed, or disadvantaged' in anyway by skin tone, and should not associate skin colour with any particular socio-economic class, ethnicity or community. Cine star and film director Nandita Das, who is often referred to as dusky, spearheaded a campaign 'Dark Is Beautiful'. Sam Balsara, Chair and Managing Director, Madison World and a former chair of ASCI, while commenting on the new addition said, 'The reason for these guidelines is to make it clear to advertisers as to what society finds acceptable and what it doesn't' (Bhatt & Balakrishnan, 2014). As brought out in Chapter 9, ASCI has taken a few steps to understand the issue more closely by aligning with UN and also commissioning an India-wide study to get insights from various stakeholders on this vexed issue and sensitize creative minds and the industry.

These are some encouraging developments both at the corporate and policy levels. Similarly, there is also an increasing discourse on gender equality and equity in academics and media. It is not just the women but also evolved men who are talking about the desired change. For instance, cine superstar Aamir Khan, in one of the series of his television programme *Satyamev Jayate* (Truth alone triumphs), examined how masculinity harmed men, revealing that many men in India still felt societal pressure to act tough, never cry and treat women as less than equal (The Conversation, 2017).

SEXIST NARRATIVE

The recent example of sexist comments by two young cricketers, Hardik Pandya and K. L. Rahul in Karan Johar's talk show created the right noise that it deserved, leading to immediate suspension of both the cricketers for a few matches and the case referred to the ombudsman. In the order published on the official website of the Board of Control for Cricket in India (BCCI), the BCCI ombudsman D. K. Jain pronounced that while there would be no further action as they had already 'served a provisional suspension and tendered an unconditional apology for their comments', both were fined ₹20 lakh each. They were directed to pay ₹1 lakh each to the 'most deserving widows of ten constables in paramilitary forces who have lost their lives through *Bharat ke Veer* App'. They were directed to deposit the remaining ₹10 lakh each in the fund created by the Cricket Association for the blind. A good beginning indeed! However, the industry association let off the producer and programme host Karan Johar of *Koffee with Karan*. The programme was not live; the indecent and misogynist comments could have been easily edited, which Johar did not do. After a few days of the broadcast of the programme, when the issue was being discussed and debated in the media, in one of the news programmes, he was heard saying that he did not realize that such comments would draw the kind of response they did (*Hindu*, 2019).

The newly placed Chief Minister of Uttarakhand, Tirath Singh Rawat, in March 2021, took a jibe at women wearing ripped jeans. In a public meeting he went about giving graphic details of a woman travelling next to him in an aircraft wearing 'gum boots' and ripped jeans. When asked 'What do you do?', he shared that he was shocked that someone running an NGO could be dressed like that. He did not stop at that; the next moment, he was judgemental about her job, wondering what people would learn from someone like her! This created a huge dissension on the social media and mainstream news channels. Well-known women put up their pictures adorning ripped jeans. Swati Maliwal, Chairperson of Delhi Commission for Women, attached her picture in shorts in the #tag.

A channel shared the picture of the chief minister's own daughter with ripped jeans, but it was sensitive enough to camouflage her face, while the father was not so sensitive making fun of a woman. Coming from someone holding a public office, to say the least, was disgusting and reflected the mindset of an elected representative. We then wonder where people get their ideas on gender from!

A young Sushmita Sen, way back in 2003, slammed a sexual harassment case under Vishaka guidelines (until the Act on Sexual Harassment of Women at Workplace [Prevention, Prohibition and Redressal] was passed on 2013, Vishaka guidelines set by the Supreme Court served as the common law) against a higher up from Coca-Cola, who tried to act fresh with her after she was commissioned by the company to play the protagonist for their brand. She not only got an out-of-court settlement compensation close to ₹1 crore, she also did not pay tax on the amount, taking up with the tax authorities that what she received was not an earning in the traditional sense, but a compensation (*Financial Express*, 2018).

The #MeToo movement in the ad sector that surfaced in 2018 is also a testimony to the fact that sexual harassment and gender-based violence in the ad sector is a reality like in any other workplace in the country. This is a worldwide phenomenon.

It is not out of place to mention here that a general perception about women working in the glam profession like modelling and advertising being 'footloose' and 'fast' is commonplace. This also finds its resonance in the stories in the mainstream cinema. The 'fallen' woman is rarely from 'honourable' professions like teaching, medicine or engineering but invariably from the glam world. Just to give an instance, the film *Phir Milenge* with a storyline surrounding the treatment meted out to people with HIV/AIDS, when there was huge stigma surrounding the syndrome, the profession of the protagonist in the film, Shilpa Shetty, was in advertising.

If, on the one hand, the proliferation of social media platforms and the onset of technology has helped connect a large population across the globe sans geographical, economic and political divide, these innovations have made women more vulnerable as target of online misogyny, hatemongering and voyeurism, on the other. Women from various streams, especially politics and media, who voice their concern on issues that hurt the interests of the powerful, are generally at the receiving end. The social media allows such men to hide behind anonymity. Today, Internet is the least-regulated phenomenon. The once-information aggregators have become huge behemoths that control the information flow in the world.

RESPONSIBILITY OF ADVERTISERS

The advertising industry transacts a business of about ₹100,000 crores that includes production and payment to celebrity endorsers. The amount obviously comes from the Corporate Inc. that sells various brands in the market. We have discussed elsewhere in the book the role of the client in deciding the ad narrative; so, let us look at how gender is included in the vision and core values of a few large companies and the industry associations.

Unilever

Unilever (in India, earlier as Hindustan Unilever), which has a number of FMCG brands including the controversial F&L and Lux that is nearing a century of being in the market, claims to have taken steps in bringing about gender inclusivity in various ways. Among many such steps taken, Unilever, in 2016, 'launched a global commitment to move our advertising away from stereotypes, recognising that they're often outdated, unhelpful and, in some cases, harmful' (Hindustan Unilever Limited, 2020).

For mainstreaming gender within their organization, its website reflects information on commissioning a study to get an understanding on 'how stereotypes affected 8000 of our employees. The results made tough reading.' A staggering 60 per cent of women and 49 per cent men shared that stereotypes had held them back at work (Hindustan Unilever Limited, 2020).

In 2020, the company shared a big announcement that it would remove the word 'fair' from its flagship brand F&L. This media report came soon after Johnson & Johnson announced that it would stop selling its two fairness products in India (India TV, 2020).

On Unilever's decision, the *Washington Post* wrote that,

> The company Unilever said it would stop promoting skin 'whitening' or 'lightening', and rebrand the skin-care line in response to critics who say the products promote harmful stereotypes around beauty and skin tone. But it won't go as far as some have demanded: ridding stores of the creams and their connotations, no matter what they are called. (Berger, 2020)

Samsung

Samsung, the Korean giant that entered India in 1995 and became one of the largest FMCG goods company with its range of electrical and electronic brands, talks about diversity and inclusivity at Samsung on its website. On the opening page under the head 'Inside Samsung', it reflects, 'Embracing diversity brings different experiences and perspectives that helps us build a better tomorrow.' Giving the percentage of women employed, the data reflects that there were 45 per cent women in 2016, but, in 2019, it came down to 40.2 per cent. In leadership positions, there were 6.5 per cent women in 2016 and 6.3 per cent in 2019. The figures, as of 2021, were not reflected when the site was visited in April 2021.[1]

The company shares its support of the girl child and also its participation in the government's Skill India Mission, by providing technical training to thousands of young Indians, besides creating employment opportunities for many of them. There is a mention of its campaign #SapneHueBade (the dreams got larger) that won the award in 'Glass: The Lion for Change' category at Cannes in 2018. The newly created category of award 'celebrates culture-shifting creativity and recognizes work that implicitly or explicitly addresses issues of gender inequality or prejudice, through the conscious representation of gender in advertising' (Samsung Newsroom India, 2018).

The film is the real-life story of a young Indian girl, Seema Nagar, from Rajasthan, who underwent many roadblocks before she got trained under the Samsung scheme and also got a job at its servicing centre. But she did not stop at that; she got the opportunity to work as a trainer in the same technical school where she studied (Samsung Newsroom India, 2018).

Tata Group

The Tata Group, a conglomerate of various companies, talks about inclusivity and diversity including employing members from lesbian, gay, bisexual, transgender and queer community. A number of videos and stories by men and women including the third sex reinforce the company's vision and practice of gender equity and diversity.[2] One has seen some TATA brands breaking stereotypes, especially through its jewellery brands, Tanishq and Mia. A few of their campaigns have been covered in relevant chapters in the book.

Now, let us study the industry associations' gender perspective.

Confederation of Indian Industry (CII)

The CII has over 300,000 enterprises from around 288 national and regional sectoral industry bodies as its members as per the information available at its website. The CII does not seem to have anything in the public domain on its views on gender equity and equality or a gender discourse on what it expects from its large array of members. Under its research head, many studies are listed but none on gender. CII runs an annual programme since 2005, called the 'CII Foundation Woman Exemplar Program' that 'celebrates the indefatigable spirit of women leaders at the grassroots. The programme is intended for last-mile grass-root level women, from either rural or urban resource-poor areas, who have excelled as social change leaders in specific chosen fields'. The website claims to have reached to more than a million beneficiaries each year through a group of 80 women changemakers, who are trained and mentored by the CII expert group. Each year, 15 women leaders from the grassroots are identified through a rigorous process of selection by eminent people. Their work thereafter is scaled to drive progress and change in the areas encompassing broadly education, health, and micro enterprise (CII, n.d.).

CII conducts research on various areas, but there wasn't any study reflected on its website that had to do with gender equality, but in 2018, it did come out with a discussion paper on the 'Declining Female Labour Force Participation in India: Concerns, Causes and Policy Options'.[3]

Federation of Indian Chambers of Commerce & Industry (FICCI)

Claiming a membership of 25,000 members and office in various states and some countries, FICCI established, in 1927, advocates 'policy change'. In its mission, there is no mention about gender equality or activity, but it does have a very active women's wing, called FICCI Ladies Organization (FLO). At a UN meet, the FLO is believed to have stressed on the 'need of true gender equality as it is intrinsically linked to sustainable development', which is 'vital to the realisation of human rights for all' (Hans India, 2018).

FICCI's Women on Corporate Boards (WCB) initiative is aimed at training and mentoring women at board level. This initiative has been taken by the Trade Association after the Companies Act, 2013, made it mandatory for companies to have at least one woman director in the board. The WCB programme is a structured mentorship programme which is chaired by a former ambassador (FICCI, n.d.).

A look at some of the large corporate organizations, especially in the FMCG sector that are the largest advertisers, and an analysis of the information put in the public domain by the two industry associations make us believe that some beginning has been made, albeit a small one, both globally and in India, whereby the companies are aiming at gender equity and diversity either because they genuinely feel the need or to be politically correct. The brand custodians are also waking up to the reality, but it is a long way to go. It is hoped that the proposed amendments in the Indecent Representation of Women (Prohibition) Act, 1986, that lapsed in Parliament in 2012 and again in 2019, shall be placed in the 17th Lok Sabha in its current tenure.

GENDER DISCOURSE IN POLITICAL ADVERTISING

Most election manifestoes of varying political parties for the 2019 election had flagged issues concerning women, so it is earnestly hoped that these do not remain on paper but are actively pursued, whether one occupies the treasury bench or sits in opposition.

Let us take a look at the salient points on women issues in the manifestos of the two major national parties, namely the Bharatiya Janata Party (BJP) and the Congress, issued before the 2019 general election.

The BJP's manifesto promised financial empowerment of women, which included preference to government procurement from the Ministry of Micro, Small and Medium Enterprises and to ensure at least 50 per cent women in the workforce, a threefold increase in childcare facilities by 2022 and a comprehensive 'women in workforce' roadmap. The BJP also promised to reduce malnourishment in women and girls by 10 per cent 'in the next five years'. The BJP manifesto talked of creating a separate Women's Safety Division under the Home Ministry. It also promised to ban the triple talaq and nikah halala.

The Congress promised that every special economic zone would have a working-women's hostel and safe transport facilities. It promised to abolish laws that prohibit night shifts for women. It also promised to strictly enforce the Equal Remuneration Act and a separate investigative agency to look into the heinous crimes against women.

While the BJP has promised to provide sanitary pads for ₹1 per pad, Congress said it would install sanitary napkin vending machines in public places.

Even though both the parties supported 33 per cent reservation for women in Parliament and Assemblies, the Congress also promised to amend the Service Rules to ensure one-third of Central government appointments would be for women (Deepalakshmi, 2020).

None of these two mainstream parties in their manifesto addressed the issue specifically of sexual harassment and gender-based violence despite the fact that the crimes against women have been on the increase.

Interestingly, a group of five organizations working on gender-related issues in the northeastern state of Assam prepared a manifesto before the state assembly election in early 2021, exhorting the various parties in the fray to address the issues.

Ostensibly apolitical, five organizations from Assam that included the North East Network, Purva Bharati Educational Trust, Women in Governance, Women's Leadership Training Centre and Xobdo, Assam, jointly prepared a manifesto before the Assembly Election in Assam in 2021, which among other things demanded that the Ministry of Health and Family

Welfare to effectively implement the 'Guidelines and Protocols relating to Medico Legal Care for Survivors/Victims of Sexual Violence' for comprehensive healthcare response when dealing with persons from vulnerable groups such as persons with disabilities, sex workers, LBTQIA+ persons, children, etc. (*Hindu*, 2019)'.

At the Centre, the BJP formed the government with other allies of NDA post 2019 general election. While action is yet to be seen on various other fronts, the government passed a law banning triple talaq, immediately after getting in the saddle.

To conclude, advertising, an indispensable tool of marketing to sell goods and services, is here to stay. There is no wishing away the multibillion industry that moves the markets and the minds. The pertinent question, however, is whether the Indian advertising industry is sensitive and responsive to the changes in society, and if so, how does it represent these changes. The action taken by the professional body ASCI in undertaking an empirical research study to understand gender issues or some global companies either withdrawing fairness creams from India or, at least, removing the word 'fair' may be small steps, but that reflects their awareness of the public mood. The corporate sector, the industry associations and brand custodians, who are both legally and morally responsible for the ad narrative, hopefully would become more sensitive and create indicators on gender sensitivity at workplace and in the commercial narrative surrounding their brands. The news media, which generally does not scrutinize the ad sector and is the direct beneficiary of the ad revenue, needs to work closely with the industry bodies to bring about necessary sensitivity in the ad discourse.

NOTES

1 See https://www.samsung.com/in/aboutsamsung/sustainability/diversity-and-inclusion/

2 See https://www.youtube.com/watch?v=A0RCVhf6TAc; see also https://www.tata.com/newsroom/careers/tata-steel-diversity-inclusion-lgbtq

3 See https://www.cii.in/PublicationDetail.aspx?enc=5BRK4n4XRBz24y5u0Y7PO5OkMhTyO/jZ83IYjeVcBsZQyepfbyM/X6Wn8pzfX78MsLo7dDwM22wmbhKmNkL8xpTUmYfy0JOfytQN6Xv0A3EdrWajCfTAAOot02AI4ELHbLRL/gjvRgi9MFavMf+KuusewUJE9Ahd+SwxEBIKl8jb1Ru2d0xy485buJqNiOKq

REFERENCES

Advertising Standards Council of India (ASCI). (n.d.). https://www.mbaknol.com/marketing-management/advertising-standards-council-of-india-asci-and-the-code-of-the-advertising-standards/

Barne, D., & Wadhwa, D. (2018, 21 December). *Year in review: 2018 in 14 charts*. The World Bank. https://www.worldbank.org/en/news/feature/2018/12/21/year-in-review-2018-in-14-charts

Beery, Z. (2017, 25 September). *The ugly truth about advertising's gender bias, and how to change it*. Campaign. https://www.campaignlive.com/article/ugly-truth-advertisings-gender-bias-change/1445593

Berger, M. (2020, 26 June). After protests, a Unilever skin cream popular in India will no longer promote a 'Fair & Lovely' look. https://www.washingtonpost.com/world/2020/06/25/after-protests-unilever-skin-cream-popular-india-will-no-longer-promote-fair-lovely-look/

Bhatt, S., & Balakrishnan, R. (2014, 11 June). New guidelines for fairness advertisements: Don't show bias on basis of skin colour, say ASCI. *The Economic Times*. https://economictimes.indiatimes.com/industry/services/advertising/new-guidelines-for-fairness-advertisements-dont-show-bias-on-basis-of-skin-colour-say-asci/articleshow/36364189.cms

CII. (n.d.). *CII Foundation*. https://www.cii.in/CII_Foundation.aspx

Deepalakshmi, K. (2020, 13 January). A comparison of BJP, Congress manifestoes. *The Hindu*. https://www.thehindu.com/elections/lok-sabha-2019/a-comparison-of-bjp-congress-manifestoes/article26792374.ece

Hindustan Unilever Limited. (2020, 4 March). *Nine ways we are making Unilever a more gender-balanced business*. https://www.hul.co.in/news/news-and-features/2020/nine-ways-we-are-making-unilever-a-more-gender-balanced-business.html

India TV. (2020, 25 June). *Fair & Lovely no longer 'fair': Hindustan Unilever to give new name to popular skin care cream*. https://www.indiatvnews.com/business/news-hindustan-unilever-removes-fair-from-fair-and-lovely-hul-johnson-and-johnson-629109#:~:text=In%20a%20major%20announcement%2C%20Hindustan,that%20are%20sold%20in%20India

Pandit, A. (2021, 24 April). Desi ads follow gender stereotypes: UN study. Times Global Page (16), *The Times of India*.

Samsung Newsroom India. (2018, 26 June). *More power to women, Samsung India campaign wins Glass Award at Cannes Lions 2018*. https://news.samsung.com/in/more-power-to-women-samsung-india-campaign-wins-glass-award-at-cannes-lions-2018

The Conversation (2017, June 19). *'I'm so sorry': When Indian advertisements turn around sexism*. http://theconversation.com/im-so-sorry-when-indian-advertisements-turn-around-sexism-79272

The Financial Express. (2018, 26 November). Payout received as compensation in case of sexual harassment not chargeable. https://www.financialexpress.com/money/income-tax/

payout-received-as-compensation-in-case-of-sexual-harassment-not-chargeable-to-tax-itat/1393991/#:~:textSen%20made%20a%20complaint%20to,compensation%20worth%20Rs%201.45%20crore.

The Hans India. (2018, 3 October). *Beyond gender equality*. FICCI. http://ficci.in/ficci-in-news-page.asp?nid=15468FICCI. (n.d.). *Women on corporate boards*. http://www.ficci-ccg.com/

The Hindu. (2019, 20 April). Hardik Pandya, KL Rahul fined ₹20 lakh each for their sexist comments on Koffee with Karan. https://sportstar.thehindu.com/cricket/bcci-ombudsman-hardik-pandya-kl-rahul-rs-1-lakh-rs-10-lakh-fine-koffee-with-karan/article26895591.ece

The Hindu. (2019, 19 March). *Assam assembly elections: Women's manifesto by right groups*. https://www.thehindu.com/elections/assam-assembly/assam-assembly-elections-womens-manifesto-by-rights-groups/article34098925.ece

Wolfe, M. (2017, 4 October). *Gender bias in advertising: Why it matters*. LinkedIn. https://www.linkedin.com/pulse/gender-bias-advertising-why-matters-michael-wolfe/

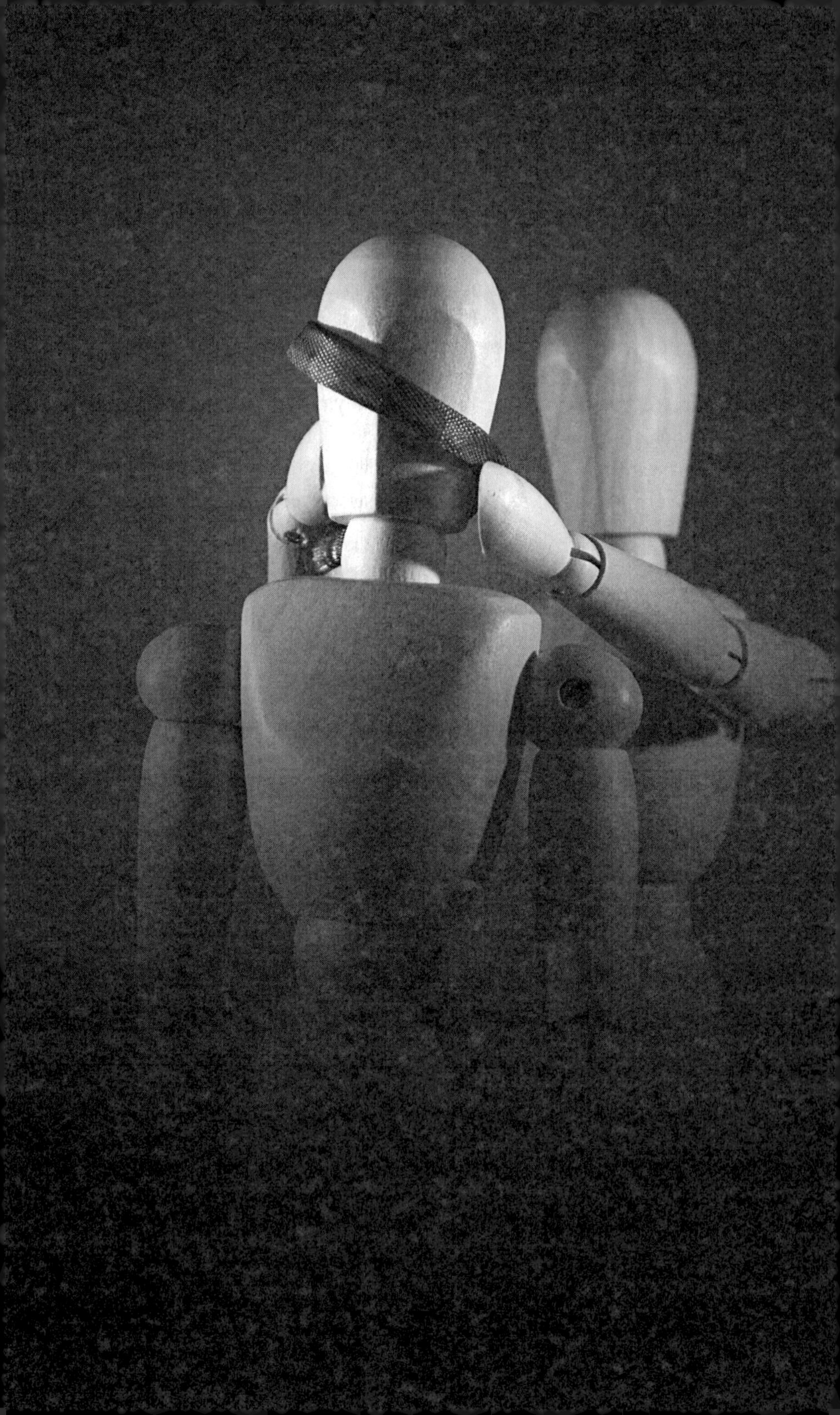

CHAPTER 11

WAKE-UP CALL FOR THE AD SECTOR

You can't sell anything if you can't tell anything.

Beth Comstock

The Consumer Protection Act, 1986, with amendments over the years, created a positive ecosystem for protecting the rights of the consumers who often found themselves not only duped by unscrupulous companies but also without much redressal mechanism to bank upon. The Consumer Protection Act, 2019, which came into operation in July 2020 replaces the earlier Act and, this time around, it has specific provision on advertising and celebrity endorsers in the liability clauses. Before the Act was passed in 2019, the issue was under immense discussion in the public domain on how the changes would affect the marketplace and the overall ecosystem. The opposition parties, in general, felt that the bill could have added many more provisions to make it more robust.

During the discussion on the bill, the Telugu Desam Party's Member of Parliament felt that by not including healthcare as a part of the services, despite a ruling of the Supreme Court mentioning it, the bill had overlooked a crucial area. He also asked why the bill was silent on surrogate advertising. Rajiv Pratap Rudy, from the treasury benches, suggested if call drops and power cuts could be added in the proposed law. Some members felt that the bill had gone for centralization, encroaching on the rights of the states (*Hindu*, 2019a).

Both the All India Trinamool Congress and Communist Party of India MPs suggested the sending of the bill to a select committee of the Rajya Sabha for a closer scrutiny, but it was rejected by the upper house. Replying to a debate on the bill, the former Minister for Consumer Affairs, Food and Public Distribution, late Mr Ram Vilas Paswan, said that the various suggestions given by members would be included in the rules framed by the ministry under this legislation, reported the media. (*Hindu*, 2019b) Despite some criticism, there is no gainsaying the fact that the Consumer Protection Act, 2019, is indeed a landmark legislation aimed at protecting consumer rights.

Before we discuss the relevant provisions in the Act that affect advertising and those who make millions of rupees by endorsing the brands without much overt responsibility, let us look at some star celebrities who endorse brands and the price they are paid for endorsements, in addition to, and more importantly, learning why more and more brands go for celebrity endorsements.

Interestingly, Section 21 of the Act that deals with endorsements was notified along with other provisions. Analysts believe that 'though part of the Act, this provision is still not an enforceable Law, and therefore gives a breather to clients, agencies and endorsers'.[1]

CELEBRITY ENDORSEMENTS

Celebrity endorsement is a marketing strategy that, in general, makes use of well-known actors and sportspersons from popular culture to create the necessary brand image. The popularity and fame of the chosen celebrity is attached to the brand to attract a certain kind of target audience. With markets turning flat and global brands doing the rounds in most countries, the discussion within agencies on whether to use a global brand ambassador or pick up someone local to find better resonance with the audience came under discussion when India entered the economic liberalization phase in the 1990s. An interesting instance can be cited of the upscale suiting brand Reid & Taylor that cast Pierce Brosnan, who plays James Bond, in the Indian version with the global tagline 'Bond with the best', but it did not seem to work. The company then changed the tone, tenor and imagery in the campaign, using the emotional route, reflecting on how children wished to celebrate their parents' silver jubilee; this also did not quite work. It was only when they brought in the invincible Amitabh Bachchan, the Big B, that the desired result was achieved (Jethwaney & Jain, 2012).

'Boost is the secret of my energy' by master blaster cricketing legend Sachin Tendulkar is believed to have done wonders to the brand in the 1990s, and later, Kapil Dev validated it by endorsing that Boost was the secret of their energies, that is, 'Our energy!' The brand has continued with the same tagline and celebrity endorsers from the cricketing world, with Virat Kohli being the brand ambassador in its current campaign.[2]

Virat Kohli is believed to be one of the largest earners on endorsements. His brand endorsements include Myntra, Wellman, Himalaya, MuvcAcoustics, Too Yumm, Manyavar and Philips India. According to industry buzz, he charges 5.5 crores per endorsement (Tewari, 2020).

Sachin Tendulkar, whose net worth is assessed at over US$150 million earns a huge amount from endorsements. The list of brands includes Pepsi, Adidas, TVS, MRF Tyres, Britannia, Canon, Philips, Visa, Reynolds, Sanyo BPL, Boost, Toshiba, G-Hanz, Sunfeast, Airtel, Castrol India, Coca-Cola and Colgate. His yearly income from brand endorsements, according to industry estimate, stands nearly at ₹17 to 20 crores (Shah, 2021).

Septuagenarian Amitabh Bachchan is undoubtedly a one-stop celebrity endorser for brands from hair oil to children's clothes, from jewellery to fountain pen, from FMCG to automobiles, the list is endless. Age has neither diminished his charm nor people's attraction towards him. His charisma is believed to turn around the brands. This even has been true when a brand may find itself on the wrong side of the law or public opinion. The case in point is the worms' controversy episode in Cadbury chocolates in 2004, a classic case of his contribution to change perceptions and bring the brand back on its feet. On the social advertising front, what Amitabh could do for the polio drops campaign in connecting with the masses, probably, has been his immense contribution in the social sector—the eradication of polio from the country in 2014.

According to industry reports, Bachchan's net worth is over US$400 million, a lot of which comes from endorsements (Celebrity Net Worth, n.d.). He is believed to charge between ₹5 to 8 crores for endorsing a brand. It is not uncommon to find him in 12–15 brand endorsements in different categories at a given time (Exchange 4 Media, 2019).

Among women celebrities, the two stars from the cinema world topping the charts are Deepika Padukone and Alia Bhatt. Of late, one also finds Kiara Advani catching up. The success in endorsements comes from the success of celebrities on the Bollywood turf.

Padukone reportedly charges ₹6–8 crore per endorsement deal and has emerged as one of the highest-paid female brand ambassadors in India. The actor has endorsed various brands such as Nescafé, L'Oreal Paris, Lux, Oppo, Royale Atmos, Tetley Green Tea, Nestlé Fruita Vitals, Jio, Axis Bank, Tanishq, Coca-Cola, Goibibo, Gillette Venus, Vistara, Britannia and Kellogg's (Exchange 4 Media, 2020).

Alia Bhat's endorsements include Manyavar Mohey (previously done by cine star Anushka Sharma with Virat Kohli before their marriage), Sunfeast Dark Fantasy, MakeMyTrip, Cornetto, Garnier, Nokia, Uber Eats, Lays, Fujifilm Instax, Frankfinn, Lux, Caprese, Sunsilk, Philips, Fruity Fizz, BlueStone, Hero Pleasure and Flipkart (Singh, 2020).

Celebrity endorsements in India run into thousands of crores of rupees. Depending on the categorization based on the market value, a day's shoot may fetch the top-ranking celebrity over ₹5 crores. As per industry insiders, the most expensive celebrity is cricketer Virat Kohli. With a brand value of over US$237 million, the *Economic Times* has put Kohli at the highest brand value in India (Laghate, 2021).

Consumers expect their favourite endorsers to be honest to their word. Unfortunately, Akshay Kumar, another popular actor and brand celebrity who endorsed Chyawanprash during the COVID-19 phase, contracted COVID. No sooner did the news break, there was a huge trolling on the social media. The ad clearly claimed 'Protection against COVID-19 with 2 spoons of Chyawanprash daily.' The ad did not stop there but further claimed, 'According to clinical study conducted across 5 centres, Dabur Chyawanprash helps in protection against COVID-19' (Tewari, 2020).

Source: https://www.dabur.com/amp/in/en-us/media/akshay-kumar-the-new-face-of-dabur-chyawanprash

The COVID-19 times has seen many brands claiming immunity, if used. Some of the examples include the following and the action taken under various Acts. The Maharashtra Food and Drug Administration, under various laws including the Disaster

Management Act, 2005, and the Drugs and Magic Remedies (Objectionable Advertisements) Act, 1954, booked the owner of Arihant Mattress after his company released an ad in a Gujarati newspaper that claimed that their mattress was 'corona resistant'. 'Eat chicken, beat corona' was the ad released by the Karnataka Poultry Farmers and Breeders Association. On a complaint filed by PETA, ASCI asked the releaser to withdraw the online ad.

Interestingly, Maharashtra Government has issued guidelines around COVID-19 that broadly requires

---

> every person/Institution/organization using print or electronic or social media for dissemination of any information regarding Covid–19 to ascertain the facts and obtain prior clearance of the Commissioner, Health Services, Director of Health Services (DHS-I & II), Director, Medical Education & Research (DMER), or Collector as the case may be. (Ranga & Tandon, 2020)

Not only that but the order also warns that the violation of any provision of these regulations 'would be deemed to have been committed an offence punishable under Section 188 of Indian Penal Code, 1860 (IPC), which prescribes punishment for disobeying any order duly promulgated by a public servant' (Ranga & Tandon, 2020).

CONSUMER PROTECTION ACT, 2019—ANALYSIS IN RELATION TO ITS IMPLICATION ON ADVERTISING

Let us now look at the provisions of the Consumer Protection Act, 2019, to understand how it is going to impact the industry and, also, celebrities who endorse brands. With its coming into force on 20 July 2020, the earlier Consumer Protection Act, 1986, stands repealed (GoI, 2020).

HOW IS 'CONSUMER' DEFINED IN THE ACT?

The consumer is defined in the Act as follows:

---

(7) 'Consumer' means any person who—

(*i*) buys any goods for a consideration which has been paid or promised or partly paid and partly promised, or under any system of deferred payment and includes any user of such goods other than the person who buys such goods for consideration paid or promised or partly paid or partly promised, or under any system of deferred payment, when such use is made with the approval of such person, but does not include a person who obtains such goods for resale or for any commercial purpose; or

(*ii*) 'hires or avails of any service for a consideration which has been paid or promised or partly paid and partly promised, or under any system of deferred payment and includes any beneficiary of such service other than the person who hires or avails of the services for consideration paid or promised, or partly paid and partly promised, or under any system of deferred payment, when such services are availed of with the approval of the first mentioned person, but does not include a person who avails of such service for any commercial purpose.

Explanation.—For the purposes of this clause,—

(*a*) the expression 'commercial purpose' does not include use by a person of goods bought and used by him exclusively for the purpose of earning his livelihood, by means of self-employment;

(*b*) the expressions 'buys any goods' and 'hires or avails any services' includes offline or online transactions through electronic means or by teleshopping or direct selling or multi-level marketing. (GoI, 2019).

WHAT ARE THE RIGHTS OF CONSUMERS?

As interpreted from the Act, the rights of the consumers include the following:

1. Right of information about the quantity, quality, purity, potency, price and standard of goods or services.
2. Protection from hazardous goods and services.
3. Protection from unfair or restrictive trade practices.
4. The right to have variety of goods or services at competitive prices (Singh, 2020).

DEFINITION OF ESTABLISHMENT

In Clause 19, the Act defines an establishment as follows:

> (19) 'Establishment' includes an advertising agency, commission agent, manufacturing, trading or any other commercial agency which carries on any business, trade or profession or any work in connection with or incidental or ancillary to any commercial activity, trade or profession, or such other class or classes of persons including public utility entities in the manner as may be prescribed.

CENTRAL CONSUMER PROTECTION AUTHORITY (CCPA)

An important operative part of the new Act is the setting up of the CCPA, whose aim would be to protect, promote and enforce the rights of the consumer. It will regulate cases related to unfair trade practices, misleading advertisements and violation of consumer rights. Headed by a director general, CCPA shall have the powers to impose penalty on the violators and pass orders to recall goods or withdraw services, discontinue unfair trade practices and ask for reimbursement of the price paid by the consumers. For facilitation of investigation into such violations, the CCPA will have an investigation wing under it.

Interestingly, the CCPA, as reflected in the government's press release, has only serving bureaucrats drawn from the concerned ministry and departments in it: the additional secretary of Consumer Affairs has been given the charge of the chief commissioner, a joint secretary as commissioner, director general of Bureau of Indian Standards as director general (Investigation) and director general, National Test House as additional director general (Investigation). The CCPA came into effect on 29 July 2020 'to exercise the powers and discharge the functions under the Act'. The release named the officers who would join the first CCPA (GoI, 2020).

Let us now operationalize various definitions as in the Act.

UNFAIR TRADE PRACTICE

A trade practice is considered 'unfair' when, in order to promote its sale, service or distribution, the concerned entity uses illegal means to mislead the public to go for deceptive goods or services or if the goods and services are portrayed as of good quality through deceptive advertising. The 2019 Act has, in fact, widened the definition of 'unfair trade practice' to take within its ambit 'misleading advertisements', the practice of selling without issuing a bill for goods and services, and failing to take back defective goods and refund the amount within the stipulated time frame (Kanth & Bhatia, 2020).

MISLEADING ADVERTISEMENT

Misleading advertisement is defined in Clause 28 as:

'Misleading advertisement' in relation to any product or service, means an advertisement, which:

1. Falsely describes such product or service; or
2. Gives a false guarantee to, or is likely to mislead the consumers as to the nature, substance, quantity or quality of such product or service; or
3. Conveys an express or implied representation which, if made by the manufacturer or seller or service provider thereof, would constitute an unfair trade practice; or
4. Deliberately conceals important information (GoI, 2019).

If we interpret Clause 28, although the Act does not use the expression 'surrogate advertising' anywhere, but by implication, this category should ideally fall in the category of misleading ads, especially those relating to tobacco and alcohol.

OFFENCES AND PENALTIES

The Act in Chapter VII (Clauses 88, 89) talks about Offences and Penalties as follows:

> Whoever, fails to comply with any direction of the Central Authority under sections 20 and 21, shall be punished with imprisonment for a term which may extend to six months or with fine which may extend to twenty lakh rupees, or with both.
>
> Any manufacturer or service provider who causes a false or misleading advertisement to be made which is prejudicial to the interest of consumers shall be punished with imprisonment for a term which may extend to two years and with fine which may extend to ten lakh rupees; and for every subsequent offence, be punished with imprisonment for a term which may extend to five years and with fine which may extend to fifty lakh rupees.

Section 21(4) uses the expression 'party to the publication', which may imply that it is meant for the advertising agency that creates ads and also releases in the media. This may also cover independent media agencies that release ads in media.

The former Minister for Consumer Affairs, Food and Public Distribution, late Mr Ram Vilas Paswan, clarified in the Parliament that the action for misleading ads would be taken against the ad agencies that created them but not media that carried the ads for publicity, as reported by the media (*Hindu*, 2019a).

Similarly, the Act has made the 'manufacturer or service provider' liable for punishment. Although not implicitly said, but by implication, the ad agency can be seen as the service provider to the manufacturer in preparing the advertisements for the brands thus manufactured.

Some analysts believe that the Act also covers under its ambit social media influencers, who will not be able to escape the liability of punitive action for misleading the public by endorsing brands (*Economic Times*, 2020).

WHAT DOES THE ACT SAY ON CELEBRITY ENDORSEMENT?

Interestingly, the Act does not use the word 'celebrity' anywhere. Instead, it has defined the term 'endorsement' in relation to an advertisement to mean: (a) any message, verbal statement, demonstration; or (b) depiction of the name, signature, likeness or other identifiable personal characteristics of an individual; or (c) depiction of the name or seal of any institution or organization, which makes the consumer believe that it reflects the opinion, finding, or experience of the person making such endorsement (Kasad, 2020).

The ASCI, a self-regulatory body created by the industry, uses the term 'celebrity'. Issued in April 2017 as Guidelines on Celebrity Advertising, the ASCI provisions are as follows:

- Subject advertisement (mentioned as 'advert') should not violate any of the ASCI code that is product/ service should be honestly represented, should not be offensive to public, should not promote harmful products or substances and observe fair competition.
- Testimonials, endorsements or opinions in advert must reflect genuine and reasonably current opinion of the individual(s) making such representations and should reflect adequate information about or experience with the product/service.
- Due diligence is done to ensure that all description, claims and comparisons made in the advert can be substantiated and are not deceptive/misleading. Celebrity can seek advertising advice from ASCI to ascertain violations in advert, if any which can be construed as due diligence.
- No product/treatment/remedy which are prohibited under the Drugs & Magic Remedies and the Drugs & Cosmetics Act should be endorsed by celebrity.
- No tobacco-based products or products bearing health warning should be endorsed by celebrity. (RNA, 2019)

Despite the advisory to endorsers by ASCI and the new Consumer Protection Act, 2019, that has created liability for the endorsers, it is not uncommon for celebrities to appear in tobacco and liquor ads without impunity through the surrogate route. These companies take the brand extension route by marketing an innocuous product in the same name to avoid legal tangle. There, however, have been instances when they were asked to explain. Critics believe that there are big lobbies working on their behalf, and as the government earns huge excise from these products, it turns a Nelson's eye. Celebrities including superstars like Shah Rukh Khan, Ajay Devgan and Sanjay Dutt, who currently appear in such ads, as well as Priyanka Chopra, Dharmendra and his sons Sunny and Bobby Deol, Dimple Kapadia and Malaika Arora have also endorsed various brands of alcohol and tobacco in the past.[3]

The Indian Institute of Human Brands (IIHB) came out with a document post the coming into force of the Consumer Protection Act in July 2020, which makes interesting observations and provides insights.

As said elsewhere in the chapter, Section 21 of the Consumer Protection Act, which deals with 'endorser' in advertising, is yet to be notified with rules and guidelines.[4]

DEFINING 'DUE DILIGENCE' ON THE PART OF THE ENDORSER

Section 21(5) of Consumer Protection Act says 'No endorser shall be liable to a penalty under sub-sections (2) and (3) if he has exercised due diligence to verify the veracity of the claims made in the advertisement regarding the product or service being endorsed by him.'

The corresponding Clause 21(6) further clarifies that

> No person shall be liable to such penalty if he proves that he had published or arranged for the publication of such advertisement in the ordinary course of his business: provided that no such defense shall be available to such person if he had previous knowledge of the order passed by the Central Authority for withdrawal or modification of such advertisement.

Clause 21(7) makes interesting reason for levy of penalty based on 'a) the population and the area impacted or affected by such offence; b) the frequency and duration of such offence; c) the vulnerability of the class of persons likely to be adversely affected by such offence; and d) the gross revenue from the sales'.

FTC, a regulatory body in USA, in 1980, made a landmark judgement in the *Cooga Mooga, Inc. versus Charles E. Boone*, a celebrity endorser case, issuing a consent agreement prohibiting him from making false advertising assertions. The commission granted him not to divulge his financial interests in the product but asked him to pay 25 cents on each of the 13,000 bottles on which the manufacturer issued a refund. It also said that for checking on the veracity of the statements, the endorser could hire an independent agency. Boone asserted that since the 'independent lab tests' had verified his assertions about the product, he would go ahead to endorse the brand in its new ad 'and I am going back on the air with it' (Rosellini, 1981).

As there are no reference points here, one would watch with interest cases that may emerge in the future in India.

WHAT ARE THE IMPLICATIONS OF THE PROVISIONS ON CELEBRITY ENDORSERS?

The report by IIHB suggests that with increased due diligence, celebrities may have to make higher indemnity provisions in their contracts with agencies to mitigate future liability, if any. The IIHB believes that this may lead to higher prices for celebrity endorsements to match with the risk associated (Rosellini, 1981).

There are scores of examples when celebrities have endorsed brands in tobacco and alcohol categories, which, on the face of it, is an illegal activity. Not all but some celebrities have used caution in the past not only on such products but also on other brands, heeding to their conscience. There is this interesting case, which happened much before the new Act came into being. The story goes that Amitabh Bachchan withdrew from endorsing Pepsi when he was faced with a moral dilemma. A young girl at a school asked him why he endorsed the product, which was 'poison', as told by her teacher in the class. Bachchan shared this story with IIM (Ahmedabad) students and faculty members in January 2014 that he was so disturbed by what the child said that he decided to withdraw from the brand after that incident.

He also told the gathering that he exercised due diligence before endorsing any product. 'I look into it ... I meet the client and ask them about it ... I don't endorse tobacco or alcohol because I don't have them ... then why I should endorse them?' he said (Dutta & Bhushan, 2014).

One has seen a growing heat against celebrities for endorsing brands that either did not stand up to the promise of quality or those that were considered ethically and morally wrong as the fairness creams. Shah Rukh Khan and Deepika Padukone were criticized for endorsing fairness creams not by only activists but also fellow actors, including Abhay Deol (Shiraz, 2020).

Post the controversy on higher content of monosodium glutamate in Maggie noodles in 2015, FIRs were filed against Amitabh Bachchan and Madhuri Dixit, among others, for endorsing the brand. After the real estate company Amrapali failed to fulfil its promise of handing over properties to home buyers, FIRs were lodged in 2016 against M. S. Dhoni who had endorsed the brand (Mtira et al., 2020).

Such litigations against celebrity endorsers for misleading or false advertising, believe analysts, are only bound to increase with the introduction of liabilities under the new Act.

There is another twist to the argument. Well-known celebrities are often roped in by the Central and State governments to endorse behaviour change ads, which many of them oblige and often do pro bono. The Act is silent on the celebrity liability on such ads, just in case something goes amiss.

Legal minds believe that the most revolutionary provision of the Consumer Protection Act is the setting up of CCPA with its own investigation wing. The other interesting feature is bringing e-commerce under Consumer Protection Act's ambit, a growing need of the hour. With many international companies in the business, future judgements based on the new Consumer Protection Act would be watched with interest. Analysts believe that the Act has been lenient on penalties on endorsers compared to the amount paid to them for endorsing brands. More clarity would come only after rules and guidelines are issued, besides the judgements from CCPA in the near future.

Analysts suggest that if CCPA works closely with the advertising sector, especially ASCI, it would become more meaningful and useful. Citing the examples of the FTC in the USA, working closely with advertising fraternity, and the Competition and Markets Authority in the UK, working in close coordination with the ASA, the cases of misleading advertisements can attract better compliance (Bar and Bench, n.d.).

In conclusion, it is hoped that with the marketing of goods and services becoming multipronged via various platforms, a plethora of competitive goods and services, and people's craze about celebrities—at least, in this part of the world—the Consumer Protection Act, 2019, would be able to come up to the expectations of millions of consumers who comprise the aspirational class in the country.

NOTES

1 Analysis by Indian Institute of Human Brands at https://brandequity.economictimes.indiatimes.com/news/marketing/the-celebrity-and-the-consumer-protection-act/77189902

2 https://www.afaqs.com/news/advertising/54409_boost-is-the-secret-of-my-energy-1-tagline-3-decades-many-cricket-champs

3 For reference on how ASCI and the now extinct MRTP Commission gave judgements on surrogate ads on liquor and tobacco ads, read the chapter 'Advertising: Laws and Ethics' in Jethwaney and Jain (2012).

4 IIHB Consumer Protection Act Report available at https://brandequity.economictimes.indiatimes.com/news/marketing/the-celebrity-and-the-consumer-protection-act/77189902

REFERENCES

Bar and Bench. (n.d.). *Law governing endorsements: The global perspective and its emergence in India.* https://www.barandbench.com/columns/law-governing-endorsements-the-global-perspective-and-its-emergence-in-india

Celebrity Net Worth. (n.d.). *Amitabh Bachchan net worth.* https://www.celebritynetworth.com/international-celebrities/indian-celebrities/bollywood-celebrities/amitabh-bacchan-net-worth/

Dutta, V., & Bhushan, R. (2014, 31 January). *Amitabh Bachchan says he stopped endorsing Pepsi after Jaipur girl called it 'poison'.* Retail.com. https://retail.economictimes.indiatimes.com/news/food-entertainment/personal-care-pet-supplies-liquor/amitabh-bachchan-says-he-stopped-endorsing-pepsi-after-jaipur-girl-called-it-poison/29642894#:~:text=He%20said%20he%20could%20not,a%20brand%20that%20Bachchan%20promotes

Exchange 4 Media. (2019, 11 October). *Shahenshah of the endorsement world turns 77 today.* https://www.exchange4media.com/marketing-news/shahenshah-of-the-endorsement-world-turns-77-today-100083.html#:~:text=At%20present%2C%20he%20has%20more,Pepsi%20and%20polio%20vaccination%20drives

Exchange 4 Media. (2020, January 6). *Birthday girl Deepika Padukone is a beloved face of brands.* https://www.exchange4media.com/marketing-news/birthday-girl-deepika-padukone-is-a-beloved-face-of-brands-101826.html

GoI. (2019, 9 August). *The Consumer Protection Act, 2019.* Ministry of Law and Justice (Legislative Department). http://egazette.nic.in/WriteReadData/2019/210422.pdf

GoI. (2020, 30 July). *Central Consumer Protection Authority established to promote, protect and enforce the rights of consumers; will function from Indian Institute of Public Administration premises*. Ministry of Consumer Affairs, Food & Public Distribution, Government of India. https://pib.gov.in/PressReleasePage.aspx?PRID=1642422#:~:text=As%20provided%20in%20section%2010,Department%20of%20Consumer%20Affairs%2C%20Smt

Jethwaney, J., & Jain, S. (2012). *Advertising management* (2nd ed., pp. 218). Oxford University Press.

Tewari, S. (2020, 3 July). Brand endorsement fees of celebrities may fall by up to 50%. *Livemint*. https://www.livemint.com/industry/advertising/brand-endorsement-fees-of-celebrities-may-fall-by-up-to-50-11593738647538.html

Kanth, G., & Bhatia, D. S. (2020, 14 January). *India: The Consumer Protection Act, 2019: An overview*. Kanth & Associates. https://www.mondaq.com/india/dodd-frank-consumer-protection-act/876600/the-consumer-protection-act-2019-an-overview#:~:text=The%202019%20Act%20has%20also,defective%20services%20and%20refund%20the

Kasad, A. (2020, 27 July). *Endorsers beware: Of endorsements & celebrities in Consumer Protection Act, 2019*. Adgully. https://www.adgully.com/endorsers-beware-of-endorsements-celebrities-in-consumer-protection-act-2019-95113.html

Laghate, G. (2021, 4 February). Virat Kohli remains India's most valuable celebrity with brand value of $237.7 mn. https://economictimes.indiatimes.com/industry/media/entertainment/virat-kohli-remains-indias-most-valuable-celebrity-with-brand-value-of-237-7-mn/articleshow/80691574.cms?from=mdr

Mtira, C., Shah, S., & Chanchani, D. (2020, 15 December). *Consumer Protection Act, 2019 and endorsers*. RGNUL Student Research Review (RSRR). http://rsrr.in/2020/12/15/liability-of-endosers-under-consumer-protection-act-2019/

Ranga, S., & Tandon, N. (2020, 15 June). Misleading advertisements during Covid-19. *Advaya Legal*. https://www.advayalegal.com/blog/misleading-advertisements-during-covid-19/

RNA. (2019). ASCI guidelines on celebrity advertising. https://rnaip.com/asci-guidelines-on-celebrity-advertising/

Rosellini, L. (1981, 29 October). Special case at the F.T.C. *The New York Times*. https://www.nytimes.com/1981/10/29/us/special-case-at-the-ftc.html

Shah, C. A. Y. (2021, 16 March). Sachin Tendulkar net worth 2021: Salary, car, income, assets. https://caknowledge.com/sachin-tendulkar-net-worth/.

Shiraz, Z. (2020, 6 June). *The real woke hero! Abhay Deol slams Indian celebrities for endorsing fairness creams while supporting anti-racism protests in America*. India.com. https://www.india.com/viral/the-real-woke-hero-abhay-deol-slams-indian-celebrities-for-endorsing-fairness-creams-while-supporting-anti-racism-protests-in-america-4050481/

Singh, H. (2020, July 23). *Consumer Protection Act, 2019: Meaning and key features*. Jagran Josh. https://www.jagranjosh.com/general-knowledge/meaning-and-features-of-consumer-protection-act-2019-1578557665-1

Singh, J. (2020, 29 January). *At the age of 26, Alia Bhatt endorses 18 popular brands*. https://winkreport.com/at-the-age-of-26alia-bhatt-endorses-18-popular-brands/

The Economic Times. (2020, 11 August). The power of celeb endorsements may be impacted under new Consumer Protection Act. https://economictimes.indiatimes.com/magazines/panache/the-power-of-celeb-endorsements-may-be-impacted-under-new-consumer-protection-act/articleshow/77458439.cms?from=mdr

The Hindu. (2019a, 30 July). Lok Sabha passes Consumer Protection Bill. https://www.thehindu.com/news/national/lok-sabha-passes-consumer-protection-bill/article28760805.ece

The Hindu. (2019b, 6 August). Rajya Sabha passes Consumer Protection Bill. https://www.thehindubusinessline.com/news/national/rajya-sabha-passes-consumer-protection-bill/article28837345.ece

CHAPTER 12

WHAT NEXT? THE AGENDA FOR TOMORROW

Men and women have roles—their roles are different, but their rights are same.

Harri Holken

After a long narrative on the state of women's representation in advertising, citing empirical data, arguments and counterarguments, laws and ethical mores, is there any hope for change? Is there a way to break the status quo? For the optimists, yes. For the pessimists, it does not matter anyway! If not this, they will find something else to brood about.

Change is the only constant. We have already seen it coming, albeit in small measures. Some more struggle, some more hand-holding, and things shall change one day.

So, what next?

Let us quickly look at the hard facts point wise on gender in the Indian ad narrative, before we a chart a road map.

1. Inappropriate and indecent portrayal of women in advertising is a worldwide phenomenon, and India is no exception.
2. Blatant stereotyping of women is found in advertisements across all brand categories in India.
3. Traditional societies like India have the double burden of stereotyping and patriarchal narrative.

4. The Indecent Representation of Women (Prohibition) Act is not a reference point in the creative process among advertising professionals.

5. Indian advertising, per se, does not reflect the social shift to represent the changing role and status of Indian women based on reality.

6. The liberalization of the Indian economy that brought various global brands and advertising agencies in India changed the ad narrative for good, which, among other things, includes the projection of bold and inappropriate woman imagery, in general.

7. Stereotyping of women is a much larger issue in Indian advertising than recognized. It is found across various brand categories like the FMCG; lifestyle; BFSI; travel and leisure and automobile. More than 80 per cent ads from a sample of over 1,160 ads from across the decades proved that this is the biggest malaise in Indian advertising.

8. Objectification of women is blatant in certain product categories, namely beauty products, apparel, tobacco, alcohol and condoms. The negative weightage went from 90–100 per cent in many cases. The redeeming thing, however, is that the current decade from 2011 onwards has reflected a 19 per cent reduction in the objectification of women across the spectrum. Despite the dip, there is still a huge negative weightage, which is a cause of worry, but some effort on the part of the industry needs to be appreciated.

9. Family, which, for long, was the mainstay of Indian advertising, has been largely relegated to the backyard, thus, reflecting the postmodern reality of the Indian society. Besides the nuclear family set-ups, which also reflect a patriarchal narrative, one also gets to see single parent ads that reflect the current reality.

10. There has been some effort on the part of some brands to project the modern uninhabited women—the reference mostly coming from the Bollywood crop—to reflect the social shift, which may or may not find resonance with the youth, but certainly not with a larger audience.

11. There are ads that create new stereotypes, like the concept of a 'superwoman', which raise the expectations from women at home and work.

12. There are no gender-sensitivity indicators on the representation of women in the advertising industry. There is no knowledge among the creative teams of the existence of any law on the indecent portrayal of women in India. Their engagement with the professional codes is also minimal.

13. Advertising professionals seem to have created a cloistered world around themselves in which they operate and create a dramatized version of 'reality', satisfying themselves that they only mirror the social reality.

14. Self-regulatory body ASCI seems to have recognized the writing on the wall and is taking steps such as commissioning a research on gender, GenderNext, and joining the Unstereotype Alliance as its founding member among other initiatives, including advisory on the skin colour in its self-regulatory code for advertisers.

15. The dwindling ratio of women in the ad industry should be a matter of great concern, which many within the industry recognize but do not make visible efforts to address the issue.

16. One of the open secrets, in general, is the gender-insensitive environment in the ad industry.

17. The Indecent Representation of Women (Prohibition) Act, 1986, that was moved twice for amendment in the last

two Parliament sessions, but lapsed on both the occasions, reflects the lackadaisical attitude of lawmakers on women's issues.

18. The course curricula of media schools, in general, are neither inclusive nor gendered.

WHAT WILL IT TAKE TO CHANGE THE PARADIGM?

Changing the attitudes of people, in general, and creating a gender-sensitive society may be a distant dream, but a few small steps in sensitizing the content creators and other stakeholders on gender discourse can be the beginning of a long journey. It is going to take a multidisciplinary effort to connect the dots on bringing about sensitivity when there is a near absence of gender training and sensitivity among all those who have a stake in advertising, as clients, as agency heads, as human resource persons and the campaign teams comprising account supervisors, account planners, creative writers and art directors, among other media specialists.

SOME RECOMMENDATIONS

Often, people do many things out of ignorance and lack of exposure. Gender debates, per se, are of a recent origin. To bring about the desired change, two things may help, bringing sensitivity around the issue and publicize policy infringement repercussions.

It is earnestly believed that if the stakeholders can have access to information—some formulae, some indicators and, most importantly, access to codes and laws on women—it could be the first step at sensitization. As the ICSSR research was a policy research, therefore, a lot of effort went into envisioning the possible ways and means to bring about change, offering solutions and making recommendations to the policymakers and the industry.

Here are a few recommendations that may pave the way for a gender-sensitive ad narrative.

MULTIMEDIA TOOLKIT FOR THE AD SECTOR

As a part of the seminal research, the research team conceptualized and produced a Multimedia Tool Kit (MMTK). The picture of its home page is given below to provide the reader with an idea on what all it contains. Web enabled, the interactive MMTK can be said to be a primer on gender discourse, a one-stop answer to most of the questions people may have on gender, like the conceptual framework, frequently asked questions, books on gender (some in PDF format and/or the listing of books) and various laws and codes, all compiled at one place either in PDF or with citation of web links. Select ads were deconstructed based on the theoretical construct of Erving Goffman's classic *Gender Advertisements* to provide the viewer with an idea on how gender sensitive or insensitive these were.

The MMTK also included a gender sensitivity test (GST), a prototype which could be applied on the creatives to gauge their gender sensitivity before releasing the ad in the media. The GST, created on Google Forms, is an interactive psychometric tool that was primarily designed as a self-assessment tool for content creators. Based on their responses to the indicators in the GST, the team could see how the ad created by them scored in terms of gender sensitivity and consider taking corrective action. The questions in the GST have been included based on researchers' understanding drawn from various theoretical constructs and research findings, but in no manner, do they claim the GST to be the 'last word'. It, in fact, is work in progress.

The GST created on Google Forms has been annexed at the end of the chapter.

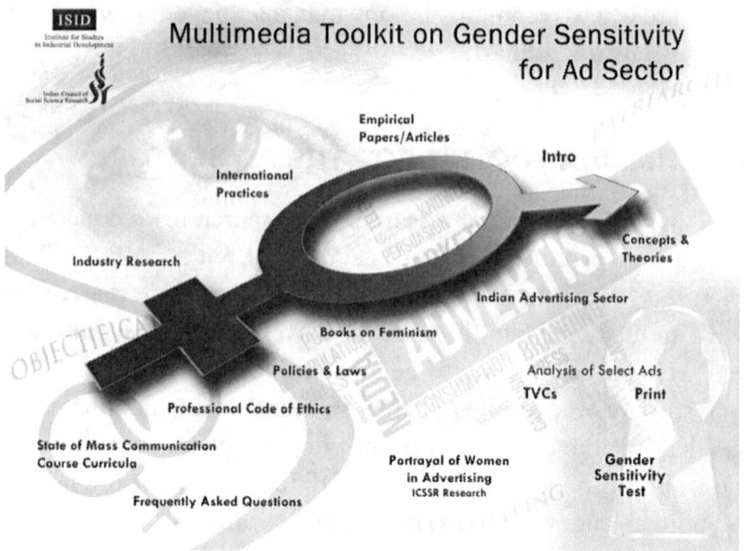

GST

The MMTK has a web-enabled GST created on Google Forms. This barometer, an interactive psychometric tool, is primarily designed as a self-assessment tool for content creators. The text of the questions has been annexed at the end of the chapter.

PROFESSIONAL CODES OF ETHICS

The various professional codes by industry bodies are ambivalent on gender norms, and therefore, these also need addressing. The ASCI, of late, has displayed a certain sensitivity to the gender issue. It is hoped that from the insights it draws from its commissioned research study, GenderNext in 2021, the ASCI will make some definitive provisions in its Code of Conduct.

MAKING MASS COMMUNICATION SYLLABUS INCLUSIVE AND GENDER-SENSITIVE

As brought out in one of the chapters, the syllabi of media schools are largely silent on gender discourse. The Ministry of HRD and UGC may actively consider making gender studies a compulsory paper or module in journalism and mass communication course curricula. To begin with, UGC may do so in the over 300 universities and institutions that teach mass communication at both undergraduate and PG levels. An interdisciplinary approach to teaching gender is recommended. Most universities have schools/departments in women studies and sociology that generally have courses in media and gender. The faculty, therefore, can be drawn from these departments, without incurring any extra expenditure. This is doable and needs to be addressed on priority.

Based on the interaction with over 25 media academics, a tentative course on gender with thrust areas is given below. As a long-term project, the HRD may consider making a paper on gender compulsory across the fields of science, arts, technology, engineering and business studies. It is only when a large, educated population is sensitized on gender at the threshold of their careers that we can bring about attitudinal change among the youth.

Suggested thrust areas:

1. To introduce relevant theories (feminist, standpoint, intersectionality, social justice and others) and select women-centric literature to make students understand women's perspectives, struggles, issues and movements—global and Indian.

2. To introduce social and cultural construct of gender.

3. To sensitize students on issues and concerns relating to women including patriarchy, culture and their concomitant impact (gender discrimination and disparities).

4. Conceptual framework of gender, power and representation (in media, popular culture and the arts, and assess the effects of these representations).

5. Gender rights and challenges (various policies and laws and their implementation mechanism, including the Indecent Representation of Women [Prohibition] Act, 1986, and the Sexual Harassment of Women at Workplace [Prevention, Prohibition, and Redressal] Act, 2013).

6. Gender-related variables as per SDGs.

7. To introduce, through case study method, the manifestation of gender insensitivity in media content, including advertising both at overt and subtle levels.

8. To introduce various laws against portrayal of women, sexual harassment at workplace and the right to equality under the Constitution.

9. To introduce various codes of conduct by professional bodies.

AREAS FOR POLICY INTERVENTION

The Indecent Representation of Women (Prohibition) Act, 1986, that was placed for amendment before the Parliament twice during the 15th and the 16th Lok Sabha terms, lapsed. The reformulated bill proposes the following amendments in the parent Act:

The bill has expanded the definition of the term 'indecent' to now include 'depiction of women as a sexual object, which appeals to the prurient interest'. Amendment in definition of the term 'advertisement' to include 'digital form or electronic form or hoardings, or through SMS, MMS, etc.'; 'distribution' to include publication, license or uploading using computer resource or communication device. Insertion made of a new definition to define the term 'publish'. Amendment in Section 4 to include that

'No person shall publish or distribute or cause to be published or cause to be distributed by any means any material which contains indecent representation of women in any form.' Penalty on the infringement of the law would now be similar to that provided under the IT Act, 2000. Creation of a centralized authority under the aegis of the NCW. This authority will be headed by member secretary, NCW, having representatives from ASCI, Press Council of India, Ministry of I&B and one member having experience of working on women's issues. This centralized authority will be authorized to receive complaints or grievances.

A policy brief on the portrayal of women in advertising was prepared and sent to various stakeholders including the Ministries of Information and Broadcasting and Women and Child Development (WCD). It has also been put in the public domain.[1] Based on empirical data and our understanding of the issue, as and when the amended bill is presented to the parliament, the below following suggestions were reflected in the policy brief.

Add 'Stereotypical Portrayal' in the Proposed Amendment

Rationale: The amendment to the Act has expanded the definition of the term 'indecent' to now include 'depiction of women as a sexual object, which appeals to the prurient interest' (taken from the IT Act). Most empirical studies in India, including the current study, suggest that while objectifying women as sex objects is an issue of great concern, it is often restricted to a certain category of brands. More commonplace phenomenon in Indian advertising is the biased, regressive and stereotypical portrayal of woman. Indian advertisements, in general, cater to the patriarchal pattern of narrative, where a woman is portrayed as subservient to man, low in intelligence, incapable of making decisions and is positioned low in social hierarchy. The ads, in general, do not reflect the social shift and the changing role of women in the Indian society. Therefore, it is recommended that the amendment may include this aspect also. Interestingly, Prasar Bharati's code specifies that ads should not portray women in a manner that 'emphasizes passive, submissive qualities and encourages them to play a subordinate, secondary role in the family and society,' but ads continue to portray women exactly like that. If this provision becomes a part of the law, it would be taken seriously by the ad industry. Therefore, it is recommended that the proposed amendment may consider including 'stereotyping' also in the definition.

The proposed amendments must also fix responsibility.

1. When it comes to responsibility, who would be held responsible for the advertisement that is deemed objectionable? Would it be the advertising agency that conceptualized the ad, the client who played a role in deciding the narrative and giving the final go ahead or the media vehicle that carried the ad? Would it be one or all of them?

2. Within the agency, an ad campaign is the result of teamwork among the account planner, account servicing person, creative writer, visualizer, art director, filmmaker and the agency head. How would the interpretation of law work for a variety of people engaged in the act of creating an ad campaign?

3. What would be the indicators for judging an ad as 'indecent', 'prurient' and, if added, 'stereotypical'?

4. In case of non-compliance, would the self-regulatory industry body ASCI be empowered to exert pressure on the concerned agency/client to withdraw or reorient the concerned ad? Would ASCI get disciplinary/penal powers?

AREAS FOR POLICY CONSIDERATION

Government

Setting Up of a Gender Committee

It is recommended to set up a body under the aegis of the Ministry of I&B that can work closely with the Ministry of WCD and the

NCW in guiding the government and the industry on representation of gender in media at various media platforms and genre, including news, advertising and entertainment. This body with well-known academics, researchers, social scientists and policymakers can aid and advise the government on policy issues.

Advisory to ASCI

Ministry of I&B may consider advising ASCI to include provision on stereotyping and, also, prepare gender sensitivity indicators after stakeholder consultations.

Preview of Advertisements by Ad Agencies

The I&B Ministry may advise the industry self-regulatory bodies like the ASCI and industry association AAAI to create a mechanism for ad agencies for preview of ads on gender sensitivity indicators before releasing in the media. The responsibility of media channels—print, electronic and digital—may also be defined.

Accreditation to Mass Communication Profession

It is recommended that the Ministry of I&B may consider accrediting the profession of journalism and mass communication in partnership with professional bodies from the media, including advertising and public relations sector. This would ensure that all those working in the media industry have professional training in the field before they join the industry. This would go a long way in ensuring professionalism in content creation as well as addressing the issue of required sensitivity towards various issues, including gender.

Advertising Industry

1. It is recommended that the Ministry of I&B, in collaboration with the industry associations, would interface with at least

the top-100 advertisers from the corporate world on the need for gender-sensitive ad content. The role of organizing such parleys can be given to industry associations like CII, FICCI and Associated Chambers of Commerce and Industry of India.

2. It is suggested that professional bodies like the ASCI and AAAI, in collaboration with the academia, as a matter of practice, would consider organizing, from time to time, orientation workshops on gender and related issues for the ad practitioners, especially creative teams.

3. It is suggested that the ASCI, in its current mobile application ASCI Online—which allows the public to report ads that exaggerate claims—may suitably incorporate gender-sensitivity ratings to map public opinion on advertisements.

4. The advertising industry may consider floating an award at the national level on the lines of Cannes' Glass Lion for rewarding gender-sensitive ad campaigns to bring the issue into focus and, also, encourage work in this direction.

In the end, it can be concluded that in spite the fact that the problem of gender sensitivity is age old and it may take a long time to achieve a gendered and inclusive society, but credit must go to the millions of courageous women and men who have fought bitter battles and spearheaded movements to bring us to a stage where the issue is debated head-on. There are policy interventions and laws in place, and some change is visible within the industry also.

'We shall overcome, one day ...,' the lines immortalized by Martin Luther King Jr resonate decades after he made it a cry for justice, an anthem for hope.

Even this, we shall overcome!

ANNEXURE

Gender Sensitivity Test

Self-analysis tool for checking gender sensitivity for your campaign.

*Required

1. Is the presence of a female character relevant to the brand? —1 point

☐ Yes

☐ No

2. Is the women in the ad portrayed as dominant or passive?* —1 point

☐ Dominant

☐ Passive

3. Who has lent the voice-over to the ad?*

☐ Male

☐ Female

☐ Not relevant

4. If female voice used, is it because it lends sensuality to the narrative (Mark 'No', if not relevant)* —1 point

☐ Yes

☐ No

5. If male voice used, it is because it lends credibility and power to the narrative.*

☐ Yes

☐ No

6. Is the woman featured in the ad as ...? —7 points

	Yes	No
An expert/advisor		
Informed/intelligent		
Decision-maker/in control		
Working professional		
Traditional role of a homemaker		
Gullible/dumb		
Decorative prop/object		

7. Is the women portrayed as someone looking for approval of a male character in the ad?*

☐ Yes

☐ No

8. Is the colour of the dress of the woman character in the ad stereotypically feminine?* —1 point

☐ Yes

☐ No

9. Is the woman character in the ad looking glamourous and picture-perfect?* —1 point

☐ Yes

☐ No

10. If yes, is it critical to the brand?*

☐ Yes

☐ No

☐ Not relevant

11. Is the woman shown in a revealing attire/showing cleavage, etc.?* —1 point

☐ Yes

☐ No

12. If yes, is it critical to the brand? (If answer to the previous question is 'No', select 'not relevant')*

☐ Yes

☐ No

☐ Not relevant

13. Is the camera positioning/angle, highlighting a particular body of the woman?* —1 point

☐ Yes

☐ No

14. If yes, is it critical to the brand narrative? (If answer to the previous question is 'No', select 'not relevant')

☐ Yes

☐ No

☐ Not relevant

15. Is the frame composed in a manner that makes the character look dominant? —1 point

☐ Yes

☐ No

16. Does the portrayal of woman character depict the way she would be in real life?*

☐ Yes

☐ No

17. Is the role of the client key to influencing the ad narrative?*

☐ Yes

☐ No

18. Is the choice of a female celebrity critical to the brand?*

☐ Yes

☐ No

19. If yes, was the choice of female celebrity made by the client?* —1 point

☐ Yes

☐ No

20. Do you think woman celebrity makes it easier to portray her an object of desire?* —1 point

☐ Yes

☐ No

21. Are you sure of the laws relevant to the profession of advertising?* —1 point

☐ Yes

☐ No

22. If yes, did you refer to the following laws and industry codes while creating the campaign: * —5 points

	Yes	No
Indecent Representation of Women (Prohibition) Act, 1986		
Consumer Protection Act, 1986		
ASCI Code of Conduct		
BCCC Code of Conduct		
Doordarshan Code for advertisers		

NOTE

1 http://isid.org.in

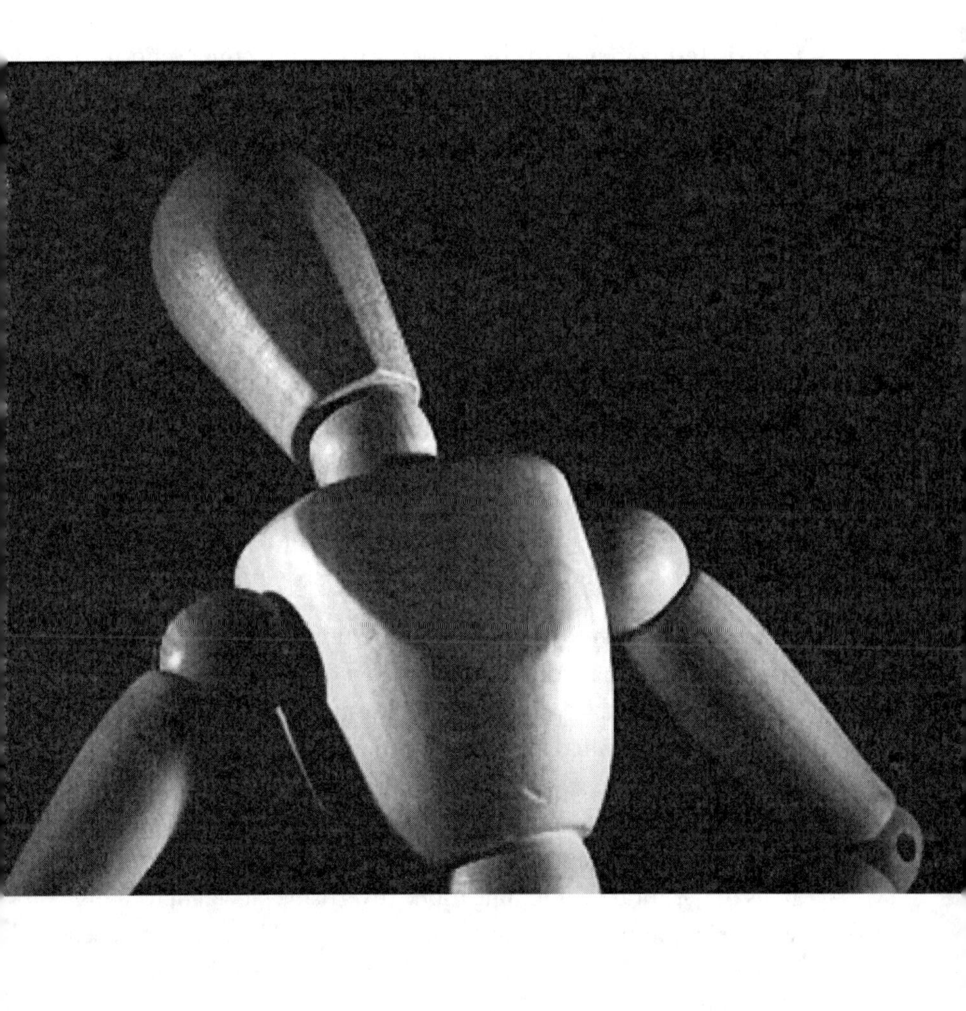

ABOUT THE AUTHOR

Jaishri Jethwaney did her doctorate from the School of International Studies JNU, in media and elections, which included extensive fieldwork in India, Germany and the USA. She did her master's in political science from the Hindu College, Delhi University; postgraduate diploma (PGD) in advertising and public relations and PGD in journalism from RP Institute of Mass Communication, New Delhi. She went to New South Wales for her fellowship in public relations. After a long stint at the Indian Institute of Mass Communication spanning over 25 years as Professor and Program Director until 2016, when she demitted office she joined the Institute for Studies in Industrial Development (ISID)—a public funded, national-level policy think tank working on media policy issues. Currently, she is a senior ICSSR research fellow based at ISID. The area of her present research is 'Wages and related issues in the news media industry in India'.

Professor Jethwaney has been a lead communication expert for many international consultancies taken on behalf of UNESCO, UNICEF, United Nations Population Fund, World Health Organization, United Nations Population Fund among others. She is on the board of studies of several central and state universities. In her long career, she has designed and anchored more than 150 training programmes of various durations in the areas of corporate communication, advertising, social marketing, disaster communication and CSR, among others. She has been a visiting faculty to many coveted organizations, including the National Judicial Academy, Bhopal, and the LBS National Academy of Administration, Mussoorie, Ordinance Staff College, Nagpur, and Power Management Institute, among others.

Among the many books she has authored and co-authored, some are *When India Votes* (2019), *Social Sector Communication* (SAGE, 2016), *Corporate Communication* (SAGE, 2018), *Public Relations Management*, 3rd edition (2015) and *Advertising Management*, 2nd edition (2012). She has contributed to the *SAGE Encyclopaedia on Corporate Reputation* in 2016 and has chapters in many books.

Among the many awards that Professor Jethwaney has received, some are the Exceptional Woman of Excellence by Women Economic Forum, 2019; Sahyog–Sahyadari (Doordarshan) award on leadership in mass communication teaching, 2014; Best Professor award by World Education Congress, 2013, and the Leadership award in PR academics from the PRSI in 2010. Detailed CV at http://isid.org.in jjethwaney@isid.edu.in

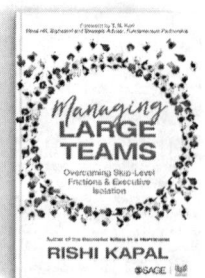

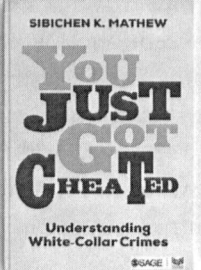